International Business and Global Climate Change

Climate change has become an important topic on the business agenda with strong pressure being placed on companies to respond and contribute to finding solutions to this urgent problem. This text provides a comprehensive analysis of international business responses to global climate change and climate change policy.

Embedded in relevant management literature, this book gives a concise treatment of developments in policy and business activity on global, regional and national levels, using examples and systematic data from a large number of international companies. The first part outlines the international climate policy landscape and voluntary initiatives taken by companies, both alone and together with others. The second part examines companies' strategies, covering innovation for climate change, as well as compensation via emissions trading and carbon offsetting.

Written by well-known experts in the field, *International Business and Global Climate Change* illustrates how an environmental topic becomes strategically important in a mainstream sense, affecting corporate decision-making, business processes, products, reputation, advertising, communication, accounting and finance. This is a must-read for academics as well as practitioners concerned with this issue.

Jonatan Pinkse is Assistant Professor at the University of Amsterdam Business School, The Netherlands. His publications have focused on strategy and sustainability, especially business responses to climate change.

Ans Kolk is Full Professor of Sustainable Management at the University of Amsterdam Business School, The Netherlands. She has published extensively on business and climate change, corporate social responsibility and corporate sustainability.

International Business and Global Climate Change

Jonatan Pinkse and Ans Kolk

In association with the European
Academy of Business in Society

Routledge
Taylor & Francis Group

LONDON AND NEW YORK

EABIS

European Academy
of Business in Society

First published 2009 by Routledge
2 Park Square, Milton Park, Abingdon, Oxon OX14 4RN

Simultaneously published in the USA and Canada
by Routledge
270 Madison Avenue, New York, NY 10016

Routledge is an imprint of the Taylor & Francis Group, an informa business

© 2009 Jonatan Pinkse and Ans Kolk

Typeset in Baskerville by
RefineCatch Limited, Bungay, Suffolk
Printed and bound in Great Britain by
CPI Antony Rowe, Chippenham, Wiltshire

British Library Cataloguing in Publication Data
A catalogue record for this book is available from the British Library

Library of Congress Cataloguing-in-Publication Data
Pinkse, Jonatan.
  International business and global climate change / Jonatan Pinkse and
Ans Kolk.
    p. cm.
    Includes bibliographical references and index.
    1. International business enterprises–Environmental aspects.
2. Climatic changes–Economic aspects.   3. Environmental policy–
Economic aspects.   I. Kolk, Ans   II. Title.
    HD2755.5.P563 2009
    658.4'083–dc22
    2008022260

ISBN10: 0–415–41552–7 (hbk)
ISBN10: 0–415–41553–5 (pbk)
ISBN10: 0–203–88710–7 (ebk)

ISBN13: 978–0–415–41552–1 (hbk)
ISBN13: 978–0–415–41553–8 (pbk)
ISBN13: 978–0–203–88710–3 (ebk)

Contents

Figures

Tables

Boxes

Abbreviations and acronyms

ACEA	European Automobile Manufacturers Association
ACX	Australia Climate Exchange
APEC	Asia-Pacific Economic Cooperation
BP	British Petroleum
CaCX	California Climate Exchange
CAFE	Corporate Average Fuel Economy
CCS	Carbon Capture and Storage
CCSP	Climate Change Science Program
CCTP	Climate Change Technology Program
CCX	Chicago Climate Exchange
CDM	Clean Development Mechanism
CDP	Carbon Disclosure Project
CEO	Chief Executive Officer
CERES	Coalition for Environmentally Responsible Economies
CFC	Chlorofluorocarbon
CH_4	Methane
CO_2	Carbon dioxide
COP	Conference of the Parties
CSR	Corporate Social Responsibility
EC	European Commission
EPA	US Environmental Protection Agency
ERT	European Round Table of Industrialists
EU	European Union
EU ETS	European Union Emissions Trading Scheme
FoE	Friends of the Earth
FT	Financial Times
GCC	Global Climate Coalition
GDP	Gross Domestic Product
GE	General Electric
Gg	Giga-gram (1,000,000,000 grams)
GHG	Greenhouse gas
GM	General Motors
GTL	Gas to Liquid
HFC	Hydrofluorocarbon
ICCR	Interfaith Center on Corporate Responsibility

IPPC	Intergovernmental Panel on Climate Change
ISO	International Organisation for Standardisation
JI	Joint Implementation
LFE	Large Final Emitter
METI	Japanese Ministry of Industry and Trade
MNC	Multinational Corporation
MoE	Ministry of Environment
MRET	Mandatory Renewable Energy Target
NAP	National Allocation Plan
NGO	Non-governmental organisation
NGAC	New South Wales Greenhouse Gas Abatement Certificate
NSW	New South Wales
NSW GGAS	New South Wales Greenhouse Gas Abatement Scheme
OECD	Organisation for Economic Cooperation and Development
OTC	Over the Counter
PCF	Prototype Carbon Fund
PFC	Perfluorocarbon
PV	Photovoltaic
R&D	Research and Development
RGA	Regional Greenhouse gas Allowance
RGGI	Regional Greenhouse Gas Initiative
SEC	Securities and Exchange Commission
SF6	Sulphur hexafluoride
UCF	Umbrella Carbon Fund
UK	United Kingdom
UN	United Nations
UNEP	United Nations Environment Programme
UNFCCC	United Nations Framework Convention on Climate Change
US	United States
WBCSD	World Business Council for Sustainable Development
WMO	World Meteorological Organisation
WRI	World Resources Institute
WSSD	World Summit on Sustainable Development
WWF	World Wildlife Fund

Preface

This book results from a long time fascination with business responses to climate change. The emergence of concerns about global warming in the international policy setting in the early 1990s was accompanied by a varied reaction on the part of companies. This included indifference, ignorance, contesting of the science (evidence) of climate change, and resistance to policy measures for fear of harm to competitiveness. A proactive response was rather uncommon at the time, and this remained so more or less until after the Kyoto Protocol was adopted in 1997. From then onwards the scene has really started to change in an unprecedented way.

Overall, in a period of less than 20 years, and particularly in the last decade, we have seen a large shift in attitudes and in the activities taken as a result. This book documents this change, outlining the policy context, which has been rather dynamic and thus also uncertain for companies, as well as the various dimensions of business and climate change. It has an international focus throughout and pays considerable attention to international companies, which are most confronted with the large variety of policy developments and societal concerns around the globe.

The book in a sense also reflects our own ongoing curiosity in how companies deal with an environmental issue that has gained such momentum. Even though one of us has seen the issue develop since the early 1990s, this course and spread, particularly amongst companies and the networks around them, exceeded any expectation. It has been a transition from scepticism and lack of attention to an incredible number of initiatives, conferences, seminars, reports and articles, and with a range of organisations and stakeholders, including investors, who have adopted the issue as a serious concern for business and society. Business schools have started to pay attention to climate change in curricula, in view of the fact that it has become an operational and financial concern, in addition to being a public policy and strategic issue. The number of researchers focusing on the topic of business and climate change has multiplied from basically two in the mid-1990s to dozens, including a considerable number of PhD projects.

Obviously we have no reason to discourage this wave of attention, as it is great that so many have become interested in the topic that has intrigued us for so long as well. Although climate change has only hit the agendas of business and management scholars quite recently, it is likely to stay there for quite a while. In the years to come, the impact of climate change on business may well increase further, when the consequences of more regular occurrences of floods, droughts, and other extreme weather conditions will be felt. The issue can also be expected to be a driving force for much of the innovation that will take place in the world in the coming decade. Besides, what climate change can do very well, also from a broader sustainability perspective, is serve as an extremely good example of how a societal (environmental) problem has become one that affects all aspects of doing business, with implications for strategy, organisation, marketing, communications, accounting, and finance. This is further explained in this book. We also indicate linkages with and spillovers to other sustainability issues where appropriate, although obviously business and climate change is the main focus.

This book could not have come about without support from others, although the contents are fully ours. Important has been the pleasant atmosphere and entrepreneurial spirit at the University of Amsterdam Business School, where colleagues from several disciplines pay attention to environmental, social and governance issues. We have cooperated over the years with several people outside our own university as well. In the field of climate change, it is worth mentioning David Levy, with whom the early fascination has been shared for more than a decade now, which also resulted in joint work. More recently collaboration has also taken place with researchers at the Swiss Federal Institute for Technology (ETH), and with many others in the framework of two international research networks: the International Research Network on Social and Environmental Aspects in Business and Management, and the Transnational Climate Change Governance Network. We would also like to acknowledge the Netherlands Organisation for Scientific Research (NWO) for funding for a project of which this is one of the results. Final words of thanks and of course the most honourable mention one could think of are for those who share our lives, but that goes well beyond the scope of this book.

Introduction

1   Introduction

Climate change is one of the environmental issues that has increasingly attracted business attention in the course of the 1990s. While public and policy interest had already started in the late 1980s, leading to a first international agreement at the Rio conference in 1992, the main driver for corporate strategic change was the adoption of the Kyoto Protocol in 1997. This event spurred the development of regulation and increased the pressure from non-governmental organisations (NGOs) on governments to ensure ratification of the Protocol, and on companies, which were urged to take appropriate steps to address global warming.

In the period leading up to the Kyoto meeting, a considerable number of large multinationals in particular had started to spend much time and effort in trying to influence, both individually and through a range of business associations, their government's stance on an international climate treaty and emissions reduction policies. With only some exceptions, companies initially opposed the adoption of such measures and regulation. Uncertainties about the economic, technological and strategic impact of an international climate policy led many of them to stress the threats to their business and the negative consequences for the economy as a whole. Especially in the US, the unresolved scientific nature of the global warming debate was often used as further argument.

When government support for an international agreement in Kyoto turned out to be more widespread than initially expected, however, the picture started to change slowly but surely, and an increasing number of companies stopped their opposition. Some did this rather reluctantly, and merely prepared to comply with expected regulation. Others openly adhered to the precautionary principle, emphasised the opportunities that a more proactive approach would bring, and started to take steps. As a result, the decade that has passed since the adoption of the Kyoto Protocol has witnessed a wave of corporate activities and initiatives to reduce emissions, through product and process improvements, co-operation with other companies, government agencies and NGOs to exchange technologies and expertise, and the exploration of options such as emissions trading.

All this has taken place against the background of a fragmentation of approaches on how to implement Kyoto (if at all). The most notable policy development has been the introduction of an emissions trading scheme in the European Union since January 2005. This is the only compulsory trading system, in addition to a number of voluntary ones, particularly in the US and Australia. For companies, the issue of climate change thus continues to be characterised by diversity in policy developments and uncertainty as to the (potential) impact on markets, technologies and organisations.

This book provides a comprehensive analysis of the policy, societal and competitive contexts faced, and partly shaped, by companies, and discusses the ins and outs of international business responses to climate change. We will use recent data to illustrate developments, but the analysis is embedded in knowledge about the history of corporate reactions to climate change in the past decade, which has seen remarkable changes. Before turning to the setup of the book (section 1.3), in this introductory chapter we will first briefly put things into perspective by giving some examples of changes in corporate positions over the years. Subsequently, section 1.2 will give some basic information on the scientific and political background of climate change to clarify the complexity of the issue and provide a background to the main topic of this book.

1.1 PATHS OF CHANGE

It is noteworthy that the timing and pace of shifts in corporate positions on climate change varied by industry and country of origin, and were also shaped by individual corporate perceptions and histories. Particularly large companies in the oil and automobile industries provide notable examples of the diversity, and of individual pathways of change. If we go back to 1998, the year after the adoption of the Kyoto Protocol, US companies Exxon and Ford were, for example, still strong opponents. Exxon particularly focused on the science of climate change.

> Ours is a company which is based on science, technology and engineering. We apply this same rigor to the issue of global climate change, which Exxon has been studying for more than ten years. What is perfectly clear is that *nothing is clear*. There needs to be a much better understanding of this extremely complex subject before governments or international bodies mandate cuts in fossil fuel use.
>
> (Exxon Perspectives, June 1998: 4; emphasis in original)

Ford Motor Company showed disapproval because of the domestic economic implications:

> Ford believes that international global climate negotiations may lead to agreements that will severely disadvantage the US economy, impair US competitiveness and lead to an outflow of US jobs.
> <http://www.ford.com/corporate-info/govt_policy/global.html>
> (Website visited on 14 September 1998)

Objections to Kyoto were shared by the Bush Government, which decided in

March 2001 to reject the Protocol. Interestingly, this has not hampered US companies from changing their position in the course of years. If we look at more current statements of the two companies mentioned above, an evolution of views turns out to have taken place in the meantime. ExxonMobil still pays attention to the (uncertain) science of climate change, but it has become more active in taking steps to address climate risks, one could say regardless of, or despite, that:

> We recognize that, although scientific evidence remains inconclusive, the potential impact of greenhouse gas (GHG) emissions on society and eco-systems may prove to be significant. To help address these risks, we are continuing to take actions to improve efficiency and reduce emissions in our operations. We are also working with the scientific and business communities to undertake research to create economically competitive and affordable future options to reduce long-term global GHG emissions while meeting the world's growing demand for energy.
>
> (ExxonMobil 2004: 14)

For Ford, corporate realities have changed dramatically since 1998:

> Climate change is a critical issue for Ford Motor Company.... We have consistently acknowledged the potentially serious consequences of climate change. The need to reduce greenhouse gas emissions is driven by many factors: greater scientific certainty, increasing interest by governments, emerging investor attention to the business risks and opportunities, growing importance to consumers and rising questions about regional energy security. We are committed to improving fuel economy and reducing greenhouse gas emissions across our range of vehicles. We will also continue working on innovative policy approaches that encourage the development of advanced technologies and lessen greenhouse gas emissions. We have set several voluntary targets to reduce greenhouse gas emissions from our plants, and we seek to achieve several industry targets for our products.
>
> (Ford 2004: 60)

In 2005, the company also issued the 'Ford report on the business impact of climate change' with a preface that stated:

> In November 2004, Ford Motor Company received a shareholder resolution from the Interfaith Center on Corporate Responsibility (ICCR) and the Coalition for Environmentally Responsible Economies (Ceres) and others requesting we release information specific to our greenhouse gases emissions strategy. Much of the information requested is reported annually in our Sustainability Report (formerly called the Corporate Citizenship Report) and we have excerpted the most recent Sustainability Report as an appendix to this report. However, we agreed to publish the industry's first report

dedicated to the issue of climate change and its effect on business as well as the automotive industry as a whole.

(Ford 2005: 1)

These two examples from the US show the different elements that have come to the fore in business responses to climate change in the past decade. These reflect the changes in the policy, societal and competitive landscape, where – besides governments (in the US also at local levels) and NGOs – other stakeholders such as investors and consumers have started to pay attention to the issue.

It must be noted that other companies from a comparable context reacted more quickly. General Motors (GM), for example, started to co-operate with the World Resources Institute, British Petroleum and Monsanto in a 'Safe Climate, Sound Business' project in February 1998. At that time GM also expressed its objective of playing a leading role in climate issues. Like Toyota, the company joined the Pew Center on Global Climate Change, which advocates active steps to deal with the problem, when it was founded in May 1998. At the same time, however, GM was still a member of the Global Climate Coalition (GCC), which strongly lobbied against binding international agreements such as Kyoto, in a desire to also stay involved in the domestic policy debate and help combat undesirable regulation. And, as a further illustration of the dilemmas of managing a large multinational amidst such a large international controversy, GM's German subsidiary, Adam Opel, pleaded for a more consensual approach in line with the European debate.

Such internal organisational differences, very relevant in the case of such large multinationals, also played a role in Shell's relatively late withdrawal from the Global Climate Coalition. In spite of the insistence of the UK and Dutch parts, Shell Oil in the US long refused to change position, hinting at the importance of its shareholders. Only after Royal Dutch/Shell increased its influence, Shell Oil left the GCC. Interestingly, Shell's 1998 report on Profits and Principles came up with two different wordings of this issue – correcting in an addendum the original text:

> Shell companies belong to many industry associations, some of which take a view on climate change and lobby regulators. The most controversial of these is the Global Climate Coalition of the USA. Shell Oil in the USA remains a member of the Global Climate Coalition, which has a style unique to the USA reflecting the political culture. Shell Oil believes it has a better chance to influence the actions of the Global Climate Coalition, and persuade its fellow members of the view held by Shell companies on climate change, if it remains a member.

(The Shell Report, 1998: 35)

> Shell companies belong to many industry associations, some of which take a view on climate change and lobby regulators. One such lobby group is the Global Climate Coalition (GCC) of the USA. Until recently Shell Oil in the USA had been a member of the coalition. Following Kyoto it became clear

that the respective views of Shell companies and the GCC were too far apart. Shell Oil withdrew its membership in April 1998. The main disagreement centred on the Kyoto Protocol which aims to cut overall greenhouse gas emissions by 5 per cent in the year 2012. The GCC is actively campaigning against legally binding targets and timetables as well as ratification by the US government. The Shell view is that prudent precautionary measures are called for.

(Addendum to The Shell Report, 1998)

Almost a decade later, Shell actively explores different energy sources, including wind and solar power, biofuels and hydrogen, and aims to become a leader in trading GHG allowances in emerging markets. British Petroleum, the first large multinational that openly changed position in May 1997 and then withdrew from the GCC, also invests in low-carbon power generation businesses, which includes hydrogen, wind, solar and gas-fired power generation.

It is of course not only the oil and automobile companies where interesting developments have taken place, although we have used these here to illustrate different paths of change. Other companies across the whole range of industries are also investing in developing new products and services related to climate change, in many cases building on the competencies already in place. The launch by General Electric of its Ecomagination campaign, in 2005, has attracted much attention, also because the company emphasised the business case.

> Ecomagination is GE's commitment to address challenges such as the need for cleaner, more efficient sources of energy, reduced emissions and abundant sources of clean water. And we plan to make money doing it. Increasingly for business, 'green' is green.
>
> (GE press release, 9 May 2005: 1)

In addition to industrial companies, the financial sector has also responded to climate change. Banks and insurance companies offer weather derivatives to hedge risks of unexpected changes in weather conditions and exposure to emissions trading schemes. Financial service providers also use their expertise of commodity markets to assist their clients in the emerging market for emissions allowances, or develop special funds for such investments. Investors are in general putting more pressure on companies in relation to climate change, as already noted in the Ford quote above, be it from a risk reduction or market opportunity perspective. They request disclosure and form coalitions that collect information, for example through the Coalition for Environmentally Responsible Economies (Ceres) and the Carbon Disclosure Project; shareholder resolutions are filed as well.

Many other examples can be given from companies worldwide, and we will do that throughout this book. For now, it suffices to point out that climate change affects companies' decisions on strategy, policy, organisation, public affairs, marketing and sales, logistics and purchasing, and finance and accounting. The various dimensions will be discussed in the chapters that follow.

1.2 SOME BASIC INFORMATION

This book is not about the science or politics of global climate change. Nevertheless this section will give some basic information on its scientific and political background because it helps in understanding why certain countries and businesses are affected more than others and how they respond. We will argue that even though climate change is a global issue, the way it is perceived differs considerably throughout the world. We will support this with country-level statistics about the level of emissions, public opinion on the salience of climate change, and potential costs and benefits of mitigation and adaptation of climate change. The aim is to clarify the complexity of the issue and to provide a background to the main topic of this book.

Behind climate change and global warming is a natural process, discovered in the early nineteenth century, that keeps the Earth habitable. The idea is that the Earth's atmosphere absorbs some of the heat radiation from sunlight that is carried back into space after it hits the Earth's surface, and thus functions as a blanket. What causes the atmosphere to have this attribute is that although most gases, including oxygen and nitrogen, are transparent and do not absorb heat radiation, there are a few gases – called greenhouse gases – that are opaque and do not let heat radiation pass. One of the major greenhouse gases and the one that was discovered first is carbon dioxide (CO_2); a main source of which is the combustion of fossil fuels. Correspondingly, the basic tenet of the human-induced climate change hypothesis is that, starting with the Industrial Revolution, by using fossil fuels humans have significantly increased the level of CO_2 in the atmosphere and thereby contributed to the warming of the Earth. This hypothesis has been supported by findings showing that during the twentieth century the CO_2 concentrations display a rising curve (Keeling's curve, see Figure 1.1). More recently, in the 1970s and 1980s, it has also been discovered that besides CO_2 several other gases, including chlorofluorocarbons (CFCs), methane, and nitrates, have an even stronger effect on global warming, but were not noticed earlier because only minuscule amounts of these greenhouse gases are present in the atmosphere (Weart, 2003).

Over the last two decades, scientific research on climate change has predominantly taken place under the auspices of the Intergovernmental Panel on Climate Change (IPCC). The IPCC was established in 1988 to assess the scientific information, the environmental and socio-economic impact, and a response strategy for climate change with the aim of achieving more credibility of the scientific community and to serve as input for policymakers (Siebenhüner, 2003). In four assessment reports – published in 1990, 1995, 2001 and 2007 – the IPCC provided the scientific basis for international climate policy to reduce GHG emissions. The main results of these assessment reports were that greenhouse gas concentrations have increased due to human activity; the global average temperature has risen significantly over the past decades; and human activity has been affecting the global climate (IPCC, 2007a).

The reason that there is much concern about climate change is that, particularly

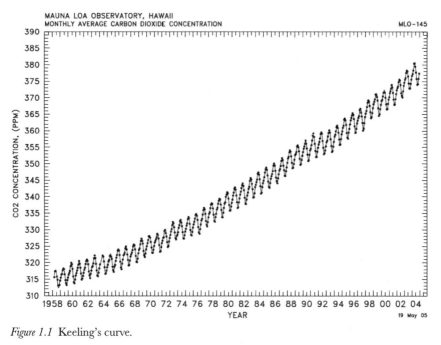

MAUNA LOA OBSERVATORY, HAWAII
MONTHLY AVERAGE CARBON DIOXIDE CONCENTRATION   MLO-145

Figure 1.1 Keeling's curve.

Source: Keeling and Whorf (2005)

due to temperature increases, it affects physical and biological systems by changing ecosystems and causing extinction of species (IPCC, 2007b). The latest IPCC report shows that there are already some observable impacts of climate change such as an increase in glacial lakes, instability of regions with permafrost, an earlier start of spring in some locations, shifts in migration patterns of plants and animals (e.g. birds), and rising water temperatures affecting survival and migration of fish. The IPCC report also points out that there are many projected effects which will increasingly have a social impact and adversely affect human health. It is expected that melting glaciers and changing precipitation patterns will lead to deteriorating availability of fresh water, crop yields will be lower in some regions, rising sea levels will cause coastal areas to be more vulnerable to storms and flooding, and there will be a wider spread of tropical diseases (IPCC, 2007b). In other words, even though climate change is a global phenomenon, its impact is different by location, and, in particular, developing countries with low adaptive capacity are affected disproportionately.

Besides the global impact, what also sets climate change apart from many other environmental issues is that it became a salient political issue within a relatively short period of time, and that this occurred on a global level. In the early 1980s, climate change got political attention specifically from international organisations such as the World Meteorological Organisation (WMO) and the United Nations Environment Programme (UNEP) (Andresen and Agrawala,

2002; Boehmer-Christiansen, 1996; Paterson, 1992; Rowlands, 1992). It was UNEP's funding of scientific research that increased the policy relevance of climate change because it changed the focus of research from the physical impact to the societal impact (Andresen and Agrawala, 2002). Since 1985, natural scientists have requested politicians to take note of the issue (Paterson, 1992), which has led to discussions about appropriate policies to act on global warming (Boehmer-Christiansen, 1996; Rowlands, 1992).

In 1988, national governments also became engaged in the international climate change debate and this year marks the point at which climate change really turned into a political issue (Andresen and Agrawala, 2002; Bodansky, 2001; Paterson, 1992; Rowlands, 1992, 1995). In this year, several events coincided that led to widespread attention for the importance of climate change: it was one of the hottest and driest summers in North America on record; James Hansen of the NASA Goddard Institute for Space Studies made headlines with a statement for the US Senate Energy and Natural Resources Committee that temperature increases during the 1980s were almost certainly evidence of global warming; and the IPCC was established (Andresen and Agrawala, 2002; Rowlands, 1995). Concurrently, the General Assembly of the United Nations asked the WMO and UNEP to set up a Framework Convention on Climate Change (FCCC).

Even though climate change was almost immediately debated on an international level, individual countries have maintained very different political standpoints on the issue. And, while national governments appeared to agree on their position on climate change on several occasions, for instance in 1992 at the United Nations Conference on Environment and Development when the FCCC was established, or in 1997 at the Kyoto Conference when the Kyoto Protocol was set up, the climate change debate has been surrounded by sharp political divergence between countries. The transatlantic divide on climate change between the US and the EU has been most salient (Busby and Ochs, 2004). Other industrialised countries, such as Japan, Canada and Australia, have been regularly changing sides, every so often joining forces with the US or the EU (Schreurs, 2002). Another divide is the split between North and South, or, stated differently, between developed and developing countries (Newell and Paterson, 1998; Roberts and Parks, 2007). Large developing countries, such as Brazil, China, and India, have stressed the historically high GHG emissions of developed countries, which make these countries also primarily responsible for climate change mitigation. In addition, developing countries have emphasised their right to development in the sense that climate policy should not delay their economic growth (Bodansky, 2001).

Various factors have played a role in explaining cross-country differences in the perception of global climate change: differences in the physical and social impact of a changing climate; in the costs of compliance to international commitments; in public awareness of environmental issues; in dependence on fossil fuels; and in the institutions that govern national politics (Bodansky, 2001; Busby and Ochs, 2004; Fisher, 2004; Kolk, 2000). One overarching factor that seems to explain political positions of countries is the level of GHG emissions that a country generates each year, because it indicates how high the burden of climate change mitigation will be for a country. As Table 1.1 shows, North American countries have seen a steep rise in their GHG emissions since 1990; a similar trend, but more moderate, has applied to Japan; emissions of the European Union have gone down, although just a little. However, within the EU the trend in GHG emissions differs considerably between Member States. Whereas Northern European countries have generally seen declining emissions, in Southern European countries emissions have increased, notably in Spain. Another important development is the sharp decrease in GHG emissions of Russia and Ukraine. This is due to the fact that these economies almost completely collapsed after the fall of the Berlin Wall. This same phenomenon partly explains the considerable decrease of German GHG emissions after the unification of East and West Germany in 1990.

Besides a country's level of GHG emissions, public opinion on how serious a threat climate change is differs as well. Looking at different global public opinion surveys, the picture emerges that perceptions in the US (still) differ from those in other parts of the world. A global survey conducted in 2006 by the Pew Research Center shows that people in the US are much less concerned about climate change than people from Europe or Japan; the only country that has a largely similar profile as the US is China (see Figure 1.2). Another survey conducted by GlobeScan in the same year sheds a comparable picture although the differences are a little less extreme (see Figure 1.3). What these results also reveal is that since 2003 public opinion has changed dramatically and opinions of citizens in different

Table 1.1 Total GHG emissions per country in Gg CO$_2$ equivalent (without land use, land-use change and forestry)

	1990	*1995*	*2002*	*2003*	*2004*	*2005*	*Change from 1990 to 2005 (%)*
EU	4,257,837	4,148,804	4,155,411	4,223,045	4,227,825	4,192,634	−1.5
France	570,949	565,748	560,767	563,363	563,394	560,695	−1.8
Germany	1,227,860	1,095,654	1,017,514	1,030,852	1,024,957	1,001,476	−18.4
UK	771,429	710,140	656,945	662,710	660,446	657,417	−14.8
Spain	287,366	318,370	402,171	409,488	425,236	440,649	53.3
Italy	516,851	530,264	557,816	572,802	577,859	579,548	12.1
US	6,229,041	6,560,936	7,047,178	7,089,204	7,189,715	7,241,482	16.3
Canada	595,954	645,654	720,418	744,952	747,350	746,889	25.3
Australia	418,275	444,656	511,253	514,515	523,590	525,408	25.6
Japan	1,272,043	1,343,636	1,354,922	1,360,230	1,356,989	1,359,914	6.9
Russia	2,989,833	2,092,063	1,996,218	2,063,203	2,086,409	2,132,518	−28.7
Ukraine	923,844	522,882	400,018	415,136	413,381	418,923	−54.7

Source: UNFCCC

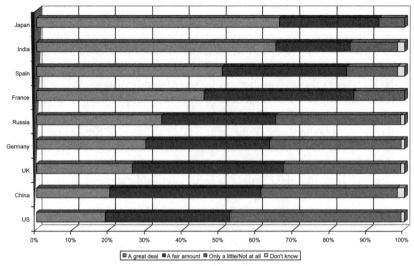

Figure 1.2 Opinion poll on personal concern about global warming.

Source: Pew Research Center (2006)

countries seem to have been converging. This is confirmed by a 2007 survey by GlobeScan, the University of Maryland's Program on International Policy Attitudes (PIPA), and the BBC. This shows that US citizens know as much about climate change as their European or Asian counterparts (see Figure 1.4), but are a

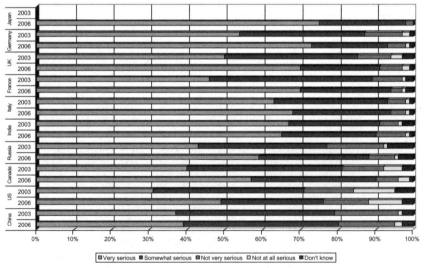

Figure 1.3 Opinion poll on how serious a problem people consider climate change to be.

Source: GlobeScan (2006)

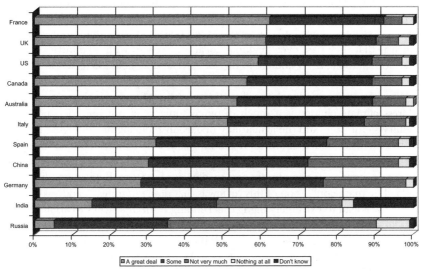

Figure 1.4 Opinion poll on whether people heard or read about global warming or climate change.

Source: GlobeScan/BBC/PIPA (2007)

little less certain that human activity is a significant cause of climate change; interestingly enough, India stands out here in terms of less 'belief' and lower awareness (see Figure 1.5). Nevertheless when it comes to taking major steps to mitigate

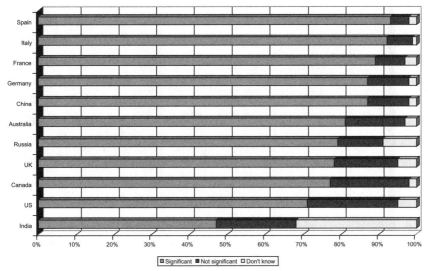

Figure 1.5 Opinion poll on whether people view human activity as a significant cause of climate change.

Source: GlobeScan/BBC/PIPA (2007)

climate change the 2007 survey still shows some differences between the US and (some) European countries (and also China); Indian respondents see much less need to act (see Figure 1.6). Obviously, such polls have their limitations, one of which is that they pass over (regional/local) differences within countries – these have, for example, been notable in the US (Byrne *et al*, 2007; Peterson and Rose, 2006).

What the economic burden will be for countries of taking such major steps to address climate change is a much disputed topic, as it not only depends on a country's emissions and the availability of carbon-reducing technologies, but also on the extent to which countries are willing and able to work co-operatively on the subject (Nordhaus and Yang, 1996). The most authoritative report on the economic impact of climate change to date is the Stern Review, published in 2006. The main conclusion of this review is that doing nothing to address climate change will lead to extremely high costs running from 5 per cent to about 20 per cent of global gross domestic product (GDP). It states that preventing climate change from happening by reducing GHG emissions to a safe level would cost about 1 per cent of global GDP each year. What is more, the report emphasises that it will be necessary to take action within the next 10 to 20 years, otherwise certain adverse impacts of climate change cannot be averted. A recent report by the University of Maryland just focusing on the US concurs with the conclusions of the Stern Review (Ruth *et al*, 2007). Whereas the Bush government has emphasised the economic burden of measures to curb climate change, this report argues that the economic costs of direct and indirect impacts of climate change will be much higher. The authors therefore conclude that not taking any policy

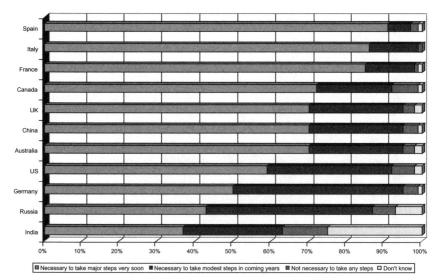

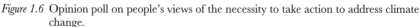

Figure 1.6 Opinion poll on people's views of the necessity to take action to address climate change.

Source: GlobeScan/BBC/PIPA (2007)

action is an even more expensive option for the US, because without efforts to reduce GHG emissions the opportunity is missed to avoid some of the adverse effects of climate change.

What is important as background information for this book are not only facts about country differences regarding climate change, but also what the issue means for different industries. Unfortunately, there is no comprehensive database yet on GHG emissions subdivided per industry or individual company. Nevertheless what contribution each industry makes to a changing climate can be approximated by looking at information on GHG emissions that has been disclosed by (part of) the Global 500, the biggest companies worldwide, through the Carbon Disclosure Project (CDP, 2007). Figure 1.7 shows an industry breakdown of GHG emissions reported by Global 500 companies for 2006 and shows that integrated oil and gas has the highest emissions (25 per cent) from production activities owned or controlled by a company (Scope 1 emissions) and from purchased electricity (Scope 2 emissions), followed by electric utilities – international (23 per cent), metals and mining (12 per cent), electric power companies – North America (10 per cent), multi-utilities and unregulated power (9 per cent), chemicals (3 per cent), and automobiles (1 per cent). All the other sectors combined account for the remainder of 17 per cent of Scope 1 and 2 GHG emissions. Although it seems that integrated oil and gas is the heaviest polluter according to CDP, it must be noted that the power generating industry has been subdivided into three categories, which combined are responsible for 42 per cent of GHG emissions. Data on so-called Scope 3 emissions – indirect emissions from purchased materials, transportation, the use of products and services, business travel, and employee commuting – is even harder to obtain, as only a very modest number of companies measure them. Based on information of the few companies that disclose Scope 3 emissions to CDP, it shows that integrated oil and gas is again topping the list (63 per cent), followed by metals and mining (22 per cent), food products (5 per cent), automobiles (4 per cent), electric utilities – international (3 per cent), and other sectors (3 per cent).

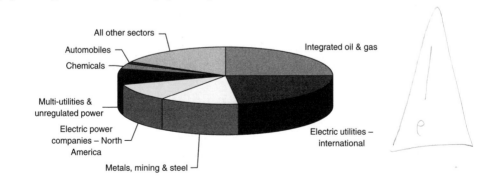

Figure 1.7 Scope 1 and 2 GHG emissions per industry.

Source: Carbon Disclosure Project (2007)

1.3 SETUP OF THIS BOOK

The book is structured as presented in Figure 1.8, and consists of eight chapters, including this first chapter and a short concluding one (Chapter 8). In between, there are two parts (I and II), both with three chapters each (respectively 2, 3 and 4; and 5, 6 and 7). Below we will outline the main tenets of the chapters in both parts. Part I is entitled 'Between regulation and self-regulation', part II 'Strategic options for business'.

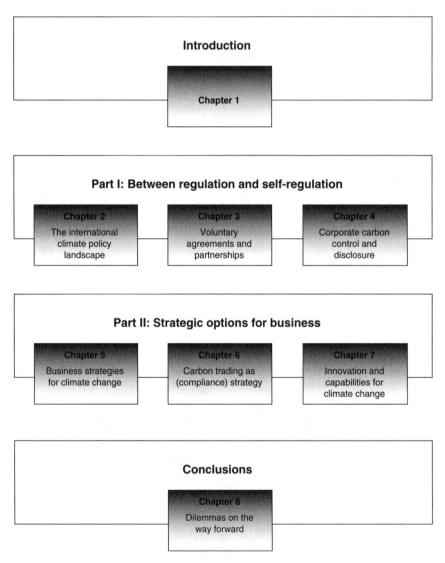

Figure 1.8 Plan of the book.

Chapter 2 gives an overview of the main international policy developments from the early 1990s onwards. The aim of the synopsis is not to provide an extensive discussion of all initiatives over the years, but merely to indicate and briefly explain the most relevant regulatory developments across the world. This covers international, regional and national climate policies. The chapter presents the main climate change policy events to understand the context in which business responses have evolved, thus setting the stage for the rest of the book. If we look at all the different climate change policy instruments that have been implemented or are in the process of being implemented, there is a complex situation for companies operating in these various countries. They face a range of initiatives at the local, national and international levels, some binding, some voluntary, and with a multitude of stakeholders involved. The issue of climate change is characterised by uncertainty as to the (potential) impact on markets, technologies and organisations, with companies helping to shape the future of climate change regimes through voluntary initiatives as well.

The next two chapters subsequently focus on these voluntary initiatives taken by companies, which have evolved against the background of these regulatory developments, and cover the other side of the continuum from regulation to self-regulation. Voluntary initiatives are frequently categorised into three types: voluntary agreements between business and government; multi-stakeholder partnerships involving various constellations of business, NGOs and/or government; and unilateral activities by companies. Chapter 3 deals with the first two categories, Chapter 4 with the third. Chapter 3 thus examines voluntary agreements between business and government; and partnerships between companies and other actors in government and society. There are a large number of existing initiatives and, particularly in the field of partnerships, a wave of emerging ones with different foci and constellations of actors. The chapter discusses nature and types of both, and gives an overview of the main voluntary agreements in a range of countries, as well as of partnerships in which multinationals are involved. While it is difficult to assess effectiveness, especially in the case of partnerships, this has not hampered their spread and growth; they are part of companies' political responses as well.

Voluntary agreements between business and government, and multi-stakeholder partnerships often involve and presuppose a good insight into company emissions, setting clear targets and reporting on progress. Chapter 4 therefore examines individual company self-commitments in the field of climate change. They aim to effectively manage GHG emissions internally and to disclose information on the risks and opportunities of climate change to investors and other external stakeholders. The chapter analyses the various aspects related to emissions management, particularly concerning measurement and target-setting, and the choices to be made in this respect, and outlines considerations and developments in carbon disclosure. It becomes clear that the whole set of business practices for tracking and disclosing climate change-related information has seen great development in the past few years. However, producing reliable information about corporate approaches to climate change still remains a very challenging task as there is a lack of standardisation. While this offers dilemmas for companies, it is also complicating matters for external stakeholders such as investors, regulators and NGOs who would like to compare different companies on their carbon footprint.

Overall, Part I shows that there is still a policy vacuum in view of the diversity of local/regional initiatives without a clear international framework that is being implemented globally. This leaves a clear role for business, and companies have voluntarily taken more responsibility for their impact on the changing climate in a variety of ways.

To explain why this has been the case, Chapter 5 first pays attention to the factors that have influenced corporate activities on climate change. It subsequently examines GHG emission-reduction options available to companies, focusing on the strategic responses that have emerged most recently, and identifies actual patterns of market-oriented actions. These business strategies for climate change consist of different combinations of the market components available to managers. We present a typology that shows that under current, rather flexible regulatory regimes, managers have the possibility of choosing between a greater emphasis on improvements in their business activities through innovation on the one hand, and compensatory approaches granted by the emerging carbon market on the other. An innovation strategy can improve a company's assets and competencies as a result of the development of new climate-friendly technologies or services that reduce emissions. Compensation involves the transfer of emissions or emission-generating activities. Companies can follow these approaches merely on their own or by interacting with external actors, be it other companies in the supply chain or industry, NGOs or government agencies. Chapters 6 and 7 then deal with the two main aims of the climate change strategies identified in the typology: Chapter 6 with compensation, Chapter 7 with innovation.

Chapter 6 examines compensatory approaches, particularly carbon trading, and companies' activities in this area in the face of a range of emerging carbon markets with different characteristics: those that are created as a result of regulatory constraints, and those without regulatory constraints (voluntary markets). Corporate responses are highly dependent on the way in which the political debate on emissions trading has unfolded in recent years and the many ups-and-downs that the emerging carbon market has witnessed so far. The chapter shows that companies have played a large role in the development of the carbon market, because they have not just waited for governments to implement trading schemes. Companies have not only tried to stay in compliance with new regulatory constraints, but have also chosen to respond strategically by avoiding such constraints, using their bargaining power to influence actors that enforce new regulations, and acting in voluntary markets to stay ahead or profit from emerging opportunities. Both compliance and voluntary markets have generated a wave of corporate activities, and the chapter gives an overview of all major trading and offset initiatives.

Although compensation is in an emergent stage, innovative approaches for climate change are even more novel and in their early stages. Chapter 7 examines the peculiarities and most notably the challenges related to innovation for climate change. It analyses which capabilities companies might develop in response to climate change and how far-reaching the influence of climate change is on core business strategies. We discuss how corporate climate change activities build on a company's existing capabilities in other areas of its operations and/or may help create new sources of competitive advantage and thus benefit the company's profitability, growth and/or survival. The overview of capabilities that may play a role in the case of climate change is followed by a discussion of some of the key challenges in successfully innovating for climate change. In identifying these challenges, we draw attention to the importance of industry peculiarities in determining the degree of innovation that might be possible at all. The impact of climate change capabilities also depends on companies' position in the supply chain and their geographical spread. In explaining these challenges, we give various examples of industries and companies where innovation and climate change capabilities seem feasible or are emergent.

Chapter 8, finally, briefly reflects on the some of the dilemmas on the way forward in the post-Kyoto setting as they have come to the fore in our study of business and climate change, and its evolution over a period of more than a decade.

Part I

Between regulation and self-regulation

2 From Rio to 'Beyond Kyoto': Synopsis of international climate policies

This chapter will give an overview of the main international policy developments from the early 1990s onwards. The aim of this synopsis is not to provide an extensive discussion of all initiatives over the years, but merely to indicate and briefly explain the most relevant regulatory developments around the world. This covers international, regional and national climate policies. The chapter describes the basic climate change policy events, giving particular attention to emissions trading, to understand the context in which business responses have evolved. Chapter 3 will subsequently focus on the voluntary co-operative initiatives taken by companies, including voluntary agreements and multi-stakeholder partnerships on climate change, that have evolved against the background of these developments.

Over the years, there has been considerable attention given to the types of environmental policy instruments available as well as their pros and cons. Generally speaking, interest has moved away from the traditional command-and-control approach, in which the government sets legally binding standards for emissions limits or the specific technology to be used, to market-based instruments – sometimes called second-wave policies, since they emerged later, in the 1980s. In climate change policies, which started in the 1990s, command-and-control has been much less important than market-based instruments.

Scholars have emphasised that market-based instruments are more cost-effective than traditional regulation to achieve the same level of effectiveness, because they rely on the efficiency of the market mechanism; they also grant companies more flexibility (cf. Hahn and Stavins, 1992; Tietenberg, 1990). In particular, an emissions trading system creates incentives to reduce emissions with technologies that are most appropriate and beneficial to companies. However, the functioning and thus the effectiveness of emissions trading depend on a number of factors related to the design of such schemes and in part the political involvement of companies. Companies have obviously tried to influence the emerging carbon market to their benefit. They have lobbied directly and through their national governments to achieve the best outcome – individually and collectively through business and industry-specific associations (for more details see Chapter 6).

In these complex lobbying processes, some companies have been better placed than others; in particular the large ones are usually more influential in view of their impact on employment and economic growth. Moreover, closely related to this, their managers have better access to politicians and know how to use their position. Companies have also helped shape the direction and contents of various policy instruments by formulating proposals and by coming up with their own individual or collective voluntary initiatives. To these, we will turn in Chapters 3 and 4. First this chapter will summarise the main policy developments over the years, as well as introducing the components of the Kyoto market mechanisms, most notably emissions trading, and the Clean Development Mechanism (CDM).

2.1 POLICY DEVELOPMENTS ON CLIMATE CHANGE

International policy on climate change started with the adoption of the United Nations Framework Convention on Climate Change (UNFCCC) at the United Nations Conference on Environment and Development in Rio de Janeiro in 1992. This agreement marked the beginning of a long process of international policy developments on climate change, as shown in Table 2.1. UNFCCC was a broad

Table 2.1 Overview of policy developments on climate change

Year	Policy/event	Elaboration
1992	Framework Convention on Climate Change	Adopted at the United Nations Conference on Environment and Development (Rio de Janeiro); expression of intent by industrialised countries to stabilise emissions at 1990 levels by the year 2000; no mandatory emission curbs.
1992 & 1995	EU carbon tax proposal	The European Commission proposed in 1992 a carbon tax that would raise prices of fossil and nuclear energy by 50%. The proposal was conditional on the introduction of a similar tax by the US and Japan. In 1995 a carbon tax was proposed without this condition. Both proposals failed because several EU countries refused to accept the tax.
1997	Kyoto Protocol (COP 3)	Agreement on reduction targets for greenhouse gases compared to 1990 levels, to be reached in 2008–2012. Differentiated targets per country/region, e.g. Australia +8%; Canada –6%; Japan –6%; Russia 0%; US –7%; EU –8%. EU overall target translated into specific ones for member countries, e.g. Germany –21%, France 0%, Italy –6.5%, Spain +15%, UK –12.5%.
1998	COP 4 in Buenos Aires	First Conference of Parties after Kyoto. Confirmation of the Kyoto agreement and adoption of a 'Plan of Action' to implement the Protocol.
1999	COP 5 in Bonn	A 'process meeting' which showed different views. Discussion points were targets for developing countries (China and India refused to accept targets) and the EU–US disagreement on restrictions on the use of the flexible mechanisms. Agreement to conclude final negotiations on global greenhouse gas emissions by November 2000.

2000	EU renewable energy proposal	Proposal of the European Commission to set 'indicative' national targets for renewable energy production with the aim to double energy consumption from renewables to 12% by 2010.
2000	COP 6 in The Hague	Failure to achieve agreement between the US and EU. Main issues concerned rules for emissions trading and the Clean Development Mechanism. The issue on which the negotiations ultimately failed was the use of forests and farmlands as carbon sinks, which was favoured by the US, but contested by the EU.
2001	IPCC 3rd Assessment Report	Third report by the Intergovernmental Panel on Climate Change (IPCC), released in January. It contained expectations that the consequences of climate change will be greater than expressed in earlier assessments.
2001	US rejection of Kyoto Protocol	In March 2001 the Bush administration declared that it would not implement the Kyoto Protocol and intended to withdraw the US signature.
2001	Launch of US alternative 'science-based' climate plan	Some 'softening' of the US stance in June, shown in the proposal of an alternative 'science-based' response to climate change. Main elements were increased research expenditure for energy efficiency improvements and voluntary measures for industry.
2001	Bonn Agreement on Kyoto implementation	Agreement by the EU, Japan, Canada, Australia, Russia, and a number of developing countries on the rules for the reduction of GHG emissions as laid down in the Kyoto Protocol. Concessions of the EU included allowing emissions trading and the limited use of forests and agricultural land as carbon sinks, which enabled Japan to meet its targets.
2001	EU emissions trading scheme proposal	Proposal by the European Commission to set up an emissions trading scheme to come into effect from 2005 onwards.
2001	COP 7 in Marrakech	2001 Bonn Agreement turned into a legal text. Further concessions won by Russia and Japan on the use of carbon sinks and the ability to sell surplus emissions credits.
2002	EU Kyoto Ratification	EU agreement to ratify the Kyoto Protocol by the end of May 2002.
2002	Launch of UK emissions trading scheme	The UK government opened a national emissions trading scheme in April. Under the scheme, companies received a limited amount of emissions allowances that served as a 'cap' on their carbon emissions, which they are allowed to trade.
2002	COP 8 in New Delhi	The eighth Conference of Parties put the position and vulnerability of developing countries central. India criticised calls for emissions targets for developing countries and stressed the growing tension between the developed and developing world on climate change.
2003	McCain-Lieberman plan	Senators McCain and Lieberman propose a bipartisan plan to introduce industry-wide caps on GHG emissions and to set up an emissions trading scheme. The bill failed

(Continued overleaf)

Table 2.1 Continued

Year	Policy/event	Elaboration
		to pass US Congress by 12 votes, which was commonly viewed as a positive sign.
2003	Opposition of US states to federal government climate policy	Twelve US states file a lawsuit against the Environmental Protection Agency for denying responsibility for GHG emissions (reflecting their opposition to the US federal policy). US Northeast states also develop (regional and perhaps later EU-linked) 'cap-and-trade' plans.
2003	Chicago Climate Exchange (CCX)	Start of this voluntary trading scheme (which is legally binding for member organisations to meet reduction targets of 6% by 2010 compared to average 1998–2001 greenhouse gas emissions).
2003	Regional Greenhouse Gas Initiative (RGGI)	Initiative in the US by Northeast and Mid-Atlantic states to discuss a regional cap-and-trade programme that will initially cover CO_2 emissions from power plants but can be extended later.
2004	COP 10 in Buenos Aires	Disagreement about future of Kyoto Protocol after 2012 (to come up with new negotiation rules/targets by 2008); weak compromise found for a 2005 seminar to exchange information.
2005	Start of EU ETS	On 1 January 2005, the EU emissions trading scheme started.
2005	Kyoto Protocol entered into force	On 16 February 2005, the Kyoto Protocol entered into force with the official ratification by Russia. In 2004, President Putin had announced that Russia intended to ratify (as a 'quid pro quo' for EU's acceptance of Russian WTO admission).
2005	New South Wales Greenhouse Plan	Australian state plan to reduce greenhouse gas emissions to 2000 levels by 2025, and realise 60% reductions by 2050.
2005	Kyoto Protocol Achievement Plan	Adopted by Japanese government; implies dissemination of technology, emissions reporting and voluntary use of Kyoto Mechanisms.
2005	COP 11 in Montreal	First meeting of the parties to the Kyoto Protocol (COP/MOP-1); Marrakech Accords were adopted and a four-track path was initiated to discuss future action on climate policy beyond 2012.
2006	US State of the Union	US President Bush called for an end to the US addiction to oil and proposed to step up development of clean technologies, e.g. ethanol.
2006	Asia-Pacific Partnership on Clean Development and Climate	Brings together Australia, China, India, Japan, South Korea and US in what has been labelled as an 'alternative to Kyoto' attempt that focuses on voluntary, non-binding steps relying on clean technology.
2006	California Global Warming Solutions Act	Mandates a cap of California's greenhouse gas emissions at 1990 levels by 2020.

2006	Stern Review	Sir Nicholas Stern, a former World Bank economist, published a report on the economic impact of climate change. It argued that not addressing climate change will lead to costs running from 5% to about 20% of global GDP, while preventing would cost about 1% of global GDP each year.
2006	COP 12 Nairobi	Lack of progress on post-Kyoto climate policy due to refusal of US and developing countries to commit to binding targets. More attention to adaptation to climate change because COP was held in sub-Saharan Africa.
2007	Launch of EU climate change targets	EU launched new targets to prevent warming of more than 2°C before 2020 including 20% reduction in GHGs (30% if other industrialised countries come aboard); 20% improvement in energy efficiency; 20% of energy use from renewable sources; 10% of transport fuel consumption by biofuels.
2007	IPCC 4th Assessment Report	Fourth report by the Intergovernmental Panel on Climate Change (IPCC), released in February. It reaffirmed findings that global temperatures are rising and that this development is very likely to have been induced by human-caused GHG emissions.
2007	California Climate Exchange (CaCX)	Launched by the Chicago Climate Exchange to developing trading instruments related to the California Global Warming Solutions Act.
2007	Western Climate Initiative	Initiative by Western states in the US and two Canadian provinces to realise a regional, economy-wide reduction target of 15% per cent below 2005 levels by 2020, using market based systems such as a cap-and-trade programme. Builds on two earlier initiatives: the West Coast Governors' Global Warming Initiative (2003) and the Southwest Climate Change Initiative (2006).
2007	US mayors' climate protection agreement	Signed by 600 mayors in all 50 US states and Puerto Rico. Involves a commitment to cut greenhouse gas emissions by 7% in 2010 compared to 1990 (which is the US Kyoto target). Initiative was started in 2005 by the mayor of Seattle.
2007	Canadian Regulatory Framework for Air Emissions	Successor to earlier plan launched by the previous government in 2005. The 2007 plan aims to realise a 20% reduction of greenhouse gas emissions by 2030 compared to 2006.
2007	Australia Climate Exchange (ACX)	Launched Australia's first emissions trading platform.
2007	Australia and New Zealand intended joint emissions trading	Announcement by Australia and New Zealand to join forces in the development of carbon-trading systems that would be compatible. Follows on earlier statement by Australia that it intends to move towards a domestic, nationwide emissions trading system per 2012.
2007	Sydney APEC declaration on climate change	Adopted by 21 Pacific Rim countries (including Australia, US, Canada, Russia, China, Japan); includes an aspirational goal of a reduction in energy intensity of at least 25% by 2030 compared to 2005, and support for a post-2012 international climate agreement.

(Continued overleaf)

Table 2.1 Continued

Year	Policy/event	Elaboration
2007	Midwestern Greenhouse Gas Reduction Accord	Initiative by the Midwestern US states Minnesota, Wisconsin, Illinois, Iowa, Michigan, and Kansas, as well as the Canadian Province of Manitoba to set a cap on GHG emissions and develop an emissions trading scheme by 2010. Indiana, Ohio, and South Dakota are also part of the Accord, but merely as observers to participate in the formation of the regional cap-and-trade system.
2007	Australia ratifies Kyoto Protocol	Early December the new Prime Minister Kevin Rudd ratified the Kyoto Protocol, making the US the only non-ratifying industrialised country.
2007	COP 13 Bali	Establishment of the 'Bali Action Plan'; an agreement to start negotiating a post-2012 internal framework for climate change policy as a follow-up to the Kyoto Protocol.

Source: Adapted/updated from Kolk and Hoffmann, 2007; Kolk and Pinkse, 2005b

plan for action, but did not set clear targets for the reduction of greenhouse gas emissions other than the objective for a stabilisation in 2000 at the 1990 level. While there were international discussions about the issue in subsequent years, it was not until 1997 that countries agreed upon more detailed, differentiated reduction targets under the Kyoto Protocol (Grubb *et al*, 1999). However, in the years following Kyoto, the negotiations about the exact rules for implementation of the Protocol have been very turbulent. This has created great complexity for multinationals in particular since the specific shape of their home and host country governments' climate policies continues to be uncertain.

The negotiations about the implementation of the Kyoto Protocol most obviously took place at the so-called Conference of Parties (COP) meetings. The first COP after Kyoto was held in Buenos Aires in 1998, where parties reaffirmed their commitment to the Protocol. However, in 1999, at the COP in Bonn, some fundamental disagreements between countries emerged. First, the US pushed for the inclusion of, and thus targets for, developing countries, which was opposed by India and China in particular. Second, the EU called for a restriction on the use of emissions trading, offset projects and carbon sinks, whereas the US favoured an approach with maximum flexibility and no limits on the use of these mechanisms.

These differences had already been visible in the years leading up to the Kyoto Protocol. The policy measure originally put forward in the EU in these years was some form of carbon tax. However, two proposals (in 1992 and 1995) to implement an EU-wide carbon tax failed due to lack of agreement between the Member States (Christiansen and Wettestad, 2003). By contrast, the US introduced the option of GHG emissions trading in the discussion, because it had good experiences with similar trading schemes for the reduction of sulphur and nitrogen oxides (Grubb *et al*, 1999). It was the conflict between the US and EU that led to the failure of the climate talks at the sixth COP in The Hague in

November 2000. The use of forests and farmlands as carbon sinks formed the central issue on which the negotiations collapsed. In March 2001, hopes that the Kyoto Protocol would enter into force soon were blown when US President Bush decided to reject it altogether, based on the argument that ratification would harm the US economy and its international competitiveness.

In the course of 2001, however, the US government experienced considerable pressure to reconsider its position towards the Kyoto Protocol. As a result, the negative stance was alleviated somewhat and an alternative, 'science-based', climate change plan was presented, which emphasised a technology-based solution to global warming that would not harm competitiveness. One month after the launch of this US proposal, negotiations in Bonn, which aimed to 'save' the Kyoto Protocol and move on without the US, resulted in an agreement between the EU, Japan, Russia, Australia, Canada and a large number of developing countries. The EU made concessions to Japan and Russia by allowing unrestricted use of the flexible mechanisms (emissions trading, Clean Development Mechanism and Joint Implementation), and to Canada and Australia by allowing (limited) use of forests and farmlands as carbon sinks. The 2001 Bonn agreement put the US in an isolated position. Shortly afterwards, the European Commission adopted a proposal to start a European Union emissions trading scheme (EU ETS) in 2005 (EC, 2003). Looking back at the negotiations preceding the Bonn agreement, it is remarkable that the EU had become the main advocate of the policy measure they rejected for years: emissions trading (Christiansen and Wettestad, 2003).

At the next COP in Marrakech, the political agreement of Bonn was turned into a legal text that enabled the ratification of the Kyoto Protocol (Den Elzen and De Moor, 2002). Since then most parties, including the EU, Japan and Canada, ratified the Kyoto Protocol, while the US and Australia have not done the same. It was only at the end of 2007, following a change of government, that Australia chose to ratify after all. After long hesitation, Russia eventually ratified in February 2005, thus putting the Protocol into force (Henry and McIntosh Sundstrom, 2007). In spite of this 'landmark', the international climate change arena has continued to exhibit changes, with implications and/or active roles for companies. At least three notable developments should be mentioned.

First, there still exists uncertainty about what will be the future of the Kyoto Protocol after 2012. Discussions about emissions reduction targets (including potentially those for developing countries) after the first commitment period (2008–2012) started in Buenos Aires (2004), but only a weak 'compromise' could be found. Since then, several meetings have reaffirmed countries' willingness to continue discussions. The COP in Montreal (2005) appeared to lead to a breakthrough, as at least a dialogue was initiated to discuss future action, which proved to be an important signal to business that Kyoto's flexible mechanisms will continue beyond 2012 (Depledge and Grubb, 2006). However, one year later in Nairobi (2006) not much progress was made (Pew Center, 2006). Only at the COP in Bali in December 2007 did participating countries finally come to an agreement to start negotiating a post-2012 global climate policy framework as a follow-up to the Kyoto Protocol.

Discussions on future action have centred on two issues. First the topic of reduction targets for developing countries has been and will be contentious. It was already raised at international climate talks in New Delhi (2002) when India repeated its refusal to impose targets, based on the argument that industrialised countries have traditionally been the main contributors to global warming and are thus responsible for its solution. A second, closely related issue has been the long-standing unwillingness on the part of the US to agree to legally-binding commitments as long as developing countries have no emissions reduction targets (Depledge and Grubb, 2006). Besides the UN, countries have also started to discuss post-Kyoto climate policy in other political arenas. Most noteworthy has been the 2007 Asia-Pacific Economic Cooperation (APEC) Sydney Declaration on climate change, which set the non-binding target to improve energy efficiency by at least 25 per cent by 2030 and to increase forest cover by 20 million hectares within 13 years. However, due to the fact that this declaration lacks a binding commitment and does not target GHG emissions directly, it has been much criticised as being just a distraction from the UN approach.

A second development is the emergence of technology-oriented agreements, which have been introduced on national and international levels (de Coninck *et al*, 2007; Philibert, 2005). A technology-oriented agreement is an alternative kind of climate policy compared to the Kyoto Protocol's binding commitment approach, which is aimed at research and development and/or transfer and deployment of emissions-reducing technologies. An international case in point of a technology-oriented agreement is the Asia-Pacific Partnership on Clean Development and Climate, launched in 2006. In the Asia-Pacific Partnership the US and Australia aim to work together with China, India, Japan, and South Korea on the transfer and deployment of technologies that improve energy efficiency and reduce air pollution and GHG intensities (Asia-Pacific Partnership, 2006). There has been quite some discussion whether this Partnership has been put in place as a substitute for or complement to the Kyoto Protocol (McGee and Taplin, 2006). While the Asian countries involved in the Partnership have argued against the fact that it is a substitute for Kyoto (Tiberghien and Schreurs, 2007), nevertheless at its launch Australia in particular positioned it as such (Crowley, 2007).

With regard to technology-oriented agreements, it has been argued that agreements aimed at knowledge sharing, research, development and demonstration, and technology transfer, although useful in their own regard, cannot form a substitute for a commitment-based approach; only a mandate for deployment of particular technologies could be just as effective environmentally (de Coninck *et al*, 2007). Technology mandates have been taking shape in many different countries recently. One example is the renewable portfolio standard that many US states have put in place (see section 2.3). However, technology-based climate policies are not limited to the US. The EU has also started to employ this approach, first with the 2001 EU Renewables Directive which set an EU-wide target to use 22 per cent renewables in electricity production by 2010 (EC, 2001) and more recently with the adoption in 2007 of an indicative target to have 20 per cent of the EU's energy consumption coming from renewables in 2020 (EC, 2007).

A third development has not been a direct change in international climate policy as such, but a string of events occurring over a period of about one year that has considerably increased the saliency of climate change and heightened the urgency of climate policy. The first of these events is the release of Al Gore's movie An Inconvenient Truth (24 May 2006). The success of this movie has had a huge impact on the public perception of climate change. What further contributed to its impact has been the fact that Al Gore won two Oscars for the movie and, together with the IPCC, received the Nobel Peace Prize in 2007. A second event was the publication of the Stern Review on 30 October 2006. The main merit of the Stern Review was that its lead author – Sir Nicholas Stern – was the World Bank's former chief-economist with no ties to the environmental movement whatsoever. As a consequence climate change was no longer seen as an issue propagated by environmental activists, but had become an important global issue which could have a huge economic impact. The third in this string of events was the publication of the IPCC's 4th assessment report in the period from February to May 2007. This assessment report reaffirmed the fact that global temperatures are rising and that it is very likely, with over 90 per cent certainty, that human-induced GHG emissions have caused this to happen.

To summarise, then, since the inception of the 1997 Kyoto Protocol global climate change seems to have become a widely salient issue appealing to voters all over the world (cf. Bonardi and Keim, 2005), especially in more recent years (Brewer, 2006). However, it is also clear that the international policy context on climate change can hardly be characterised as a 'level playing field' in the post-Kyoto period. It is not only difficult to keep track of the exact details of climate policy on an international level, but also on a national level. Even though many countries have ratified the Kyoto Protocol, it is still not evident in most cases how national governments intend to meet their targets. This means that there is ample room, and perhaps also necessity, for companies to try to influence the direction and contents of climate change measures, at national and international levels. Most concretely, they have done this by helping to shape the emergent market mechanisms included in the Kyoto Protocol, particularly the emissions trading schemes.

2.2 INTERNATIONAL CLIMATE POLICIES

Climate change policies, which started in the 1990s, have mostly been based on market-based instruments instead of the then prevailing command-and-control regulation. The main market-based instrument for climate change is emissions trading through a 'cap-and-trade' system. It was the Kyoto Protocol that first established emissions trading for the purpose of climate change mitigation. Under the Protocol participating countries are allowed to exchange part of their obligations with another party (Grubb *et al* 1999). This intergovernmental emissions trading regime, which enables *countries* to transfer GHG emissions, has led to the creation of domestic systems to trade emissions at a *company* level. This means that companies need a permit to emit greenhouse gases and governments allocate allowances that determine how much ('the cap'). If individual countries launch similar 'national' emissions trading schemes, in theory the two can be linked and companies can engage in cross-border trade of emissions allowances (Blyth and Bosi, 2004). However, in practice this has not occurred yet, as the implementation of company-level emissions trading schemes has seen great diversity across the world (see Chapter 6 for more details).

In addition to emissions trading, the Kyoto Protocol also established two projected-based instruments: Joint Implementation (JI) and the Clean Development Mechanism (CDM). They allow countries to reduce emissions resulting from cross-border investments (Grubb *et al* 1999). JI can only be used between two countries that both have an obligation to reduce emissions; they have to agree on how to divide the 'reduction credits'. In the case of CDM, the receiving country of a cross-border investment is a developing country that does not have an obligation to reduce emissions (yet). The investing country can thus use all obtained credits for compliance with its own commitment. CDM was introduced in the negotiations of the Kyoto Protocol as a compromise towards developing countries. As a consequence, the goal of CDM is not only to enable developed countries to engage in projects in developing countries and thus lower their mitigation costs, but also to use these projects for promoting sustainable development and transferring emissions-reducing technologies to developing countries (Lecocq and Ambrosi, 2007).

Notably, CDM credits from early project activities (from 2000 onwards) could already be used for compliance in the first commitment period (2008–2012). Consequently, CDM became operational already before the Kyoto Protocol came into force (Streck, 2004) and has already become an active market within a few years (Lecocq and Ambrosi, 2007). Both JI and CDM are important mechanisms for business, because investments in such projects are not limited to national governments but allow industry involvement (private investments). To illustrate, although at the outset the World Bank and the Government of the Netherlands were main participants in the CDM market, in 2006 already 80 per cent of all transactions were by private companies (Lecocq and Ambrosi, 2007). CDM is particularly attractive to companies because this mechanism enables companies to deploy existing climate-friendly technologies to developing countries. It is the extra revenue generated by the CDM credits that makes these technology transfers commercially viable in a developing country context, which might not be the case without CDM (Arquit Niederberger and Saner, 2005).

Although the Kyoto Protocol has established emissions trading between countries as well as JI and CDM, it does not require participating countries to also implement a domestic emissions trading scheme applying to companies (Blyth and Bosi, 2004). After ratifying the Protocol, countries have to draw up a plan specifying how they intend to meet their Kyoto target, but a domestic emissions trading scheme is just one of the options. As a consequence, governments across the globe have implemented a wide variety of policy instruments as part of their domestic climate policies, many of which are aimed at companies, but many also promote emissions reductions from households, transportation, and agriculture.

What is more, policy instruments to reduce company-related GHG emissions not only include (plans for) implementing a domestic trading scheme and facilitating private involvement in CDM and JI, but also measures to promote energy efficiency, the use of renewable energy, diffusion of climate-friendly technologies, and development of cleaner vehicles. What many climate policy instruments have in common is that in addition to emissions trading most are currently also to some extent market-based using market forces to enhance cost efficiency (Oikonomou and Jepma, 2008), and granting companies considerable flexibility in complying.

2.3 REGIONAL AND NATIONAL CLIMATE POLICIES

2.3.1 The European Union

At the centre of the EU's climate change plan to comply with the Kyoto Protocol is the European Union emissions trading scheme (EU ETS). The EU ETS started in January 2005 and is particularly aimed at energy-intensive activities as it only covers CO_2 emissions (Egenhofer, 2007; Haar and Haar, 2006). While it is meant to ensure harmonisation of emissions trading across the EU, the detailed plans for the allocation of allowances (National Allocation Plans) and for monitoring participants' emissions data are left to the individual Member States. Through a 'linking directive', credits earned with JI and CDM can be used to fulfil the obligations under the EU ETS. It is again up to Member States whether a limit will be imposed on the use of such credits (EC, 2004). Although the EU ETS is the main policy instrument in the EU climate change plan, several other instruments have also been adopted to target a wider range of sectors in addition to greenhouse gases.

A comprehensive outline of EU climate policy was presented early on in 2007 when the EU launched new targets to prevent warming of more than 2°C before 2020 (EC, 2007). The EU conveyed the intention to achieve 20 per cent reduction in greenhouse gases (30 per cent if other industrialised countries come aboard); 20 per cent improvement in energy efficiency; 20 per cent of energy use from renewable sources; and 10 per cent use of biofuels for transport fuel consumption (all by 2020). These targets mainly fall in line with or build on several directives that have been passed over the years. For example, in 2001 the EU implemented the above-mentioned directive on renewable electricity, which sets an indicative target to use 22 per cent renewables in electricity production by 2010.[1] The EU intended to harmonise the 'support schemes' each country uses to achieve this renewable electricity target, but failed to realise this.

Regarding support schemes, the EU had a preference for a market-based tradable certificates model where utilities have the choice to either generate renewable electricity themselves or buy it from others in the form of green certificates. However, several countries had already adopted alternative models, e.g. Germany

---

1   It must be noted, however, that this target is a European average, as specific targets differ per Member State (Rowlands, 2005).

uses a 'feed-in tariff' which obliges utilities to buy a certain amount of renewable electricity at a set price, which they were not willing to replace by a market-based policy instrument (Rowlands, 2005). With regard to energy efficiency, policy measures have already been put in place in response to the oil crises of the 1970s, but predominantly on a national instead of an EU level (Geller *et al*, 2006). Nevertheless, the EU still tries to have a role in the promotion of energy efficiency and in 2006 passed a directive on energy end-use efficiency and energy services (EC, 2006). The EU has also implemented separate policies to reduce other GHG emissions. For example, in 2006 the EU passed regulation controlling three so-called F-gases – hydrofluorocarbons (HFCs), perfluorocarbons (PFCs), and sulphur hexafluoride (SF6) – which have a very high global warming potential because they stay in the atmosphere much longer than CO_2.

What becomes clear when looking at European climate policy is that although the EU plays a central role in drawing up broad-based policies, often accompanied by indicative and/or binding targets, much activity also takes place on a national level. While it might seem that this predominantly applies to policies to promote energy efficiency and renewable electricity, emissions trading has also seen some national initiatives. The EU established an emissions trading scheme in 2005, but this step had already been taken earlier by Denmark and the UK. Denmark launched a CO_2 emissions trading scheme for electricity producers in 1999 (suspended at the end of 2004), while the UK introduced a scheme in 2002 that covers more industries and GHGs (almost completely suspended in March 2007).

2.3.2 Japan

Other industrial countries that ratified the Kyoto Protocol have not yet created climate policy instruments as elaborate as the EU ETS. To start with Japan, although the Kyoto Protocol has had a huge impact on the public interest for climate change in this country and was the most important stimulus to develop domestic climate change policies, progress in implementing specific measures for GHG emissions reduction has been rather slow. What is of particular importance for understanding the situation that Japan finds itself in is the fact that it has committed to a 6 per cent reduction target, because it followed the US which had a 7 per cent reduction target (Kameyama, 2004). However, this target is generally seen as too ambitious because marginal costs for Japan to reduce emissions are the highest in the world, mainly because it lacks a large energy industry involved in the production of crude oil (Jung *et al*, 2005), meaning that there is no 'low-hanging fruit'. One of the reasons why Japan nevertheless supported the Kyoto Protocol is the symbolic value of the fact that the protocol carries the name of a Japanese city. As such, it has been argued that Kyoto has come to stand for a bigger role of Japan in global environmental politics. However, even though Kyoto as a symbol for global climate change led to ratification, it did not have the same effect on the implementation of policy measures to reduce GHG emissions (Tiberghien and Schreurs, 2007).

Almost directly after the Kyoto Protocol, Japanese climate policy took off with the establishment of the Global Warming Prevention Headquarters, which in 1998 launched a Guideline of Measures to Prevent Global Warming (Kameyama, 2004) followed by a revised version in 2002 (Jung *et al*, 2005). However, what had already become visible at the negotiations of the Kyoto Protocol and has held back the implementation of more comprehensive climate policy instruments ever since, is a fundamental disagreement between the Ministry of Environment (MoE) and the Ministry of Economy, Trade and Industry (METI) on how to tackle climate change (Schreurs, 2002; Tiberghien and Schreurs, 2007). To illustrate, in 2004, the MoE proposed a voluntary emissions trading scheme as well as a carbon tax, but Japanese companies strongly opposed such a voluntary scheme because they feared it might become obligatory, with METI underlining the harmful effect for Japanese companies' competitiveness (Arita, 2004; Watanabe, 2005).

Japan's climate policy is set down in the 2005 Kyoto Target Achievement Plan (GWPH, 2005), which sets emissions reductions targets for the most important industrial sources of GHGs. One of its main components is a voluntary, but non-binding target already put in place in 1997 by Japan's most important business federation – the Keidanren – to stabilise CO_2 emissions at the level of 1990 by 2010. In addition, it contains the Top Runner Programme (originally launched in 1998 as part of the Energy Conservation Law), which demands that all new products need to become just as energy-efficient as the most efficient product in its product class (Geller *et al*, 2006). The plan also aims to promote the utilisation of JI and CDM, an intention which later led to setting up a carbon credit procurement programme (Watanabe, 2005). Compared to emissions trading, these flexible mechanisms can count on much more support from Japanese industry, because CDM in particular is viewed as a cost-effective way to take advantage of prior investments (Arita, 2005).

However, although no agreement has yet been reached to introduce a carbon tax, there has been more activity in Japan with regard to emissions trading. Both MoE and METI conducted pilot projects to test the workings of emissions trading, and the MoE followed this up with the launch of a voluntary emissions trading scheme in 2005; a scheme which combines emissions trading with subsidies for emissions-reducing projects (Watanabe, 2005). Some companies such as Matsushita and Konica also set up internal trading schemes. The only fundamental aspect of climate policy that the MoE and METI could agree on was the introduction of GHG reporting standards in 2005, demanding large Japanese companies to publicly report their annual CO_2 emissions (Watanabe, 2005).

2.3.3 Canada

Canada's way of dealing with the Kyoto Protocol bears many similarities with that of Japan. Up until the Kyoto Protocol, Canada had always sided with the US. This is not surprising as Canada's level and increase of GHG emissions is comparable to the US (Rabe, 2007) and both economies are highly interdependent due to international trade (Harrison, 2007). As with Japan, Canada's commitment to a 6 per cent reduction under the Kyoto Protocol was set after consulting the US government which committed to a 7 per cent reduction. Nevertheless, within the country Canada experienced much resistance against this commitment. Important in this respect has been the role of the province of Alberta, whose economy largely depends on its oil industry that is winning oil from tar sands (Brouhle and Harrington, 2007; Harrison, 2007; Rabe, 2007). However, in the process of ratifying the Protocol, Canada's path parted from the US. This was due to the fact that Canada profited from concessions the EU made to Japan. But what may have been even more important is Canada's political system which enabled the Prime Minister to ratify the Protocol in spite of resistance from provinces, industry and other political parties (Harrison, 2007).[2] Still, it seems that domestic resistance has affected Canada's plans to meet its Kyoto target. Although the positions of Canada and the US are different with regard to the Kyoto Protocol, the type of climate policy instruments that have been implemented are still quite similar, as both countries rely on investments in climate change research, voluntary targets for industry and a few tax incentives (Harrison, 2007).

Canada launched several plans over the years to specify how it intended to meet its Kyoto target. To develop these plans, the Canadian Federal Government has been engaged in a large number of consultation processes and round tables. In 2002, this finally led to the 'Climate Change Plan for Canada', which gave a rough idea by what process Canada would stabilise and reduce GHG emissions, and contained a proposal for developing a domestic emissions trading scheme at some point in the future (Rabe, 2007). However, this climate change plan has been predominantly characterised as a 'plan to develop a plan', lacking specifics and without making any budgetary commitments for the projects it announced (Harrison, 2007: 17). In 2005, the Federal Government issued a follow-up plan called Project Green (Canadian Government, 2005). This contained emissions targets focusing on mining and manufacturing, oil and gas, and electric utilities, designated as large final emitters (LFEs).[3] Although the plan proposed that companies may purchase emission reductions from other LFEs with excess reductions, no exact rules for such trades were indicated. What is more, it did not constitute a real 'cap-and-trade' system, but mainly a different form of granting subsidies (Harrison, 2007). The plan also established a Climate Fund that buys credits from

2   To compare, in the US the Clinton–Gore Administration was not able to ratify the Kyoto Protocol as its ratification depended on US Congress which was highly opposed to it (Harrison, 2007). Pivotal in this regard has been the Byrd–Hagel resolution, which states that no international climate treaty would be accepted unless it showed proof of meaningful developing country participation and commitment. This resolution was passed unanimously (95–0) by the Senate just before the Kyoto negotiations (Selin and VanDeveer, 2007). Since its failure to pass the Senate was known beforehand, the Protocol was 'dead on arrival' and was never sent to Congress (Rabe, 2007).

3   Since March 2004, major emitters (more than 100 kilotonnes of GHGs per year) are also obliged to report their emissions. These mandatory reporting rules were extended in 2005 and were supposed to form the basis for a more elaborate mandatory reporting scheme for the LFE programme by 2008.

emissions reduction projects on behalf of the Canadian Government; its focus was domestic reduction or offset projects, but international projects (under JI or CDM) were not excluded. Compared to the EU ETS, the Canadian plan envisaged a much larger intermediary role for the Government in the carbon market. However, this 2005 plan was never put in force and was seemingly replaced by a 'made-in-Canada' strategy towards the Kyoto Protocol (Rabe, 2007).

Since the start of 2006, with the Conservatives winning the elections, Canada's standpoint vis-à-vis the Kyoto Protocol has become very turbulent (Stoett, 2006). In April 2006 the then environment minister for Canada dismissed the Protocol and expressed a preference for the approach the US is taking, relying on voluntary measures by industry. In addition the budget for climate change programmes was cut by 40 per cent. In October of the same year a new Clean Air act was presented which reflected this new stance of the Canadian Government, outlining the 'made-in-Canada' approach. However, this plan received so much criticism that it ultimately led to the resignation of the environment minister, particularly because it became apparent that climate change was to be one of the main issues in upcoming elections. In April 2007 the new environment minister proposed a plan which supposedly envisaged a reversal of the previous plan. However, this was also heavily criticised because the GHG emission reduction targets were not set compared to 1990, but instead to 2006, thereby disguising the fact that Canadian emissions have increased immensely since 1990, and for being unclear on how the targets were to be achieved. One of the main features of the plan are emissions intensity targets for heavy industry, but these are believed to result in much lower emissions reductions than the LFE regulations proposed by the previous government in 2005 (Bramley, 2007). As it currently stands, Canada is far from being on target for meeting its Kyoto Protocol commitment, nor does it seem to be willing to keep itself to this commitment, and, to date, no comprehensive climate change policy instruments have been implemented either (Rabe, 2007).

2.3.4 The United States of America

Despite the US rejection of the Kyoto Protocol, there has not been a complete lack of climate policy in this country. The cornerstone of US climate policy is the Global Climate Change Initiative, launched in February 2002 (White House, 2002). This plan set a voluntary emission reduction target to lower the intensity of GHG emissions per economic output at a rate of 18 per cent over a period from 2002 to 2012. However, because it involves an intensity target, it could very well still lead to increased emissions over this period in an absolute sense (Byrne *et al*, 2007; Gardiner and Jacobson, 2002). It appears that the historical trend of GHG emissions from 1990 to 2001 already reflected an 18 per cent improvement in intensity, meaning that the 'new' target is nothing more than a continuation of 'business-as-usual' (Christiansen, 2003). What is more, the plan lacks any specific details on how responsibility for meeting the target is delegated to each sector of the economy (Gardiner and Jacobson, 2002). Other elements of the plan were incentives for industry to voluntarily disclose information on GHG emissions to the Federal Government, and increased expenditure on climate research and technology development.

For example, to stimulate research on the science of climate change as well as the development of emissions-reducing technologies, two programmes were launched: the Climate Change Science Program (CCSP) and the Climate Change Technology Program (CCTP) (Victor, 2004). The CCTP particularly focuses on the development of a new generation of coal-fired power plants that use coal gasification to enable capture and storage of CO_2 underground, and the development of a hydrogen economy based on hydrogen-powered fuel cell cars. Both programmes have been criticised though; the CCSP for a lack of funding, and the CCTP for the fact that similar programmes have performed rather badly in the past. Moreover, it is questionable whether public investments in technologies have an effect when there is no incentive for companies to invest in low-carbon technologies as well (e.g. by putting a price on carbon with an emissions trading scheme) (Victor, 2004).

However, there has been a growing tension within the US regarding the Federal Government's position on climate change (Selin and VanDeveer, 2007). In 2003, senators McCain and Lieberman launched a bipartisan plan to set industry-wide caps and create an emissions trading scheme; this proposal failed to pass Congress by 12 votes. However, it reflected a divergence of views between the US Congress and the Bush Government, which seems to have further increased since (Brewer, 2005a). Moreover, differences emerged between the federal and some state governments (Rabe, 2004; Peterson and Rose, 2006). A number of US states implemented stricter policy measures to combat climate change than required by the Federal Government; others are preparing for emissions trading and a decreased reliance on fossil fuels (Byrne *et al*, 2007). Most notable have been the Regional Greenhouse Gas Initiative (RGGI) of the North-eastern states, the Western Climate Initiative, the California Global Warming Solutions Act, and the Midwestern Greenhouse Gas Reduction Accord. What all these initiatives have in common is an approach of using market-based policy instruments – emissions trading – to achieve reductions for realising a binding target.

Besides, a large number of states have implemented policy measures to enhance energy efficiency and promote the use of renewable energy (Rabe, 2004). By 2006, for example, 24 states had passed legislation for a renewable portfolio standard, while 14 states had proposed such legislation (Byrne *et al*, 2007). In addition, US companies faced increased pressure from shareholder groups who asked them to take climate change seriously, and from institutional investors who called for disclosure requirements on climate risks (Monks *et al*, 2004). This movement built on the unease that had been growing in some US companies after Bush's rejection of the Kyoto Protocol, and who started to take steps, such as the creation of a pilot project for carbon emissions trading in 2003: the Chicago Climate Exchange (CCX).

All this activity on climate change has not left the Federal Government unaffected either. Although it goes a bit too far to say that the Bush Government has made a U-turn on climate change, as it is still against binding commitments, the Federal Government's attention for the issue has increased considerab' Bush's 2006 State of the Union the US President proposed to end the US addi.u.. to oil and to invest more in clean technologies, for example to develop zero-emission coal-fired power plants and to step up the production of ethanol and develop ethanol from non-food crops (e.g. switchgrass). Bush reinforced these intentions in his 2007 State of the Union, and on 31 May 2007 even called for action to reduce GHG emissions just before a G8 summit. This sea change is most clearly illustrated by a statement of Condoleezza Rice, US Secretary of State, at a meeting in September 2007 of the 16 countries with the highest GHG emissions (Harvey, 2007a: 1):

> If we stay on our present path, we face an unacceptable choice: either we sacrifice global economic growth to secure the health of our planet or we sacrifice the health of our planet to continue with fossil-fuelled growth.

2.3.5 Australia

Australia's target under the Kyoto Protocol looked rather favourable in comparison to most other industrialised countries, as the target allowed an increase in GHG emissions of 8 per cent. The reason was that Australia is highly dependent on fossil fuels and is home to one of the world's largest (exporting) coal industries (Kent and Mercer, 2006). Nevertheless, Australia decided not to ratify the Kyoto Protocol, thus siding with the US. Besides not ratifying Kyoto, what Australia also has in common with the US is that it is one of the highest per capita emitters of GHG emissions in the world (Crowley, 2007; Hunt, 2004). The main arguments of the Australian Government for not ratifying were that large emitters such as the US, India and China did not participate and the lack of targets for developing countries (Griffiths *et al*, 2007). It is striking, though, that Australia is still on target to meet its commitment under Kyoto. However, this is not because it has been able to reduce emissions from energy, industry or transport, but just because it is profiting from the favourable rules with regard to land use. In other words, it is mainly due to measures of reducing the pace of land clearing for agriculture that growth in emissions has slowed (Crowley, 2007; Hunt, 2004). To illustrate, UNFCCC data show that in 2005 the increase in GHG emissions compared to 1990 was 25.6 per cent (see Table 1.1 in Chapter 1), but merely 4.5 per cent including land use emissions; a very different trend than other developed countries.

Just before Kyoto, the Australian Government launched a plan – Safeguarding the Future. Australia's Response to Climate Change – which aimed to reduce emissions by one-third over the period from 1990 to 2010. This plan also led to the establishment of the Australian Greenhouse Office which was to manage the Government's climate policy (Kent and Mercer, 2006). In 1998, however, Australia introduced an alternative climate change plan to replace the Kyoto commitment called the National Greenhouse Strategy. This plan mainly consisted of voluntary measures and did not contain a climate policy instrument that puts a price on carbon, such as a carbon tax or an emissions trading scheme. Important for industry were the Greenhouse Challenge (1995–2005) and its follow-up Greenhouse Challenge Plus (2005–present), by which the Government tried to stimulate voluntary measures to reduce GHG emissions. However, it seems that these voluntary programmes have not led to any significant reductions in industry-generated GHG emissions (Crowley, 2007; Griffiths *et al*, 2007).

Besides mostly voluntary measures, the 2001 Renewable Energy (Electricity) Act also contained a mandatory renewable energy target (MRET), under which electricity retailers and wholesale electricity consumers have to source from renewable resources, partly with the aim to reduce GHG emissions. The MRET is a market-based instrument as it creates Renewable Energy Certificates that are tradable (Kent and Mercer, 2006; MacGill *et al*, 2006). However, the only regulatory requirement to reduce GHG emissions is an emissions trading scheme that operates on state level instead of federal level (Griffiths *et al*, 2007; MacGill *et al*, 2006). In 2003, the New South Wales Greenhouse Gas Abatement Scheme was launched by the state government (NSW, 2005). It is mandatory for electricity generators, retailers and large market customers; and voluntary for other companies. State-level reduction and offset activities stand central; international projects are not mentioned.

Strong indications that the international debate on climate change has changed considerably of late, has also left its marks on Australia. Australian Prime Minister John Howard became more approving of implementing more sophisticated climate policy instruments on a federal level (Crowley, 2007). In June 2007, for example, he announced the intention to establish an emissions trading scheme on a federal level by 2012. In addition, in the same year a bill was passed that requires companies to report their GHG emissions from 1 July 2008. Besides the influence of international trends, early movements by state governments similar to those in the US seem to have had its effect as well in changing the national policy debate on climate change (Griffiths *et al*, 2007). This has culminated in Australia ratifying the Kyoto Protocol in December 2007 after the Labor Party had won the national elections. Subsequently, plans to introduce an emissions trading scheme on a national level have been moved forward as well, now aiming at a start in 2010.

2.4 CONCLUDING REMARKS

Looking at all the different climate change policy instruments that have been implemented or are in the process of being implemented, there is a complex situation for companies operating in these various countries. They face a range of initiatives at the local, national and international levels, some binding, some voluntary, and with a multitude of stakeholders involved. As a consequence, the issue of climate change continues to be characterised by uncertainty as to the (potential) impact on markets, technologies and organisations, with companies helping to shape the future of climate change regimes through voluntary initiatives as well. The next chapters will pay more attention to these voluntary activities undertaken by companies.

3 Beyond regulation: Voluntary agreements and partnerships

After having set the general stage in the introductory chapter, and the evolution of climate policy in Chapter 2, this chapter will now focus more on the broader range of responses that has developed, thus covering the other side of the continuum from regulation to self-regulation. Since command-and-control and particularly market-based mechanisms have been discussed in the previous chapter, attention here shifts to other instruments, in which emphasis lies on business and on the voluntary and co-operative nature of such initiatives. Voluntary initiatives are now generally regarded as the third broad category of environmental policy instruments besides command-and-control and market-based regulations (OECD, 1999). However, we do not view these initiatives as encompassing a third phase (cf. Prakash and Kollman, 2004; Tietenberg, 1998), but rather as complementary to the other policy instruments. Indeed, voluntary initiatives have been important in helping shape emissions trading schemes, and fomenting public opinion on the desirability and/or feasibility of government action.

As Chapter 1 set out, after the negotiations of the Kyoto Protocol many companies stopped their opposition – demonstrated by the breakdown of the Global Climate Coalition – and shifted to a more proactive position. Industries organised themselves in associations in favour of climate change regulation (e.g. the US Business Council for Sustainable Energy and 'E7'). This not only included companies producing sustainable forms of energy, but also 'traditional' electric utilities that started to invest more in natural gas, nuclear, wind and solar energy (Kolk, 2001). In addition, companies in the banking and insurance sectors also increasingly supported climate policy initiatives, e.g. through participating in the UNEP Finance Initiative (Dlugolecki and Keykhah, 2002; Kolk, 2001). The Kyoto Protocol also formed the onset of new business initiatives in support of measures for GHG emissions reduction, such as the Pew Center on Global Climate Change.

The wave of voluntary corporate climate change activities and initiatives that has emerged is part of a broader trend where companies are not only following laws and regulations set by governments or international organisations, but have also started to create their own rules and norms with regard to global environmental issues (Pattberg, 2005). In other words, due to globalisation and the concomitant emergence of non-State, private actors – including business *and* non-governmental organisations (NGOs) – governance patterns have changed considerably. This has resulted in new forms of governance that more strongly emphasise cross-sector co-operation between business, NGOs and governments as well as self-regulation by companies (Arts, 2006; Börzel and Risse, 2005; Knill and Lehmkuhl, 2002; Pattberg, 2005). Consequently, governance of climate change is no longer just a function exercised by governments and international organisations; business and NGOs now play an increasingly large role in furthering implementation and consensus-building on international frameworks and domestic policies (Arts, 2006; Pattberg, 2005; Witte *et al*, 2003).

While there are several categorisations of voluntary initiatives, they generally make a distinction between voluntary agreements between business and government; multi-stakeholder partnerships involving various constellations of business, NGOs and/or government; and unilateral activities by companies (Mazurkiewicz, 2005; OECD, 1999). Although we follow this categorisation, in this chapter we will only discuss co-operative activities most relevant for the issue of climate change, that is voluntary agreements and multi-stakeholder partnerships. As a consequence, we will cover individual voluntary company self-commitments such as emissions targets and management that are not directly needed for compliance as well as information provision (disclosure) by companies on climate change in the next chapter.

3.1 VOLUNTARY AGREEMENTS

3.1.1 Defining voluntary agreements

In recent years, a wide variety of concerted efforts between business, governments and/or NGOs have emerged to tackle climate change. However, it is difficult to label each of these efforts exactly, because such voluntary, co-operative initiatives have been defined in many different ways. Moreover, there is a grey area between initiatives that, even though they are voluntary, are still some form of government policy, and initiatives that are completely voluntary with no relation to government policy at all. In the literature, therefore, a distinction has been made between voluntary agreements (this section) and multi-stakeholder partnerships (section 3.2). The main difference between the two is that in the case of voluntary agreements responsibility for implementation of climate change measures mainly rests with the companies involved under the aegis of the government, while in multi-stakeholder partnerships this responsibility is shared equally between all participants (Mazurkiewicz, 2005).

A voluntary agreement is a policy instrument set up by the government to motivate companies to engage in voluntary activities with regard to the environment (Delmas and Terlaak, 2001). Such agreements are generally used to deal with pollutants for which no other regulations exist yet (Morgenstern and Pizer, 2007). There are several reasons that explain why governments prefer to 'regulate' via voluntary agreements. One is that it is a suitable method to gain experience with a new environmental issue (Morgenstern and Pizer, 2007). In other words, voluntary agreements are a pragmatic way to start regulating a new environmental issue on a relatively short notice, without the high costs and legislative burden of more stringent instruments, such as a tax or an emissions trading scheme (Khanna and Ramirez, 2004). Still, the voluntary agreement would typically function as a precursor of more stringent regulations, which will replace or complement the voluntary agreement in due course (Brau and Carraro, 2004). However, it has also been argued that voluntary agreements might be applied because the government has already failed or believes it will fail to launch mandatory forms of environmental regulation (Morgenstern and Pizer, 2007).

Basically, there are two kinds of voluntary agreements: *negotiated agreements* and *public voluntary programmes* (OECD, 1999). A *negotiated agreement* is a contract between the government and an industry (or sometimes individual companies) which usually involves a target and a timetable for reaching the target (Thalmann and Baranzini, 2004). It is particularly the negotiated agreement that is introduced as an alternative to stricter regulation, e.g. an environmental tax, and negotiated as a collective agreement with an industry association. However, such agreements are not completely without risk to participating companies either, as a failure to meet the conditions set under the agreement generally means that stricter policies will be implemented instead. Negotiated agreements are sometimes also launched in addition to existing regulations to grant companies more flexibility in complying with the latter. This type is typically negotiated with individual companies instead of industry associations (Delmas and Terlaak, 2002). *Public voluntary programmes*, on the other hand, are set up by the government alone and are open to companies to take part in on a voluntary basis. By participating, companies agree to a certain standard, for example to implement certain technologies or to reduce emissions to a particular level, and in return receive benefits such as technical assistance or subsidies (OECD, 1999).

Besides co-operating with the government, both forms of voluntary agreements also mean some form of co-operation between the various companies taking part in the agreement. However, this usually does not go beyond sharing some basic 'best practices' on how to reduce emissions. Real co-operative efforts in reducing environmental impact by and large do not develop as part of the agreements, because companies still keep their competitive position in mind (Thalmann and Baranzini, 2004). How this will work out with the global sectoral agreements for energy-intensive industries that have been adopted at the December 2007 Bali conference as part of a post-Kyoto framework, remains to be seen. The idea there is precisely that it would eliminate competitive disadvantages related to divergent reduction targets for global companies as a result of different countries of origin (most notably between those operating in Europe, the US or developing countries).

3.1.2 Motives for involvement in voluntary agreements

Voluntary agreements have been hailed for the benefits they grant participating companies as well as the government. One argument to introduce a voluntary agreement is that it is a flexible, cost-effective way to reach environmental goals that makes use of specific knowledge of companies. In other words, a voluntary agreement values the fact that companies are not simply entities causing environmental problems through harmful emissions, but might actually possess the knowledge to come up with a solution to the problem (Harrison, 1999). For companies this means that participation can relieve the burden of environmental regulation because they are more flexible in the way they comply. What is more, due to the greater flexibility, companies have more leeway to develop innovative solutions to an environmental problem, and there is the possibility of gaining public recognition through participation (Delmas and Terlaak, 2001). It also gives companies the opportunity to influence at what level a target for emissions reductions is set and how the regulation is implemented (Delmas and Terlaak, 2002; Welch *et al*, 2000).

However, the influence that companies can have on the target-setting process is often also looked at with some care. Voluntary agreements may fall victim to 'regulatory capture', which means that companies are able to convince regulators to agree with a target that does not go beyond a 'business-as-usual' scenario (Morgenstern and Pizer, 2007). A typical example of regulatory capture is the case where the agreement entails a target on GHG emissions intensity or energy intensity, instead of absolute emissions or energy reductions. Since it is easier to comply with intensity targets, agreements merely requiring such a target often have a considerably higher number of participants (Thalmann and Baranzini, 2004). For the government, the main advantage of a voluntary agreement is that it requires less involvement and might therefore compensate for a lack of regulatory capacity (Mazurkiewicz, 2005). Moreover, it enables the government to create a common understanding with business about the environmental issue and improve relations between them (Harrison, 1999; Morgenstern and Pizer, 2007).

Still, an essential attribute of these kinds of co-operative policy instruments is their voluntary nature. Even though voluntary agreements generally have lower compliance costs than other instruments, there still has to be some sort of benefit to counterbalance these costs (Khanna and Ramirez, 2004; Morgenstern and Pizer, 2007; Welch *et al*, 2000). More often than not, these benefits are an explicit part of the voluntary agreement and basically function as a carrot to attract companies to participate. In many cases these explicit benefits that governments have put in place to promote the agreement also function as the main motive for companies to become part of the agreement.

One of the most often used benefits is that participation leads to regulatory relief from other policy instruments (Harrison, 1999; Khanna and Ramirez, 2004; Morgenstern and Pizer, 2004; Thalmann and Baranzini, 2004). For example, participation may result in exemption from a CO_2 or energy tax or the possibility of opting out of an emissions trading scheme. Still regulatory relief is not always that explicit in the voluntary agreement, but companies may nevertheless believe that their participation reduces the regulatory threat of the implementation of more stringent policy instruments. Moreover, it may even be so that participating in a voluntary agreement on climate change leads to regulatory relief in some other environmental areas, such as acid rain (Welch *et al*, 2000).

In addition to relief, the government can provide technical assistance to companies in achieving the emissions target set under the agreement. Participation thereby functions as a new source of knowledge with regard to the way that climate change can be dealt with (Thalmann and Baranzini, 2004). Finally, the government undertakes promotional activities to create public recognition for those companies that participate in the agreement and thus helps improve the environmental image of these companies.

However, besides the regulatory incentive of gaining from benefits that the government has put in place, companies may have other motives as well, more closely aligned with company self-interest. Since reduction of energy consumption is one of the primary ways to tackle climate change, there is a clear cost motive for companies in making production activities more energy efficient. However, even though companies might have market incentives to improve environmental performance, regardless of government involvement, they may still choose to take part in a voluntary agreement (Harrison, 1999). For example, a company may use participation to improve credibility of climate change initiatives vis-à-vis customers. Being able to show customers that it takes climate change seriously improves the environmental reputation and makes a company's products more appealing to customers that have specific green preferences (Thalmann and Baranzini, 2004). It can also be the co-operative nature of the voluntary agreement that makes it attractive to companies. If close competitors all take part in the same agreement they form one front against external parties such as environmental NGOs that criticise corporate environmental behaviour. They agree what the collective norm is regarding to what extent climate change is dealt with, which need not be the most ambitious norm. In other words, when a voluntary agreement is used to stave off criticism from outside and participation alone is enough to relieve the adverse relationship between companies and NGOs, this also means that the incentive to actually reduce GHG emissions may vanish (Khanna and Ramirez, 2004; Morgenstern and Pizer, 2007). A voluntary agreement can also be a cover for anti-competitive behaviour as it creates the opportunity to agree on more than environmental activities alone. The agreement may actually be used to increase market concentration or act as barrier to potential new entrants (Brau and Carraro, 2004).

3.1.3 Overview and analysis of voluntary agreements on climate change

Given the relatively recent regulatory attention to climate change, it is not surprising that voluntary agreements have been used on a considerably large scale to deal with this issue. As Chapters 1 and 2 showed, there has long been considerable uncertainty about climate change with regard to the scientific evidence on the danger of the problem and the impact on ecosystems and society, and how the international community would deal with the issue. Consequently, due to a potential lack of public support and the fear of a loss of competitiveness if other countries would not move in the same direction, it would be rather precarious for national governments to go ahead with stringent climate policies. What is more, GHG emissions are rather complex to regulate because there are many different sources that generate emissions, and mitigation means something different depending on the type of greenhouse gas and the specific production activity that generates emissions (Brouhle and Harrington, 2007). For all these reasons *and* the relative flexibility of voluntary agreements, this type of policy instrument has been the ideal platform for governments to start developing policy on climate change.

However, the role that voluntary agreements have played in the overall climate policy mix has seen great diversity across the globe. It seems that the exact motives that governments have used to introduce voluntary initiatives for climate change are rather different. In other words, whether voluntary initiatives have been launched to gain experience with this 'new' environmental issue or used as an alternative after (or possible future) failure to launch stricter climate policies (Morgenstern and Pizer, 2007), has depended to a considerable extent on the way in which the national public debate on climate change has unfolded. Hence, this has led to the implementation of different kinds of agreements which vary in objective as well as benefits of participation for companies. In fact, the flexibility that is inherent to voluntary agreements means that the impact on corporate climate change activities can vary considerably, depending on the specifics of an agreement. Table 3.1 gives an overview of voluntary agreements on climate change that are currently up and running. It must be stated that the list is not complete as there are a considerable number of voluntary agreements that indirectly aim to contribute to climate change mitigation (e.g. the US EPA has several agreements such as the Energy Star, Green Lights and Waste Wise programmes; see Gardiner and Jacobson (2002) for an overview). Besides, there are some programmes that have already been finalised (e.g. Canada's Industry Program for Energy Conservation, Sweden's EKO-Energy Programme, the Declaration of German Industry on Global Warming Prevention, the Dutch Long Term Agreements on Industrial Energy Efficiency, and the US Department of Energy's Climate Challenge Program) and some of which the current position is rather uncertain (e.g. Canada's Large Final Emitters Program).

Table 3.1 Voluntary agreements on climate change

Country	Voluntary agreement	Period	Objective	Incentive
Australia	Greenhouse Challenge Plus (follow-up of Greenhouse Challenge, 1995–2005)	2005–present	• Reduce GHG emissions • Accelerate energy efficiency improvements • Integrate climate change in decision-making • Improve GHG reporting	• Greenhouse Friendly™ certification • Fuel tax credit • Government and public recognition • Technical assistance

Belgium	Benchmarking Covenant on Energy Efficiency – Flanders	2004–2012	• Improve energy efficiency to be among the 10% most energy-efficient companies in the world by 2012	• Exemption from any extra specific national measures on energy conservation or CO_2 reduction
China	Top 1000 Industrial Energy Conservation Programme	2006–present	• Establish energy conservation organisation, formulate energy efficiency goals • Establish energy use reporting system • Conduct energy auditing • Formulate energy conservation plan • Invest in energy efficiency improvements • Adopt energy conservation incentives, training	• Financial support for energy conservation • Other incentives not yet implemented
Denmark	Industrial Energy Efficiency Agreements	1996–present	• Submission to energy audit • Implement certain standard projects • Report energy-accounting activities to Danish Energy Agency	• A total reimbursement of the CO_2 tax that was introduced in 2003
Finland	Agreements on the Promotion for Industrial Energy Conservation	1997–present	• Carry out energy audits or analyses in own properties and production plants • Draw up an energy conservation plan • Implement cost-effective conservation measures	• Subsidy for energy audits and analyses, as well as energy conservation investments fulfilling certain criteria
France	AERES Voluntary Agreements with Industry to Reduce GHG Emissions and Conserve Energy	2002–present	• Absolute or relative targets for all six Kyoto Protocol GHGs • Improve energy efficiency of production sites • Reduce emissions linked to buildings under responsibility and transport patterns	• If objectives are not achieved by the milestone dates of 2004 and 2007, companies will have to pay a fine

(*Continued overleaf*)

Table 3.1 Continued

Country	Voluntary agreement	Period	Objective	Incentive
France (*cont.*)			• Use flexible mechanisms under the Kyoto Protocol	
Germany	Agreement on Climate Protection (follow-up of Declaration on Global Warming Prevention, 1995–2000)	2000–present	• Achieve a specific reduction in CO_2 of 28% as compared to 1990 by the year 2012 • Reduce the specific emissions of all six GHGs referred to in the Kyoto Protocol (CO_2, CH_4, N_2O, SF_6, HFC and PFC) by a total of 35% by the year 2012 compared to 1990	• The German Government will not take any command-and-control measures if targets are achieved
Japan	Keidanren's Voluntary Action Plan for the Environment	1997–present	• Stabilise GHG emissions at 1990 levels in absolute terms by 2010 • More specific targets are different depending on the industry	• Regulatory threat that additional policy instruments such as an environmental tax or emissions trading might be implemented
Netherlands	Benchmarking covenants (follow-up of Long-term Agreements on Industrial Energy Efficiency, 1989–2000)	2001–2012	• Improve energy efficiency to be among the 10% most energy-efficient companies in the world by 2012	• Exemption from any extra specific national measures on energy conservation or CO_2 reduction
South Korea	KEMCO Voluntary Agreement for Energy Conservation and Reduction of CO_2 emissions	1998–present	• Energy efficiency enhancement target • GHG emission reduction target • Detailed process design	• Low interest loans and tax incentives to promote energy conservation and GHG reduction • Technical support • Public Relations promotion

Sweden	Programme for Improving Energy Efficiency Act	2005–present	• Introduce and obtain certification for a standardised energy management system • Submit to an energy audit and analysis • Report on the energy audit, the energy management system and the list of measures	• Tax exemption on electricity consumption if action is taken to improve energy efficiency
Switzerland	CO_2 Law Voluntary Measures	2000–2010	• Formal commitment to limit absolute CO_2 emissions	• Exemption from CO_2 tax
UK	Climate Change Agreements	2001–2010	• Negotiated targets which vary per industry in absolute or relative carbon or absolute or relative energy • Interim targets for the years 2002, 2004, 2006, and 2008 • The Climate Agreements were launched together with an energy tax and a voluntary emissions trading scheme	• A 80% tax exemption from the Climate Change Levy if negotiated agreement is met by 2010
US	Climate Leaders	2002–present	• Set a corporate-wide GHG reduction goal • Inventory of emissions to measure progress	• Standardised tools to assist in inventory of GHG emissions • Technical assistance • Public recognition

Sources: International Energy Agency Climate Change Policies and Measures Database; European Climate Change Programme (ECCP) Database on Policies and Measures in Europe; Baranzini *et al* (2004); Glachant and De Muizon (2007); Glasbergen (2004); Khanna and Ramirez (2004); Krarup and Millock (2007); Morgenstern and Pizer (2007); Price (2005); Price and Wang (2007); Wakabayashi and Sugiyama (2007)

The voluntary agreements listed in Table 3.1 basically fall in two categories as to how they are used in the overall climate policy mix. *The first category* consists of countries in which voluntary agreements have a key role in the climate policy mix (Thalmann and Baranzini, 2004) and essentially function as a substitute to mandatory climate change regulations (Khanna and Ramirez, 2004). In these situations, it seems that instead of using voluntary agreements to pre-empt stricter regulations, they have been proposed as there was simply too much resistance to stricter policy instruments such as a carbon tax (Lyon and Maxwell, 2004). It has been in those countries that either did not ratify the Kyoto Protocol (the US), were very late in ratifying (Australia), or that undergo substantial internal resistance against the target set under Kyoto (Canada and Japan) that voluntary agreements have been put in place as the primary component of national climate policy. What is more, on the whole, most of these countries have also specifically used public voluntary programmes that are completely voluntary in the sense that not participating in the agreement has no real consequences for a company (Price, 2005), except for maybe missing out on a potential improvement of public image.

To illustrate, over the past decade the main programmes in Australia have been the Greenhouse Challenge (1995–2005) and its follow-up the Greenhouse Challenge Plus. The aim of both programmes has been to stimulate climate change activities such as conducting energy audits, the purchase of green energy and to offset car vehicle emissions, but not to achieve a predetermined emissions target (Griffiths *et al*, 2007). Slightly different, although also completely voluntary, is the US EPA Climate Leaders programme, which does require companies to set a corporate-wide GHG emissions reduction target. Nevertheless, the level at which the target is set is completely at a company's own discretion, and not meeting the target does not involve any penalty or reward either, except perhaps a loss of face. As a consequence, the only common thread between companies taking part in the Climate Leaders programme is the fact that they have set a target (although many participants have their target still under development), but not the stringency and/or geographical scope of the target. For example, healthcare company Abbott has pledged to reduce total US GHG emissions by 2 per cent from 2006 to 2011, cement company Holcim to reduce US GHG emissions by 12 per cent per ton of cement from 2000 to 2008, and chemical company DuPont to reduce total global GHG emissions by 15 per cent from 2004 to 2015.[1] As these public voluntary programmes are often just a weak bid from the government, and the benefits do not go much further than providing some soft incentives such as technical assistance, it may not come as a surprise that they seem to be powerless instruments in terms of environmental effectiveness and do not put much pressure on companies to modify their behaviour from 'business-as-usual' (Griffiths *et al*, 2007; Lyon and Maxwell, 2004).

The role that voluntary agreements play in Japan is somewhat different, compared with programmes in the US and Australia. First of all, Japan has a very large number of relatively small-scale agreements, but with regard to climate change, one programme, that is, the Keidanren Voluntary Action Plan on the Environment,[2] is most comprehensive (covering a range of industries), and forms

---

1   For an overview of climate change targets set as part of the EPA Climate Leaders programme, see <http://www.epa.gov/climateleaders>.

2   It must be noted that the Keidanren Voluntary Action Plan on the Environment does not only include measures to combat climate change, but also other environmental measures such as waste management and the promotion of ISO 14001 certification (Khanna and Ramirez, 2004).

one of the central pillars of Japanese climate policy (Wakabayashi and Sugiyama, 2007). At the outset the Keidanren Voluntary Action Plan was a unilateral initiative of Japan's most influential business association. It was launched just before the Kyoto Protocol, and the target that the Japanese Government agreed to under the Kyoto Protocol was partly based on consultations with the Keidanren. Although, in essence, the targets set under the Plan were voluntary and non-binding, the general benefits of Keidanren membership for Japanese companies (i.e. being part of the business community) did put a lot of pressure to comply (Wakabayashi and Sugiyama, 2007). However, after Japan's negotiation of the Kyoto Protocol, government involvement in the programme increased considerably, because an additional feature was introduced, called 'step-by-step'. This step-by-step approach allows the Japanese Government to implement additional mandatory policy instruments if the current voluntary method is not sufficient to comply with Kyoto (Wakabayashi and Sugiyama, 2007). Unlike, the Australian and US programmes, the regulatory threat of mandatory instruments is therefore more real, because it has been formalised as part of the agreement. Nevertheless, up till now, the Japanese Government has not used this additional feature (see Chapter 2).

The second category includes countries where voluntary agreements have been implemented as part of a broader climate policy mix, also containing mandatory policy instruments such as a tax or emissions trading scheme (Price, 2005). It is not surprising, then, that, particularly in European countries, voluntary agreements have been implemented in this way. In all EU Member States, voluntary agreements currently operate side-by-side with the European emissions trading scheme. However, as the European Union emissions trading scheme (EU ETS) only started in 2005, this has not always been the case, because many voluntary agreements were already put in place years before that. Initially the situation was much more similar to the current situation in the US and Australia. That is to say, the voluntary agreements that started in the mid-1990s (e.g. Denmark's Industrial Energy Efficiency Agreements and Finland's Agreements on the Promotion for Industrial Energy Conservation) were launched in response to a failure to implement an EU-wide carbon tax (Khanna and Ramirez, 2004), not to pre-empt a European carbon tax. Nevertheless, one important difference is that most (although not all) European voluntary agreements on climate change have taken the shape of negotiated agreements instead of public voluntary agreements. As a consequence, participation is less voluntary because these agreements are usually negotiated with business associations representing whole industries, and once agreed the terms are binding. In other words, it appears that European governments have more political will to come up with a climate policy mix that puts substantial pressure on companies to reduce GHG emissions and voluntary agreements are therefore also used with this idea in mind.

Taking stock of the voluntary agreements in Europe (see Table 3.1) reveals that they use different types of incentives, and several agreements have several benefits at once. A first type of incentive used in Europe is somewhat similar to Japan's Keidanren Plan, that is, the use of threat to implement mandatory policy instruments when conditions are not met (Khanna and Ramirez, 2004). This is the case with the German Agreement on Climate Change as well as the Dutch and Belgian Benchmarking Covenants. A second type is the use of a monetary incentive or disincentive. For example, in Finland companies receive a subsidy for energy audits and specific energy conservation investments, and in France, if they are not meeting the target agreed under the AERES Voluntary Agreements, companies have to pay a fine. Monetary incentives have also been implemented as part of a more comprehensive policy mix that either involves a tax, an emissions trading scheme, or both. For example, in Sweden and Denmark voluntary agreements are directly linked to an energy or carbon tax, where meeting the targets set under the agreement means that companies are exempted from or receive a reimbursement of an electricity and CO_2 tax, respectively. Finally, the most sophisticated way in which a voluntary agreement has been integrated in an integral climate policy mix is the UK's Climate Change Agreement, which combines the agreement with an energy tax – the Climate Change Levy – and an emissions trading scheme (Price, 2005; Morgenstern and Pizer, 2007).

However, even though in Europe the voluntary agreements that are currently in place appear to be relatively more binding than most non-European counterparts, some doubts can be raised as to their function, and then particularly the relation with the EU ETS, and the related *effectiveness*. To what extent would companies still put effort in complying with a voluntary measure without a very clear penalty, when there is also a mandatory measure where non-compliance has clear financial consequences? In addition, it is not only the interaction with the EU ETS that raises doubt about the effectiveness of voluntary agreements. Not even taking into account how voluntary agreements interact with other climate policy instruments, empirical research has so far cast considerable doubt on the general effectiveness of such agreements.

There is quite a broad literature on the effectiveness of voluntary agreements in bringing down emissions harmful to the environment (see Khanna and Ramirez (2004) for an overview). However, most of the research is not related to CO_2 emissions from energy-related activities, but instead deals with toxic emissions. It is rather questionable, whether findings of studies on voluntary agreements on toxic emissions that on the whole show a positive influence on the environmental performance of companies (Khanna and Ramirez, 2004), are also valid for voluntary agreements for climate change. There are several reasons why voluntary agreements for climate change cannot be expected to have the same positive effect. First of all, CO_2 comes from energy consumption, and since energy already has a price, companies have the incentive to reduce emissions, also without an agreement (Morgenstern and Pizer, 2007). By contrast, toxic emissions were basically free before voluntary agreements were put in place. Consequently, it is quite likely that in the case of CO_2 a voluntary agreement does not create an extra incentive beyond already existing initiatives to cut costs from energy. What is more, any extra effort to cut energy use is probably more costly in a marginal sense, because there is no low-hanging fruit, as in the case of toxic releases.

Another difference is that cutting back toxic emissions often has an immediate local effect and can thus be used to improve public image vis-à-vis local communities, while the effect of less CO_2 emissions is not as visible (Morgenstern and Pizer, 2007).

The few empirical studies that have been conducted on the effectiveness of voluntary agreements for climate change are not promising either. An early study on the effectiveness of the US Department of Energy's Climate Challenge Program (Welch *et al*, 2000), for example, finds that participation in the programme either has no effect or a negative effect on the reduction of CO_2 emissions. The authors of the study argue that it seemed that the utilities that took part in the programme had considerable bargaining power and were therefore able to influence the regulators in setting the target. In addition, participation alone was already enough to silence criticism as public scrutiny was specifically focused on other (toxic) pollutants, where the effect on human health and the environment was more unequivocal at the time (Welch *et al*, 2000). A more recent collection of case studies on the effectiveness of voluntary agreements across the globe (Morgenstern and Pizer, 2007) is more promising in that the authors found that on average the agreements resulted in a 5 per cent reduction of GHG emissions. However, the main problem they encountered in establishing this percentage was in choosing what to compare the emissions reductions with. One methodology is to estimate emissions scenarios that would follow a business-as-usual trend, while the other is to compare the level of emissions of participants with non-participants. Because both methodologies have their shortcomings, the authors that synthesised the case study findings are cautious in drawing conclusions. Still, their findings give some indication that programmes with a stronger incentive in the sense that there is a clear regulatory threat (e.g. Japan's Keidanren Plan) or are integrated in a climate policy mix with a tax or trading system (e.g. UK's Climate Change Agreements), seem more effective than programmes with weaker incentives, such as those that exist in the US and Australia (Morgenstern and Pizer, 2007).

It thus seems that there are some differences in effectiveness between programmes depending on theoretically derived factors such as the credibility of the regulatory threat, the lower costs of the voluntary agreement compared to complying with a mandatory policy instrument, and the influence that a company has on the regulator that sets the targets of the agreement (Khanna and Ramirez, 2004). But, on the whole, it appears that it may be wise not to expect too much from voluntary agreements in actually bringing down emissions in the short run. This is not to say, however, that the so-called 'soft effects' of creating awareness of the climate change issue and changing the attitude of managers to take reduction of GHG emissions into account in decision making will not have a positive effect on climate change mitigation in the long run (Harrison, 1999; Morgenstern and Pizer, 2007). Multi-stakeholder partnerships that we will look at next more often than not focus on such soft effects, as they are regularly used to gain experience with the climate change issue and how best to deal with it. But, as we will see later, because such partnerships particularly concentrate on such soft effects, it is even more problematic to establish how effective they are at achieving their goals.

3.2 MULTI-STAKEHOLDER PARTNERSHIPS

3.2.1 Defining partnerships

Although there is a thin red line between voluntary agreements and multi-stakeholder partnerships, the latter are different in several regards. Partnerships for sustainable development have been referred to as 'collaborative arrangements in which actors from two or more spheres of society (state, market and civil society) are involved in a non-hierarchical process, and through which these actors strive for a sustainability goal' (Van Huijstee *et al*, 2007: 77). More generally, partnerships have been defined as 'the voluntary collaborative efforts of actors from organizations in two or more economic sectors in a forum in which they co-operatively attempt to solve a problem or issue of mutual concern that is in some way identified with a public policy agenda item' (Waddock, 1991: 481–482). Both definitions highlight the fact that partnerships cut across sectors, and that it is a non-hierarchical process, meaning that it is based on the idea of shared responsibility (Mazurkiewicz, 2005) and no single actor – e.g. the government – regulates other actors' behaviour.

Because of the assumed equality between the actors involved in a multi-stakeholder partnership, compared with a voluntary agreement, participation will generally be less risky for companies, because the threat of regulation is much smaller. What is more, multi-stakeholder partnerships can be formed around a relatively narrow topic (Waddock, 1991), e.g. developing a specific emissions-reducing technology such as biofuels or hydrogen technology, and one company can be involved in many different partnerships at the same time. Voluntary agreements, on the other hand, are generally formed around broad themes such as energy efficiency or GHG emissions reduction for the whole company, and participation typically precludes involvement in other, similar initiatives. In addition, a company has a much wider choice of potential actors to partner with; not only the government, but also NGOs, international organisations, or even other companies.

Departing somewhat from the definitions above, we argue that a collaborative effort between companies could also be seen as a partnership as long as the main goal is to address a public policy concern. Such collaborations between companies have been called 'post-partnerships', referring to the fact that companies have started to follow this approach only after similar efforts in conjunction with NGOs had failed (Egels-Zandén and Wahlqvist, 2007). In fact, it is precisely this type of post-partnership that has become quite common in the climate change arena. In view of all this, it is not surprising, then, that in the broad field of climate change there are many more multi-stakeholder partnerships than voluntary agreements.

Partnerships have received particular attention in the field of sustainable development, as a result of the inclusion in the Millennium Development Goals, which list as the eighth goal the creation of a global partnership for development. At the 2002 World Summit on Sustainable Development (WSSD) partnerships were recognised as crucial implementation mechanisms for sustainable development, in order to make progress on the many ideas launched a decade earlier at the Rio conferences that had failed to be translated into concrete measures. Partnerships in a sense aim to address different forms of 'governance' failure that are characterised by retreating governments and a 'regulatory gap', in a setting where companies and NGOs on their own are also incapable of achieving desired (public) objectives, such as protection of the environment (Biermann *et al*, 2007; Braithwaite and Drahos, 2000; Fransen and Kolk, 2007).

3.2.2 Motives for involvement in partnerships

While the WSSD route has not been used often, companies have become involved in multi-stakeholder partnerships by other means. Over the past few years it seemed that a new partnership on climate change was announced in the media almost every day, and these usually involved one or more companies. This is not surprising as one of the main arguments to explain the upsurge in partnerships is that many sustainability issues are too complex for one single actor to solve on its own (Selsky and Parker, 2005; Waddock, 1991; Witte *et al*, 2003). In other words, companies need actors from other sectors to be able to successfully address the issue at hand. This is typically the case with climate change, and companies often argue that they cannot solve this problem single-handedly because of its sheer complexity. The explanation that climate change is so complex that it necessitates co-operation across sectors (and countries) suggests that the stakes that all partners have in the partnership are equal because they share a common goal: to solve the sustainability issue at hand.

However, participants in multi-stakeholder partnerships might also have more strategic motives in mind. Although partnerships are seen as a way for different actors to bundle their knowledge and resources (Googins and Rochlin, 2000; Witte *et al*, 2003), this is not necessarily merely with the goal to solve the issue at hand (Waddock, 1991). For companies it may well be a means to learn new skills or acquire tacit knowledge that partners possess (Rondinelli and London, 2003; Selsky and Parker, 2005). Besides, by working with NGOs or governments, companies typically gain a valuable resource, that is, the reputation that these partners have in the eyes of the public regarding their positive influence on sustainability (Van Huijstee *et al*, 2007). Partnerships can also reduce risks related to climate change, which can be regulatory, reputational, commercial or financial in nature (Innovest, 2002; Wellington and Sauer, 2005). On the other hand, partnerships are not always without risks, as NGOs can draw on business to acquire financial resources and take advantage of corporate skills to create a market for sustainable products (Van Huijstee *et al*, 2007). For example, Greenpeace used the near-bankrupt German refrigerator manufacturer Foron Household Appliances to its own advantage to launch ozone-friendly 'Greenfreeze' refrigerators. At first, this led to a successful co-operation for both participating actors. However, after the collaboration Greenpeace basically gave away the ozone-friendly technology to Foron's competitors, thereby destroying Foron's strategic advantage, in the end leading to its bankruptcy (Stafford *et al*, 2000).

Research by the authors on partnerships for climate change by the Global 500 reveals that there are different, sometimes competing motives behind such involvements. First, companies use partnerships to influence the direction and shape of the climate change debate. Unlike the political activities in the 1990s when antagonistic approaches prevailed, partnerships serve to show that companies are willing and able to work co-operatively with other actors on this issue. Besides, companies are also becoming aware that not only regulatory but also societal attention to climate change is increasing. As a consequence, partnerships can play a role in anticipating corporate loss of legitimacy in the eyes of the public by demonstrating concrete action rather than only taking a position in the policy debate. Finally, climate change has started to affect markets in which companies operate (Kolk and Pinkse, 2004; 2005a; Levy and Kolk, 2002). Climate change induces a market transition that works against carbon-intensive products and production processes, thus inducing the development of more climate-friendly technologies (Hoffman, 2005). Hence, companies can become involved in partnerships with political, legitimacy, or market-oriented intentions in mind, though not necessarily at the same time and to be met in one and the same partnership.

3.2.3 Overview and analysis of climate change partnerships

To obtain more insight into existing partnerships for climate change, a closer look has first been taken at the database of 331 partnerships that have been introduced alongside the WSSD.[3] This shows, however, that these types of partnerships do not play a large role in engaging business in cross-sector initiatives in general (Bäckstrand, 2008; Biermann *et al*, 2007). Most partnerships are either led by intergovernmental organisations (often UN-related), international NGOs based in Western countries, or OECD-country governments (Bäckstrand, 2006). What is more, even though 33 WSSD partnerships have climate change as a primary theme and another 61 as a secondary theme, the involvement of business in these climate-specific initiatives is even more limited. In the climate change arena, it thus also seems that companies do not see the need to get involved in partnerships that have a relation to the WSSD (or the UN for that matter). In other words, this route towards 'private governance' (Pattberg, 2005) is not working the way it was supposed to, as it is still dominated by the powerful actors that were already involved in the intergovernmental arena, namely international organisations, governments, and large international NGOs (Biermann *et al*, 2007). Illustrative is the fact that the Asia-Pacific Partnership on Clean Development and Climate (see Chapter 2) used to be included in the database, and even while one of its goals is to stimulate private sector technology development (McGee and Taplin, 2006), its lead partners merely consist of national governments, not companies (Bäckstrand,

---

3   For the complete WSSD database on partnerships, see <http://www.un.org/esa/sustdev/partnerships/partnerships.htm>.

2007). On the other hand, it is also not that much of a surprise either, because the WSSD particularly focused on sustainability in a developing-country context. While there is unmistakably a developmental component to climate change activities (see for example the Clean Development Mechanism), for many multinationals reducing GHG emissions is still predominantly an activity that takes place in Western countries where they are located and subject to pressure from governments and NGOs.

Still there are some partnerships in the WSSD database worth mentioning. Although they are not lead partners, a large number of companies in agriculture, coal mines, landfills, and natural gas and oil systems (including multinationals such as BHP Billiton, Mitsubishi Heavy Industries, Nippon Steel, and Rio Tinto), are taking part in the Methane to Markets Partnership,[4] launched in 2004. In this partnership, companies collaborate with a wide variety of other actors, including industry associations, NGOs and research institutes. The aim of Methane to Markets is to reduce emissions of methane, a greenhouse gas 23 times more potent than CO_2, by recovering it for use as an energy source instead. The only WSSD partnerships with climate change as a primary theme that have corporate lead partners is one led by Germany-based WIP, a company specialising in renewable energy technology, to stimulate bio-energy implementation in Africa, and the Refrigerants Naturally Initiative. The Refrigerants Naturally Initiative[5] was set up in 2004 by three multinationals, McDonald's, The Coca-Cola Company, and Unilever, together with Greenpeace and UNEP. In 2006, Carlsberg, IKEA and PepsiCo joined the initiative of which the main goal is to replace F-gases, such as CFCs, HCFCs and HFCs, by natural refrigerants that are used to cool products at the point where they are sold to the end customer. Since major climate policy instruments, including the EU emissions trading scheme, do not take care of reducing GHG emissions other than CO_2, it can very well be argued that these initiatives that focus on methane and F-gases do fill a regulatory gap and thus have added value as a complement to existing climate policy.

To find partnerships for climate change with more extensive corporate engagement, we chose to analyse in what kind of partnerships Global 500 companies, which have reported their climate change activities to the Carbon Disclosure Project, are participating.[6] Using a variety of corporate and external sources, we found 183 companies (45 per cent from North America, 45 per cent from Europe, and the remainder from Asia) that were involved in a total of 224 different climate change partnerships. This set was used to discern trends in partnerships for climate change. It must be noted that it is near to impossible to come up with a full comprehensive list of climate change partnerships, also because such partnerships

4 For more information, see <http://www.methanetomarkets.org>.
5 For more information, see <http://www.refrigerantsnaturally.com>.
6 For this analysis, we took the fourth CDP survey, of which findings were released in September 2006, as our starting point. This provided insight into climate change activities of 355 of the largest companies worldwide that are listed in the Financial Times Global 500. The actual collection of full data and analysis of the partnerships took place in the period July–November 2007.

are a rather dynamic phenomenon (Waddock, 1991); new partnerships are launched constantly but many also die a slow death within a few years. But our overview gives a reasonable indication of what is going on.

If we look at the types of partners that companies co-operate with, it is interesting to note that more than one-third of all partnerships are with the government. The fact that the government is still a main partner confirms that there is some value in the argument that partnerships are a new governance form that replaces or at least supplements government regulation. There are other factors at play as well, however, as we see in the finding that a university/research institute as partner is just as common as an NGO – both account for one quarter each. The involvement of research partners suggests that many companies are looking for expertise outside their own organisation. To close this 'knowledge gap', they thus tap into climate change-specific knowledge of research institutes and universities to remain ahead of the curve in technological development. In a much more limited number of partnerships (one tenth of total), companies prefer to work with other companies only to further a public policy goal, often mediated by a business association, such as the World Business Council for Sustainable Development. Engaging consumers or the public only happens in a limited number of cases (4 per cent), which is not unexpected given the fact that, unlike the other potential partners, this group is not as organised and therefore difficult to address.

In addition to the partners, it is also interesting to identify the main aim of each partnership as this provides an overview of their nature. Looking at the predominant focus, five types can be distinguished: partnerships for (1) policy influence; (2) emissions reduction; (3) research; (4) product launch; and (5) public education. Although some partnerships had multiple goals, we chose to classify them according to their primary focus. Collaborative efforts that involve research activities (41 per cent) are by far the most common aim of climate change partnerships. Next in line are co-operative programmes to reduce GHG emissions (26 per cent), closely followed by partnerships to influence climate change policy (20 per cent). Partnerships to launch new, climate change-related products can also be found (9 per cent); initiatives to educate the public occur less often (4 per cent). It must be said, though, that, if we look at the number of companies involved in the various types, policy-influence partnerships become much more important (42 per cent of companies are engaged in them; and research partnerships less, 20 per cent) because of the fact that policy-influence partnerships are generally broad forums in which many companies participate together with others. For example, partnerships with the highest participation rates in our sample all have policy-influencing as their main goal: the Global Roundtable on Climate Change; the Pew Center's Business Environmental Leadership Council; Earthwatch's Corporate Environmental Responsibility Group; The Climate Group; the UK's Corporate Leaders Group on Climate Change. Companies choose to form broad coalitions to present a united front vis-à-vis policy makers and to increase their political clout (Kolk and Pinkse, 2007a). Box 3.1 gives some examples of policy-influence partnerships.

Box 3.1 **Some examples of policy-influence partnerships**

3C – Combat Climate Change
'The goal is to underline the need for urgent action by the global community and to influence the post-Kyoto process by demanding a global framework supporting a market based solution to the climate change issue. This can be achieved by getting as many companies as possible aboard and by getting our common platform well known and well understood.' Had 49 members by mid-December 2007.
<http://www.combatclimatechange.org>

USCAP – United States Climate Action Partnership
'United States Climate Action Partnership (USCAP) is a group of businesses and leading environmental organizations that have come together to call on the federal government to quickly enact strong national legislation to require significant reductions of greenhouse gas emissions. USCAP has issued a landmark set of principles and recommendations to underscore the urgent need for a policy framework on climate change.' Had 33 members by 15 December 2007.
<http://www.us-cap.org>

The Climate Group
'The Climate Group works to accelerate international action on global warming with a new, strong focus on practical solutions. We promote the development and sharing of expertise on how business and government can lead the way towards a low carbon economy whilst boosting profitability and competitiveness.' Had 43 members by 15 December 2007.
<http://www.theclimategroup.org>

Business Environmental Leadership Council
'The Pew Center's Business Environmental Leadership Council (BELC) was created at the Center's inception under the belief that business engagement is critical for developing efficient, effective solutions to the climate problem. We also believe that companies taking early action on climate strategies and policy will gain sustained competitive advantage over their peers.' Had 45 members by 15 December 2007.
<http://www.pewclimate.org/companies_leading_the_way_belc>

Global Roundtable on Climate Change
'The Global Roundtable on Climate Change brings together high-level, critical stakeholders from all regions of the world – including senior executives from the private sector and leaders of international governmental and non-governmental organizations – to discuss and explore areas of potential consensus regarding core scientific, technological, and economic issues critical to shaping sound public policies on climate change.' Had 151 participants by 15 December 2007.
<http://www.earth.columbia.edu/grocc/>

In research partnerships, companies are in some cases also involved with a wide range of other actors, including other companies. A typical example is the development of complex technologies such as carbon capture and storage (e.g. the Carbon Sequestration Leadership Forum and the US Department of Energy's Regional Carbon Sequestration Partnerships) or the development of a hydrogen infrastructure to facilitate fuel cell vehicles (e.g. Clean Urban Transport for Europe) that require government support due to the sheer size of such projects. But, more often than not, companies become involved in research partnerships on a unilateral basis. With this type of partnership, companies predominantly try to develop new technologies or products that directly or indirectly contribute to a reduction of GHG emissions. As it often involves developing strategically valuable knowledge

---

Box 3.2 **Examples of other climate change partnerships types**

Emissions reduction

'RESOLVE (**R**esponsible **E**nvironmental **S**teps, **O**pportunities to **L**ead by **V**oluntary **E**fforts) initiative seeks to have every company in every sector of the economy undertake voluntary actions to control greenhouse gas (GHG) emissions and improve the GHG intensity of the U.S. economy.'
<http://www.businessroundtable.org/TaskForces/TaskForce/issue.aspx?qs=6EC5BF159FF49514481138A6DF61851159169FEB56A3FB0AE>, consulted 15 December 2007.

Public education

'The mission of the National Energy Education Development Project is to promote an energy conscious and educated society by creating effective networks of students, educators, business, government and community leaders to design and deliver objective, multi-sided energy education programs.'
<http://www.need.org/>, consulted on 15 December 2007.

Research

'The Cooperative Research Centre for Greenhouse Gas Technologies (CO_2CRC) is one of the world's leading collaborative research organisations focused on carbon dioxide (CO_2) capture and geological storage (geosequestration).'
<http://www.co2crc.com.au>, consulted on 15 December 2007.

Product launch

Fuelling A Cleaner Canada Association: 'In June 1999, Petro-Canada, Ballard Power Systems and Methanex Corporation announced the signing of a memorandum of understanding to work together to prepare for the establishment of a commercially viable fuel distribution network to meet the expected market demand for fuel cell vehicles.'
<http://www.api.org/ehs/partnerships/environmental/partnercleanerfuels.cfm>, consulted on 15 December 2007.

on specific technologies it makes sense that companies go for a unilateral approach because this makes it much easier to create a first-mover advantage based on deployment of a new, climate-friendly technology. Box 3.2 gives examples of a research, emissions-reduction, product-launch and public-education partnership.

Looking at the geographical characteristics, the majority of the climate change partnerships (61 per cent) has a national orientation and one-third an international one, which is not surprising as we took a set of multinationals to collect our data. Only 6 per cent of all partnerships have a local focus and most of these are found in the US, where some activity regarding partnerships takes place on a state level. The geographical origin reveals that partnerships are not a phenomenon that just takes place in one single part of the world only. What can be observed is that European companies are more often engaged in policy-influence partnerships and less in emissions-reduction efforts than their North-American counterparts. This suggests that North-American companies are more likely to go for self-regulation due to the absence of stringent climate change regulations in this region. As to industry participation in climate change partnerships, those industries for which climate change is a particularly salient issue – automobiles, electric utilities, and oil and gas – are also the ones most active with regard to collaborative efforts. Companies in these industries engage in different types of partnerships, although, as the general trend already reflected, they are most active on policy-influence and research partnerships, and, except for electric utilities, also emissions-reduction ones. In other industries with less activity on partnerships, policy influence receives most attention, followed by emissions reductions (see Table 3.2).

As the partnership phenomenon is rather novel, it is hard to say something about *effectiveness*. Compared to voluntary agreements, it is even more complicated to assess effectiveness of partnerships for climate change, because partnerships usually do not have a clearly defined target. Since many are not directly aimed at emissions reduction, but have a range of 'softer' targets instead, such as the development of a specific technology or to persuade policy makers to move in a certain direction, it is not always clear how successful the partnership has in fact been. Indicators that might be used to analyse effectiveness include looking at the lifetime of a partnership and the satisfaction of participants with the way it has been functioning, and comparing achievements with the original aims. The wide range of objectives and partners complicates a straightforward judgement – this is something that also applies to partnerships for sustainable development more broadly. While still a mostly unexplored field of research, the prominence that partnerships have gained over the last few years in the climate change arena begs for more attention in the years to come.

Table 3.2 Industry overview of climate change partnerships*

Sector (n = number of firms investigated)	% of firms in partnerships	% of partnerships in specific type**				
		Research	Product launch	Emissions reduction	Policy influence	Public education
Automobiles & parts (n=12)	83	30	5	35	30	0
Banks & specialty finance (n=61)	34	18	8	24	47	3
Chemicals (n=7)	71	36	29	7	29	0
Electric utilities (n=33)	73	27	8	15	44	6
Food, beverages & tobacco (n=16)	50	8	8	31	54	0
General manufacturing (n=33)	48	7	13	27	47	7
Electronic & electric equipment (n=11)	55	30	10	20	40	0
IT hardware (n=20)	55	5	15	25	55	0
Insurance (n=19)	58	32	5	11	47	5
Mining (n=7)	43	14	0	43	43	0
Oil & gas (n=29)	76	23	11	28	26	11
Pharmaceuticals & biotech (n=20)	45	0	0	50	44	6
Retail (n=17)	35	31	0	31	31	8
Services (n=29)	45	13	17	30	39	0
Telecommunication services (n=24)	42	23	0	15	62	0
Total (n)	**183**	**71**	**32**	**85**	**145**	**15**

* Only those sectors where number of partnerships exceeded 5 have been included
** Percentages may not add up 100% due to rounding

3.3 CONCLUDING REMARKS

This chapter examined voluntary agreements between business and government; and partnerships between companies and other actors in government and society. There are a large number of existing initiatives and, particularly in the field of partnerships, a wave of emerging ones with different foci and various constellations of actors. While it is difficult to assess effectiveness, especially in the case of partnerships, this does not hamper their spread and growth so they apparently serve a purpose. The next chapter will focus on a third type of voluntary initiatives: individual voluntary company self-commitments such as emissions management and internal trading that are not directly needed for compliance as well as information provision (disclosure) on climate change.

4 Carbon control: Emissions measurement, targets and reporting

This chapter will focus on individual company self-commitments related to emissions management (measurement and target-setting) as well as corporate information provision (disclosure) on climate change. These topics are connected to the voluntary initiatives discussed in Chapter 3, as voluntary agreements between business and government, and multistakeholder partnerships often involve and presuppose a good insight into company emissions, setting clear targets and reporting on progress. Compared to the co-operative initiatives, where political dimensions often play a large role, internal company activities are more operational in nature. They aim to effectively manage greenhouse gas (GHG) emissions internally, and to disclose information on the risks and opportunities of climate change to investors and other external stakeholders. We label all these initiatives to manage climate change 'carbon control', reflecting the tendency that a growing number of companies are starting to take climate change into account when making managerial decisions and/or feel the incentive to become accountable to stakeholders on the topic and need information on these matters. To obtain more insight into the way that climate change is (or can be) integrated into operational activities, this chapter will look at aspects related to organisational control systems that companies have implemented to keep track of their carbon footprint. In the process, we also indicate difficulties and choices related to measurement and target setting, and reporting developments.

In a sense, climate change is comparable to other strategic business issues (Porter and Kramer, 2006; Reinhardt, 1999) in that being able to manage it effectively requires (new) control systems that keep track of how a company is doing and where it is going. More generally, control systems have been defined as 'the formal, information-based routines and procedures used by managers to maintain or alter patterns in organizational activities' (Simons, 1994: 170). It has been argued that also for environmental issues this necessity to set up formal, information-based routines and procedures exists, even though much of the information is of a non-financial nature, unlike the more traditional control systems in companies that predominantly focus on financial information (Perego, 2005). To illustrate, it is quite common to have an environmental management system in place, which is often also ISO 14000 certified (Kolk, 2000). However, many of the environmental management systems in place have a mostly internal focus and do not go much beyond assessing the environmental impact of companies' own production activities (Margolick and Russell, 2001). Compared to other environmental issues, however, climate change is more often seen as a strategic issue creating financial risks for companies, thus requiring a control system that has specifically been set up to manage these risks (Sundin and Ranganathan, 2002).

The urgency to acquire and disclose information about climate change as a means of changing patterns in existing business activities has been acknowledged by many companies. This is illustrated by the fact that the first important step that they have taken is conducting an inventory of GHG emissions to be able to put an organisational and informational infrastructure in place for assessing, measuring, and managing GHG emissions and their associated impacts (Hoffman, 2006). As a next step companies have committed to an energy use and/or emissions reduction target (Margolick and Russell, 2001). Finally, it also becomes increasingly more common to report the outcomes of activities and performance on climate change. It is these three steps that we will cover in this chapter, discussing issues and developments related to emissions inventories; emissions reduction targets; and corporate carbon disclosures, respectively. In the process, the chapter also gives insight into the various aspects (and choices) that play a role in carbon control (see Table 4.1 for an overview), and decisions that companies may have to take in design and implementation of systems. Especially for international business, there are a quite a number of factors to consider. While it is certainly not our intention to focus too much on the technicalities, an overview of peculiarities and dilemmas is worthwhile to have as background for the more strategic decision making related to climate change discussed in subsequent chapters, particularly when it comes to emissions trading (Chapter 6).

4.1 EMISSIONS MEASUREMENT AND INVENTORY MAKING

4.1.1 An emissions inventory as standard business practice?

The most common first step towards action on climate change is conducting an inventory of GHG emissions (Sundin and Ranganathan, 2002), as companies need to know their current situation for a start. Although keeping track of energy use has been an activity that has already taken root in many companies a few decades ago (mostly in response to the oil crises of the 1970s), this is not true for GHG emissions (Hoffman, 2006; Margolick and Russell, 2001). As we have seen in the first two chapters, only since the late 1990s have an increasing number of companies started to realise that the climate change issue might not go away. Typically, it is only after companies have come to this conclusion that they begin to track the amount of emissions released from their production activities. However, there are still companies, including some of the world's largest, that are not

Table 4.1 Issues related to corporate carbon control

Issue	Possible considerations
(1) Emissions inventory	
Decision whether or not to set up an inventory	• Actual climate impact • Stakeholder pressure and perceptions • Company strategy • Management priorities and values
Decisions as to measurement methodology	• Type of GHG protocol/standard • Specific purpose for having an inventory (whether for emissions trading scheme and/or climate change registry and/or internal purposes in terms of better management of GHG emissions)
Decisions as to the organisational boundaries	• Only company itself or also (parts of) supply chain • Only 100% ownership or also partly owned subsidiaries and/or joint ventures (in case of the latter selection to be made between equity share and control approach)

Decisions as to scope of emissions	• Which GHG sources to include
	  O Direct: Scope 1 (owned/controlled by company)
	  O Indirect: Scope 2 (generation of purchased electricity)
	  O Indirect: Scope 3 (other sources not owned or controlled)
	• Which types of GHG emissions to include: only CO_2 or all six Kyoto gases, or somewhere in between
	• In the process, accurate consideration of accounting principles related to relevance, completeness, consistency, transparency and accuracy

(2) Target setting	
Decision as to whether or not to set a target	• Leadership and reputation issues • Possibility of cost savings due to efficiency focus • Assessment of whether targets are a sina qua non for reduction programmes and measures or not • Stakeholder (including investor) pressure and perceptions • Management assessment of whether company-wide target may be too limiting compared to more flexible portfolio or industry(wide) voluntary target, and of complexities of target-setting in a context of regulatory and market uncertainties • Potential usefulness in managing risk of non-compliance
Decisions as to type of target	• In the process, consideration of implications related to specific purpose for which target is set (internal and/or external; reckoning with possible sensitivities and outside scrutiny) • Nature of the target: absolute (in emissions) or relative (per unit of output, energy intensity) • Target coverage: energy use and/or GHG emissions • Organisational scope: direct and/or indirect • Geographic scope: local and/or global or a combined, differentiated approach
Decisions as to level of target	• Overall degree of stringency aimed for, considering historical achievements, growth paths, and future plans of the company in industry and (inter)national contexts • Baseline year • Duration (target year)

(Continued overleaf)

Table 4.1 Continued

Issue	Possible considerations
(3) Carbon disclosure Decisions concerning external reporting	• Engage in carbon reporting or not • Which form(s)/avenues of disclosure to choose (via stand-alone or integrated CSR reporting, SEC filings and/or separate Carbon Disclosure reporting) • How to ensure harmonisation between various means of disclosure • Which aspects to include, reckoning with internal, operational and strategic, as well as external implications

measuring GHG emissions, as they apparently think that their business does not have a significant climate change impact or they assess the importance of it differently.

For example, until 2007 the Walt Disney Company had not made a company-wide inventory. It only tracked emissions in Disneyland Paris, because that was required by the French Ministry of Environment. Recently, however, the company appointed a Greenhouse Gas Emissions Manager whose task will be to co-ordinate such an inventory for the first time. While this relatively late response of an entertainment company as Walt Disney is not that surprising in a sense in view of their limited direct climatic impact, General Electric, for example, which has received much recognition due to its 'Ecomagination' campaign, made its first inventory only a few years ago, in 2003. It seems that this company has particularly been focused on the strategic opportunities of some of their product lines to enable their customers to reduce emissions, while the impact of emissions released from their own production activities had started to receive attention only somewhat earlier in the process.

Still, a Ceres[1] report published in early 2006 on the corporate governance of climate change of 100 companies from the 10 most carbon-intensive industries (with substantial operations in the US) shows that an inventory is quite a common practice nowadays. As Figure 4.1 reveals, 79 companies had already conducted an inventory by the end of 2005 (Cogan, 2006). Most striking is the disparity between two fossil-fuel producing industries: the petroleum (and gas) industry and the coal industry. Almost all companies in the petroleum industry have tracked their emissions on a company-wide scale with the exception of four US-based oil

1   Ceres is a US-based coalition of investors, environmental groups and other public interest organisations which puts pressure on companies to address climate change (as well as some other sustainability issues) through different forms of shareholder activism. Ceres for example directs the Investor Network on Climate Risk, a group of more than 50 institutional investors from the US and Europe concerned about corporate climate change behaviour (for more information see <http://www.ceres.org>).

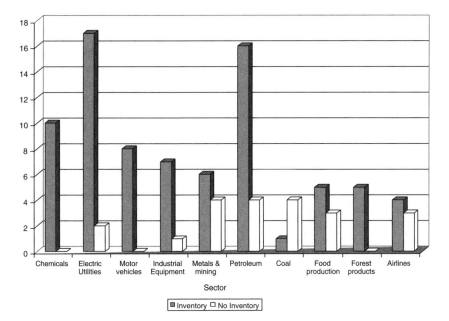

Figure 4.1 Number of companies with GHG emissions inventory.

Source: Based on Cogan (2006)

and gas companies. Since then, of these four companies, one – Murphy Oil – has performed an inventory and two others – Tesoro and Williams – are in the process of doing the same. The fact that two companies – Apache and Devon Energy – with an inventory chose not to disclose this information suggests that it is nevertheless viewed by some as strategically sensitive information. By contrast, only one UK-based coal company in the sample – Rio Tinto – had an inventory, while the other four US-based coal companies – Arch Coal, Consol Energy, Foundation Coal Holdings, and Peabody Energy – had not done the same at the time, or since. On the whole, all four show very limited action on climate change apart from support for government-sponsored clean-coal technology research efforts. Nevertheless, they do recognise that climate change could prove to be a serious threat to the coal industry (Cogan, 2006).

The apparently 'late responses' of some carbon-intensive companies can also be explained from the fact that it is not very easy to make a good and reliable inventory. Only in the past few years have several standards and protocols emerged that facilitate tracking and registering companies' GHG emissions. Currently, the most widely used standard is the WBCSD/WRI GHG Protocol which was first launched in 2001 and renewed in 2004. This GHG Protocol has also been used as the foundation for the new ISO 14064 standard for GHG accounting and verification that was released in 2006. The aim of this ISO standard is to improve the credibility and reliability of GHG accounting, because to date companies have tended to use many different measurement methods to account for their GHG emissions (Boiral, 2006; Weng and Boehmer, 2006; Fransen *et al*, 2007).

4.1.2 Methodology and scope of an emissions inventory

Even though various (non-)governmental bodies strive for further standardisation of GHG measurement, part of it is up to managerial discretion. In making an inventory companies make a choice as to how to measure GHG emissions exactly. What the outcome of these decisions is, and thus also of the inventory, depends on the *purpose* for which companies intend to use the inventory. If it is directly related to participation in an emissions trading scheme (e.g. the European Union emissions trading scheme (EU ETS) or the Chicago Climate Exchange) or a climate change registry (e.g. the California Climate Action Registry or the Canadian GHG Challenge Registry), there is limited (or no) managerial discretion. In the case of trading schemes, the allocation of allowances usually depends on historical emissions (called grandfathering, see Egenhofer, 2007) or, in some cases, on some form of industry benchmark. It is therefore critical that emissions are measured in a consistent way across companies. For example, the EU ETS only deals with CO_2 emissions from specific in-house activities such as power generation, production and processing of ferrous metals, and the production of cement, glass, pulp and paper (see Chapter 6). If an inventory is made for the purpose of joining a registry, there is a little more discretion. The aim of registries is to protect companies that have achieved emissions reductions before a regulatory scheme comes into play. By registering historical emissions, companies try to prevent being penalised by a new regulation that is introduced in a later stage which only takes emissions reductions into account achieved after a particular date (Phillips, 2004). However, as the exact details of potential future regulations are generally not known yet, companies have more flexibility as to which emissions to register exactly.

Nevertheless, companies will usually not just include emissions in their inventory that are regulated by a trading or reporting scheme, because they would in this way not get the full picture of their climate change impact and thus miss potentially important GHG risks and opportunities (Sundin and Ranganathan, 2002). If the inventory not only serves the purpose of regulatory compliance, but also has the strategic aim to manage GHG emissions optimally, companies will take a broader look at the inventory. In other words, to be able to identify where in the supply chain reductions can be achieved most cost-effectively, companies will try to measure all types of emissions that are generated through the complete supply chain. Consequently, the decision where to draw the line in measuring and/or taking responsibility for GHG emissions depends on the strategic importance companies attach to climate change and how eager they are to reduce their climate change impact. Therefore, a standard such as the GHG Protocol recommends companies, in conducting an inventory, to set organisational as well as operational boundaries to GHG measurement (WRI/WBCSD, 2004).

Setting *organisational boundaries* deals with the question of how to account for emissions of parts of the company that are partially owned, such as a joint venture or a subsidiary. How emissions from such operations are consolidated has quite some influence on the outcome of the inventory and the GHG Protocol suggests two potential approaches – the equity share approach and the control approach, corresponding to financial accounting rules – to decide upon this. With the equity share approach, companies only account for emissions according to their equity share. This might be preferred if a company wants to dampen its total emissions, because a company only consolidates the fraction of emissions in proportion to its equity share, and not all emissions released by an organisational subunit. However, if, for example, a joint venture is responsible for massive emission reductions, the company might go for the control approach instead, because with this approach companies account for the full 100 per cent of the emissions.

Early experiences of oil company BP in setting up an internal emissions trading scheme illustrate how shared ownership of operations can create problems in controlling GHG emissions. One of BP's business units, Prudhoe Bay, was operated together with Exxon and ConocoPhillips; BP only had a 26 per cent stake in the oil field. To successfully take part in the internal trading scheme this business unit had to invest in emissions-reducing projects, but it needed the consent of the other two oil companies, unless it was willing to cover all the costs itself. However, covering all costs was not beneficial for the BP business unit because the company had, at the corporate level, decided that it could only account for 26 per cent of the reductions achieved with such projects as it used the equity share approach for consolidation (Victor and House, 2006).

Setting *operational boundaries* involves determining for which GHG sources a company takes responsibility. First, a distinction can be made between direct and indirect GHG sources. Direct or Scope 1 GHG emissions come from sources that a company owns or controls.[2] This generally includes emissions from fossil fuel combustion for electricity, heat or steam generation, production processes for cement and steel manufacture, transportation by company-owned vehicles or aeroplanes, and fugitive emissions, such as refrigerants and methane (Phillips, 2004). Which sources account for direct emissions thus also depends on the consolidation method, because organisational boundaries affect what activities are owned or controlled. Indirect emissions, on the other hand, come from sources where the point of release is not within the company itself, but either upstream or downstream in the supply chain. Within the category of indirect emissions a distinction is made between Scope 2 emissions from the generation of purchased electricity and Scope 3 emissions from other sources not owned or controlled. Whereas Scope 2 emissions are still well-defined, this is not the case with Scope 3 emissions, because it is at a company's discretion how far up and down in the supply chain emissions are tracked. Examples of activities that could fall under

2   The classification in Scope 1, Scope 2, and Scope 3 GHG emissions is derived from the GHG Protocol.

Scope 3 are extraction and production of purchased materials and fuels, transport-related activities (e.g. distribution of sold products and waste transportation), outsourced activities, use of sold products and services, and waste disposal (WRI/WBCSD, 2004).

One reason for distinguishing between the different scopes is to avoid double counting, which is essential when the inventory has a role in regulatory compliance. For example, for an electricity company the CO_2 emissions from power generation are Scope 1 emissions, while for the company purchasing the power they fall within Scope 2. Generally speaking Scope 1 and 2 emissions are relatively unproblematic to measure, but for many of the sources falling under Scope 3 this is much more difficult. To cope with such measurement difficulties in conducting an inventory, and deciding how broad the inventory will be, a basic set of principles has been proposed for GHG accounting (derived from financial accounting): relevance, completeness, consistency, transparency, and accuracy (Fransen *et al*, 2007; WRI/WBCSD, 2004). Deciding which Scope 3 activities to track is typically a trade-off between relevance and accuracy (Phillips, 2004; Sundin and Ranganathan, 2002). To illustrate, measuring emissions from upstream activities depends on the information companies receive from their suppliers, which might not be as accurate, but still relevant if the climatic impact is very high. The same problem exists with downstream emissions, because the exact level often changes with the way products and services are used in practice, thus lowering accuracy. Still it is quite clear that tracking the amount of emissions released from the use of products such as automobiles is highly relevant for controlling emissions of the whole supply chain.

The principles of relevance and completeness surface in deciding which types of GHG emissions will actually be taken into account. Notwithstanding the fact that a standard such as the GHG Protocol prescribes tracking all six Kyoto gases (CO_2, SF_6, CH_4, N_2O, HFCs, and PFCs), in practice there are considerable differences with regard to which greenhouse gases companies monitor. Although many measure carbon dioxide (CO_2), as it is relevant for almost each type of business activity, far less also track other gases such as methane, HFCs (refrigerants) and PFCs (a synthetic industrial gas used in the manufacturing process of semiconductors), and thus fail in terms of completeness. This is particularly important with regard to non-CO_2 emissions. Even though the absolute release might not be that high, which could be a reason not to monitor them, the global warming potential is generally much larger (with some extreme cases). For example, methane has 25 times the potential of CO_2 (over a 100-year time horizon) and HFC-23 even 14,800 times (IPCC, 2007a). This difference in potential has already caused considerable problems in the accounting of GHG emissions, as it has enabled carbon traders to financially exploit the Clean Develop Mechanism (see Chapter 6).

Finally, transparency means that in disclosing their emissions performance companies specify which methodology has been used for measurement. A closely related principle is consistency, which implies that the same methodology is used over time, or that the consequences of changes in the methodology are made explicit. Both principles are essential to be able to compare performance across companies and over time. Until now, it seems that in reporting their emissions performance companies have struggled quite a bit in establishing a satisfactory methodology, let alone one that is transparent and consistent. As a result, comparing performance between close competitors or of a single company over time has to some degree still been a matter of comparing apples and oranges. Only when companies converge in their methodologies used will a comparison become more meaningful (CDP, 2007). The fact that emissions inventories do not produce the same quality of data as financial accounting systems, will thus affect the value of these data for decision-makers within the company as well as those outside, such as financial analysts and institutional investors (Hesse, 2006).

4.2 EMISSIONS REDUCTION TARGETS

4.2.1 Reasons to set a target, or not

One of the main reasons for measuring GHG emissions and conducting an inventory is that it produces information necessary for companies to draw up climate change programmes that include targets for emissions reduction (or stabilisation). In fact, over the past years, setting targets to reduce corporate climate change impact has been the main way for companies to show the public their commitment to helping 'solve' this issue. Nevertheless, whether setting a target is helpful in managing climate change and what would be appropriate in terms of target type and stringency are all very sensitive issues on which companies hold different views, as there are many factors to consider (Margolick and Russell, 2001). This is not surprising since, as we discussed in Chapter 2, whether or not to commit to binding commitments is also a very contentious issue for governments in the international political debate on climate change. Corporate initiatives to set climate-related targets are simply a reflection of this.

An important externally-oriented reason for committing to a target is to show leadership on the issue and thereby improve corporate reputation (Hoffman, 2006; Margolick and Russell, 2001). Showing leadership has been a key motive for early movers on climate change, for whom committing to a target has been a way of proving that they have moved in the direction of a more proactive approach. For example, the first thing British oil company BP did after stepping out of the Global Climate Coalition in 1997 was to establish a target to reduce internal emissions by 10 per cent by 2010 (other steps were setting up partnerships with Environmental Defense and the Pew Center for Global Climate Change) (Levy and Kolk, 2002). The company emphasised that their target was tougher than those of most industrialised countries under the Kyoto Protocol. The BP case on climate change has also become one the most widely-cited best practices in corporate climate change initiatives, because BP managed to achieve its 10 per cent reduction goal at the end of 2001 and also claimed to have generated US$600 million in cost savings. This also lays bare a more internally oriented reason for setting a target, that is, it can lead to cost savings, as a reduction in emissions generally goes hand in hand with a more efficient use of (energy) resources (Margolick and Russell, 2001; Porter and Van der Linde, 1995). Du Pont is another company that prides itself on having achieved cost savings through an emissions reduction programme. This chemical company claims that even though the costs to achieve emission reductions exceeded US$50 million, cost savings amounted to more than US$3 billion between 1990 and the end of 2005.

Compared to conducting an inventory, corporate views on setting company-wide targets for emissions reduction are far more disparate. To illustrate, the Ceres report on the climate change governance of 100 carbon-intensive companies shows that a much lower number, i.e. 49 companies, has set a company-specific target for GHG emissions reduction (Cogan, 2006). As Figure 4.2 illustrates, while almost all companies in industries such as electric utilities and petroleum, for which climate change is clearly a very salient issue, have an inventory, just half of these have also set a target. For US-based utilities the main reason is that many have gone for a collective approach instead, supporting the electric power sector's voluntary commitment under the US Department of Energy's Climate Vision programme to reduce sector-wide GHG emissions intensity rates by about 3–5 per cent by 2010 to 2012 (compared with 2000 to 2002 levels). Unlike the EPA Climate Leaders programme to which many US utilities have also ascribed (see Chapter 3), Climate Vision does not require an individual target or the conducting of an inventory. Similarly, an oil company like ExxonMobil supports the

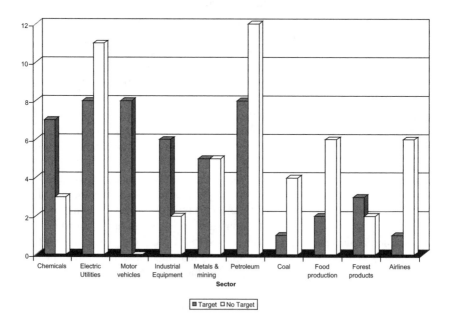

Figure 4.2 Number of companies with an emissions target.

Source: Based on Cogan (2006)

voluntary energy-efficiency target of the American Petroleum Institute, also part of Climate Vision, but has not set an overall emissions reduction target.

Even though many companies have not set a separate climate-related target, this does not necessarily mean that there is no emissions reduction programme in place. In reply to the 2006 Carbon Disclosure Project, ExxonMobil also explains that, while there is no overall target, 'all of [their] businesses have forward projections for GHG emissions on an absolute and intensity basis'. The reason for choosing this approach is that it sees that 'there are a number of factors that influence future emissions, including business growth and intensity changes such as heavier feed slates, higher quality products, regulatory changes and heavy oil developments'. The company thus argues that their 'forward projections of GHG emissions recognize the uncertainties in growth and intensity factors, as well as the impacts of [their] energy efficiency improvements and flaring reduction'. Accordingly, some companies without a target do report on such programmes and show what reductions they have achieved. What ExxonMobil's reply also illustrates is that uncertainty about factors that influence future emissions causes difficulties in setting a target. This is a possible explanation for the fact that a considerable number of other US-based companies in the electric utility, metals and mining, coal and airline sectors have neither set a target. They are very likely to be affected by future regulations on GHG emissions, about which no details are known yet, however. If a company sets a voluntary target and would have to take rather costly measures to achieve it, then it runs the risk of losing competitiveness if the government does not provide the regulatory back-up to reward early action. On the other hand, the risk of future regulation could also be a reason to choose a target because it enables a company to learn more about how to control GHG emissions. In that sense, a voluntary target can thus also be a way of preparing for future regulations (Margolick and Russell, 2001).

It must be noted, however, that not all targets are completely voluntary. Even when a regulation does not prescribe a specific target, the pressure of having to comply with regulation can be reason enough to set a target, as it is a way to make sure that the issue is also addressed within the organisation. In other words, while regulatory uncertainty might be a reason to defer a target, managing risk of non-compliance can be a motivation to set a target. The fact that the car companies in the sample all have targets for the fuel efficiency of their vehicles supports this line of reasoning (see Figure 4.2). In the US this industry has been facing the Corporate Average Fuel Economy (CAFE) standards for decades now (An and Sauer, 2004). For car companies in Europe the situation is quite similar, since the European car industry, via the European Automobile Manufacturers Association (ACEA), agreed, in 1998, with the European Commission, to voluntarily improve average car emissions to 120 grammes in 2012. This required car companies with operations in Europe to also work with targets to achieve this goal. However, because the European Commission judged that most companies were not on track in achieving this voluntary target, at the end of 2006 it started changing this voluntary commitment into a legally-binding target.

Using targets to manage regulatory risk has also become reality for utilities and other heavy users and producers of fossil fuels in Europe. Over the past years, uncertainty with regard to the regulatory approach that the EU would follow has diminished considerably with the introduction of the EU ETS in 2005.[3] This is nicely illustrated by the changing position of German-based utility E.ON. In early 2007 this company still argued on its corporate website that it had 'chosen not to release specific emissions-reduction targets at this stage due to regulatory uncertainty, particularly uncertainty surrounding the design of the EU's Emissions Trading Scheme beyond 2012 and the re-evaluation and use of nuclear energy'. By the end of 2007, however, it had posted the following statement: 'On May 31, 2007 we therefore set an ambitious enterprise-wide climate protection goal for ourselves. By the year 2030 we want to cut our specific CO_2 emissions by 50 per cent to 0.36 t/MWh compared to 1990'. Nevertheless, the level of risk does not always just stem from regulatory developments; it is also closely entwined with the way in which a company develops strategically. Scottish Power, for example, sees that 'due to the changing nature of our operations, our regulatory obligations and growth rates – it would be inappropriate to set group-wide absolute emissions reductions targets that can be tracked on a year to year basis. Our Environmental Vision states our objective to "achieve lower levels of CO_2 per GWh across our portfolio to help combat global climate change"'. This company sees a company-wide target as too much of a straitjacket, not allowing for a more flexible approach regarding specific business segments.

Regulation is not the only source of external pressure to motivate companies to set a climate-related target. Other important agents of external pressure are investors concerned about the risk that climate change poses for carbon-intensive companies in which they invest (Hoffman, 2006).[4] An overview of all shareholder resolutions related to corporate social responsibility in the period 2000 to 2003 shows, for example, that climate change and renewable energy alternatives had the strongest shareholder support of all social and environmental issues (Monks *et al*, 2004). What is more, with shareholder resolutions investors have been shown to be able to force US electric utilities in coming forward on climate change by disclosing their emissions and implementing emissions reduction programmes and targets. In 2003, for example, American Electric Power and Cinergy were put under great pressure by large American institutional investors to be more transparent about their strategy to reduce greenhouse gases and other emissions. For Cinergy this pressure has been decisive in deciding to disclose risks from climate change regulation and to implement a plan for an emissions reduction programme with targets (Hoffman, 2006).

---

3   It must be noted, though, that political turmoil surrounding the exact details about the EU ETS allocation and trading rules have caused considerable difficulties in predicting the future price of carbon, thus leaving some regulatory uncertainty intact.

4   Ceres is actually an important player in bringing together various investors to put organised pressure on companies by such measures as shareholder resolutions and reports about corporate climate change performance.

4.2.2 Determining the specifics of a climate-related target

Similar to an inventory, determining the specifics of a climate-related target, particularly aspects concerning type (absolute or relative; energy use or GHG emissions; direct and/or indirect; local and/or global), and level (stringency; baseline year; timetable), also depends on the way in which companies plan to use it (Hoffman, 2006; Margolick and Russell, 2001). When a company intends to use the target predominantly for internal purposes to control emissions, energy use, and achieve cost savings, the type of target will be different from one that is implemented to manage external impressions and improve reputation. Also, local conditions can require a different type of target than one that is set company-wide on a global level. Basically, setting a company-wide reduction target can be complicated because there are many controllable and uncontrollable company- and context-specific factors that affect a company's choice about what would be an appropriate target. Moreover, deciding about target type and stringency are very sensitive to outside scrutiny. Whereas the outcome of an inventory can be confidential (as the examples of Apache and Devon Energy illustrated), achievement towards a target is almost by definition a public matter.

Companies can make a range of choices in deciding about what kind of target to implement. With regard to *target type* there is large variation in the nature of the target, target coverage, and organisational and geographic scope (Margolick and Russell, 2001). The *nature of the target* refers to whether it is defined in absolute terms, i.e. a reduction in tonnes of emissions, or relative to an economic variable, e.g. per unit of output or as energy intensity target. When considered from the perspective of environmental effectiveness, an absolute approach is the only way to ensure a real reduction of emissions and contribution to climate change mitigation in all instances. Moreover, it is in line with commitments governments made under the Kyoto Protocol, where they agreed to reduce their emissions (phrased as percentages compared to the 1990 baseline). In other words, because of the higher certainty that a company with an absolute target will play a part in helping governments to meet their commitment, public acceptance is likely to be higher as well (Khanna and Ramirez, 2004; Margolick and Russell, 2001).

Nevertheless, a large number of companies has decided to adopt a relative target instead that relates reductions to an economic variable. The clear advantage of a relative target is that achieving it does not stand in the way of company growth and economic success. It will generally be easier to meet a relative target within a set time frame (Thalmann and Baranzini, 2004). However, this is also where the risk is; it may very well be the case that achieving a relative target does not mean that a company has reduced emissions in an absolute sense or moved away from a business-as-usual scenario. More often than not, technological advances cause emissions per unit of output to decrease over time anyway. A relative target therefore does not necessarily incite a company to put extra effort into reducing emissions, which is the basic idea behind committing to a target in the first place. In 2006, Procter and Gamble had, for example, achieved a reduction of 16 per cent in emissions intensity since 2001. Nevertheless, this reduction did not stand in the way of an increase in absolute emissions from 2.9 to 3.2 million tonnes in 2005 as production increased by 29 per cent (partly due to an acquisition). When output is measured in monetary terms, effectiveness of a target becomes even shakier, as it now also depends on economic factors such as inflation, changes in the product mix and quality of the product, which all have a bearing on prices and output value (Khanna and Ramirez, 2004).

The main issue with regard to *target coverage* is whether the target aims at reducing GHG emissions or energy consumption. Targets to reduce energy use in a company have a much longer history and as a consequence are much better institutionalised. It is an aspect that is managed on a local level, e.g. through the environmental management system, and has become common practice because performance on an energy-efficiency indicator leads to cost savings (Hoffman, 2006; Margolick and Russell, 2001). By contrast, the economic effectiveness of a reduction in GHG emissions is much less evident; in the short run, it often first leads to a cost increase instead. In addition, emissions reduction targets are generally set on a company-wide level without clear guidance as to how this translates to the local level and is often an initiative of the environmental department. All these factors combined lead to a situation where it is quite difficult for top management to convince employees across all ranks and levels of the appropriateness of such an emissions goal (Hoffman, 2006). It is thus much easier to adopt an energy-efficiency goal. Still, our analysis of 331 companies that replied to the 2006 cycle of the Carbon Disclosure Project (CDP) shows that 63 companies have set an absolute emissions target and 39 an emissions intensity target, and that only 21 companies report an absolute target on energy use and 32 have an energy-efficiency goal. Nevertheless, this is probably not an accurate reflection, because an emissions goal is typically used for the external purpose of communicating to stakeholders, whereas goals for energy use have a much stronger internal control focus. What is more, achievement towards energy-efficiency goals is sometimes regarded as confidential (Hoffman, 2006) and thus not disclosed through the CDP. Finally, it must be noted that many companies have emissions and energy targets simultaneously; the first on a company-wide level and the second more often differentiated by location (Hoffman, 2006).

The third choice in deciding about type of target is the *organisational scope*. For carbon-intensive companies it is obvious to focus on emissions generated by their own production activities. As most regulations aim at internally-generated emissions, it is sensible for companies under such pressure to first aim for a reduction of these, before looking any further throughout the supply chain. Besides, reducing direct emissions is not as vulnerable to uncontrollable factors as indirect emissions and it is therefore less risky to commit to a target for direct emissions. Still, some companies stretch the scope of targets beyond organisational boundaries, for example, because internal production does not always account for the highest proportion of total emissions that they can be seen as bearing responsibility for. It could very well be that upstream or downstream activities are much more influential in some cases. An obvious example of a huge downstream impact of a product, and one which we have already discussed, is the use of cars. Partly due to regulatory pressure, practically all large car companies have set targets accordingly to improve fuel efficiency or reduce average CO_2 emissions of their fleet. However, in an industry such as oil and gas, where product use also leads to very high emissions, one cannot observe similar kinds of targets for product use. The explanation probably lies in the fact that car companies produce technologically-intensive end-products and have (some) control over emissions from the use of their products by adjusting these technologies. Oil companies, on the other hand, produce a commodity where differentiation in the emissions generated by its use is very limited. One rather rigorous option is to switch from oil towards the production and distribution of natural gas; a switch that is occurring, though not only for environmental reasons, but also to deal with energy security.

Non-carbon-intensive companies sometimes also adopt a target for indirect emissions. There are quite some companies that have decided to reduce emissions from outsourced activities such as transportation of raw materials, distribution of end-products and business travel. British retailer Tesco, for example, has set a target for reducing CO_2 emissions per case of delivered product. Another target that is used by carbon-intensive and non-carbon-intensive companies alike is a goal for increased purchase of electricity from renewable sources, which has been made possible by the recent liberalisation of electricity markets throughout the world. The Coca Cola Company set a target for its North American operations to purchase 2 per cent of electricity from renewable sources; Du Pont has the aim to source 10 per cent of global energy use from renewable resources by 2010; the Dutch bank/insurer ING has committed to a 50 per cent energy consumption from renewable sources in 2006 and 100 per cent in 2007; and Pfizer wants to meet electricity needs with 35 per cent use of clean energy technologies by 2010. There are hardly any goals for any other emissions generated in upstream activities, which is not surprising since, as we discussed in the previous section, it is rather problematic to determine how far up and down in the supply chain a company's responsibility goes.

This aspect is becoming even more complex when the *geographical scope* is included as well. Multinational corporations (MNCs) face the choice as to whether to set a range of local (or even regional) targets, to have one universal global target, to apply an average target globally, allowing differentiation across countries, or to take another approach that reckons with specificities of business units in whatever geographical setting (Christmann, 2004; Dowell *et al*, 2000). One example of a company with local targets only is French retailer Carrefour. Carrefour has a policy where business units are themselves responsible for their specific target and emissions reduction programme. A risk of such a high degree of local responsiveness is a lack of co-ordination and consistency across business units, as well as difficulty in communicating progress to outside stakeholders. However, setting a universal target globally is also not ideal, because the prospect for reducing emissions typically differs per business unit (Hoffman, 2006). Still, a company such as Cadbury-Schweppes has opted for the approach of setting a group-wide target, requiring all manufacturing sites to reduce the amount of energy per finished product by at least 1 per cent each year for the next 10 years.

A global goal allowing differentiated targets seems to be the best of both worlds, but requires well-developed co-ordination and control systems to prevent conflict among business units regarding the targets that each will have to meet. To illustrate, in achieving a global average target, Unilever has followed a bottom-up approach, starting with local targets for each business unit. Based on an aggregation of local targets to a global level, Unilever has subsequently set a five-year global target in 2005 to reduce CO_2 emissions by 10 per cent. Another way in which MNCs have considered interorganisational differences is through internal emissions trading schemes which allow for flexibility in targets (and compliance) reflecting specificities of particular settings. This has been piloted in BP and Royal Dutch/Shell, but this method has to some extent become obsolete as companies can now use the external carbon market to shift 'emissions reductions' between business units and across borders. In a sense, as pharmaceutical company Roche notes, a global presence can be an advantage as 'measures for reducing emissions should be taken at those places where the most significant effects have been evaluated. For a multinational company this means to generate emission certificates in places where maximum effects are expected with minimum costs and then having the possibility to transfer these to sites where the situation for modifying installations is less favourable'. How this translates into adequate target types (and levels) is a complex issue, however.

Hence, apart from deciding upon type of target, companies also need to make a choice regarding the *level of the target* (Margolick and Russell, 2001). Due to the legitimising role of a climate change target, the potential loss of face when targets are not met will be quite high. In other words, target-setting for emissions reduction is a rather risky exercise and depends on many strategic decisions. This is reflected in the different levels of stringency that companies apply. The level of stringency depends on factors such as what (baseline) year to compare future emissions with, in which year the target will have to be achieved, and how fast emissions would rise under a business-as-usual scenario. What is more, determining baseline year, duration and thus stringency of the target is highly sensitive to factors such as political developments on climate change, a company's activities in the past and (near) future, as well as company growth. To stay in tune with (geo)political developments on climate change, where targets also play an important role, a target with a short duration is prudent because it can be adjusted on relatively short notice. In addition, reputation-wise a short-term target has the advantage of being able to show outside stakeholders that commitments are achieved on a regular basis. Still, strategic direction and company growth complicate matters considerably. While a target with a short duration can be quickly adapted to new activities, for example when a shift in activities takes place as a result of acquisitions or divestures, a long-term target gives flexibility in waiting for what new technological developments will bring in terms of options for mitigation. Particularly in taking account of an expansion of the company, setting a credible baseline also depends on reliability of historical emissions data of the company that has been taken over. A recent baseline year may therefore also be the result of the pragmatic reason that there is simply no way to compare current emissions with emissions in past years when emissions can only be estimated.

To avoid making a decision about the level of a target, a company can of course choose to just follow government regulation and set targets according to government and/or industry standards. This is the approach of many US-based companies supporting their business association's participation in the US Climate Vision programme. Another example is Finnish utility Fortum, which has adopted the absolute emission caps set upon their installations that fall under the EU ETS as reduction target. It does not see the need to formulate a company-wide target valid across all ranks and levels of the company. However, for this utility it is relatively easy to follow this approach because it has a limited geographical spread (about 10 countries, mostly in Europe). Highly internationalised MNCs face many different country standards which complicates matters considerably. Geographically, an MNC's home country government Kyoto commitment (and ensuing regulations) is just one contextual factor affecting the specifics of a target; host countries' positions on climate change can be of influence as well.

4.3 CARBON DISCLOSURE IN CORPORATE REPORTING

In the preceding sections, much attention has been paid to measurement and target setting mostly from an internal perspective to shed light on crucial dimensions of carbon control. However, how effective carbon control is also depends on the way in which companies use the information that thus comes available. A number of companies intends to use the resulting indicators on climate change performance in such a way that it also links to external interests. For example, companies including BG Group, Norsk Hydro, Novo Nordisk, BHP Billiton, and Munich Re all (plan to) include emissions indicators in investment decision processes, partly influenced by investor attention to and concerns about the risks of climate change. In the same vein, Santander Central Hispano has integrated these indicators in the credit decision-making process. This reflects a tendency that external stakeholders, including regulators, investors and non-governmental organisations (NGOs), have also become interested in carbon information and related views of companies on their exposure to climate change and their performance in cutting back GHG emissions. In other words, due to their stake in a company such stakeholders need this information because it has become 'material' for making decisions with regard to the company (Chan-Fishel, 2002). For example, if a company will be impacted heavily by new regulations such as the EU ETS, investors would like to know about the exact risk they run when investing in the company. Therefore, besides developing accounting mechanisms to track emissions, companies have also started to disclose the ensuing information to external audiences. Even though such reporting is still in its infancy, it has started to mature considerably, particularly in carbon-intensive sectors such as electric utilities. This is reflected in the fact that, over the past five years, three different avenues have evolved by which companies have started to fulfil this informational need of stakeholders and disclose their exposure to direct (physical) and indirect (regulatory) effects of climate change. This final part of the chapter will first discuss developments in types of disclosures, followed by some factors that may explain different reporting patterns.

4.3.1 Three avenues for climate change disclosure

A *first avenue* where carbon disclosure has become notable is sustainability or corporate social responsibility (CSR) reporting. Research on the Fortune Global 250 shows that 59 per cent of the companies that published such a report in 1999 mentioned climate change; the percentages for 2002 and 2005 were 79 per cent and 85 per cent respectively (KPMG, 1999, 2002, 2005). It must be noted that the number of disclosing companies in the set of 250 companies overall has grown over the years as well, from 88 in 1999 to 112 in 2002 and 161 in 2005. Besides the growth in percentages and numbers, the type of information provided about climate change has clearly changed. In 1999, for example, 48 per cent of companies reported on emissions performance related to its own business activities. By 2005, this had risen to 67 per cent. In addition, by then measurement and reporting on indirect emissions from the purchase of electricity had emerged (33 per cent), although many companies were rather unclear about the types of emissions involved. Indirect emissions from other sources such as transportation or product use were reported by 26 per cent in 2005. The flexible mechanisms of the Kyoto Protocol, which were rather new in 1999, received explicit attention in 2005: 24 per cent mentioned exploring the consequences of emissions trading, while 13 per cent referred to (possible) involvement in carbon reducing projects (e.g. the Clean Development Mechanism). A constant has been corporate descriptions of product innovations to address climate change concerns, improve energy efficiency and reduce dependency on fossil fuels. However, it is not always clear, particularly when it comes to product aspects, where to draw the distinction between incremental activity spurred by climate change and 'normal innovation'. It is also sometimes difficult to distinguish real activity from marketing – public affairs play an important role in these types of reports.

A *second avenue* that companies have used for carbon disclosure is addressing it in filings to the Securities and Exchange Commission (SEC), particularly in the US. All publicly listed companies in the US are required to provide information to the SEC of instances 'where a trend, demand, commitment, event or uncertainty is both presently known to management and reasonably likely to have material effects on the registrant's financial condition or results of operation'. As climate change might create situations in which a company's financial condition or operational results are seriously affected, it can very well be argued that companies are likely to address climate change in these filings (Chan-Fishel, 2002). Because disclosure through SEC filings is aimed at a narrower audience than sustainability or CSR reporting, that is, particularly investors, this type of carbon disclosure

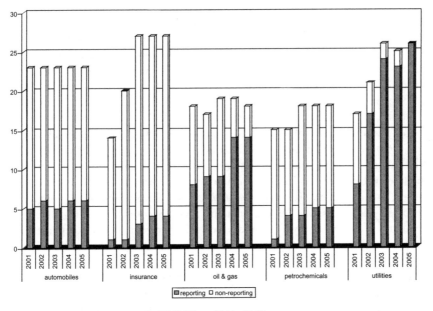

Figure 4.3 Carbon disclosures in SEC filings 2001–2005.

Source: Based on Chan-Fishel (2002, 2003, 2004, 2005, 2006)

gives some indication whether or not companies view climate change as a factor with an impact on their bottom line.

Environmental NGO Friends of the Earth (FoE) analysed the SEC filings of five carbon-intensive sectors – automotive, insurance, oil and gas, petrochemicals, and utilities – on an annual basis over a period of five years: 2001 to 2005 (Chan-Fishel, 2002, 2003, 2004, 2005, 2006).[5] The overall trend in this period is a clearly increasing number of companies that acknowledged the financial impact of climate change on their organisation and decided to disclose their carbon exposure to shareholders via this route. In 2001, 26 per cent of the companies in these sectors reported on climate change, while percentages for 2002 to 2005 were 38 per cent, 39 per cent, 47 per cent and 49 per cent respectively. The studies also demonstrate great diversity across the sectors. As Figure 4.3 shows, it is particularly in the electric utilities industry that climate change reporting in SEC filings has picked up steam. While only 47 per cent of the utilities in the sample reported in 2001, this immediately jumped up the next year to 81 per cent, reaching 100 per cent reporting in 2005. Oil and gas has also witnessed a steady increase,

5 The number of companies analysed changed slightly over the years: while the first survey included 87 publicly traded companies, for the next four surveys this amounted to 96, 113, 112 and 112 companies, respectively. It must also be noted that even though these companies were listed in the US this does not mean that their headquarters were located there as well: the surveys included a considerable number of non-US-based companies from Europe, Canada, Asia and Latin America (Chan-Fishel, 2002, 2003, 2004, 2005, 2006).

although not as rapid as utilities, growing from 44 per cent in 2001 to 78 per cent in 2005. Progress in insurance and petrochemicals has been considerably less, however, as both started with only 7 per cent reporting companies in 2001; and whereas petrochemicals jumped to 27 per cent the next year, there has been no increase since. Growth in reporting of insurance companies has been even slower, since only one company – Chubb – reported the first two years, and was only accompanied by three additional companies in 2005. Finally, in automobiles the same five or six companies reported each year. Of the Big Three US-based car manufacturers – General Motors, Ford, and DaimlerChrysler – General Motors was the only one that waited until 2004 before it addressed climate change in its SEC filings, while the other two reported each year. Another finding of the FoE analyses is that non-US-based companies have persistently reported more than their US counterparts. For example, in 2001 only 15 per cent of US companies reported while this was 56 per cent for non-US companies. This difference remained in existence over the years, with 33 per cent of US companies and 89 per cent from other industrialised countries reporting in 2005 (Chan-Fishel, 2002, 2006).

With regard to the quality of disclosure, at first climate change information in SEC filings was quite limited as most companies merely provided some qualitative information such as discussion of relevant climate change regulations, financial impact on the sector as a whole and on the company in particular, and the corporate response to these regulations (Chan-Fishel, 2002). Over the course of this period, this improved considerably, however, as companies also started to disclose the results of their inventory and level of and progress towards their climate change targets. What is particularly interesting, in view of the fact that this reporting channel is aimed at investors, is how companies perceive the financial impact of climate change on the company, to what extent financial value can be attached to it, and whether the issue is material, meaning that it is significantly affecting financial results. The views expressed have been very diverse indeed. Findings of the 2005 analysis show that of the 55 reporting companies, 9 give no information, 5 believe it is not possible to estimate the impact, 8 expect a mixed impact, 27 acknowledge an adverse impact, and 5 companies say that even though there is likely to be an impact this will not be material. It is noteworthy that this latter category contains two oil companies – BP and Suncor – that were among the few that gave quantitative information on the financial impact, but nevertheless concluded that the impact of climate change on the price of an oil barrel will still be marginal compared with other factors affecting global energy demand (Chan-Fishel, 2006).

A *third avenue* of disclosure, one specifically aimed at climate change and there-fore also providing the most comprehensive information, is the Carbon Disclosure Project (CDP). Launched late 2000 in London, it has concentrated on requesting annual information from companies around the world on GHG emissions, in the process raising both corporate and investor awareness. CDP has requested information about how companies deal with climate change by sending out a questionnaire, including questions on aspects such as perceived opportunities and risks of climate change, amount of greenhouse gases emitted, emissions reduction targets and programmes, and approach taken towards emissions trading. As stated on its website, the goal of CDP is 'to create a lasting relationship between share-holders and corporations regarding the implications for shareholder value and commercial operations presented by climate change. Its goal is to facilitate a dialogue, supported by quality information, from which a rational response to climate change will emerge'.[6] Basically, CDP represents an effort to develop standardised reporting procedures for companies concerning their climate-related activities, in a form intended to complement annual financial accounts and pro-vide information relevant to investors relating to the business risks and opportun-ities from climate change. CDP was established by the US charity Rockefeller Philanthropy Advisors as a London-based co-ordinating secretariat for insti-tutional investors who want to obtain insight into the climate risk profiles of the Financial Times 500 (FT500) companies. The first CDP inventory, published in 2003, only targeted the Financial Times 500; the fifth (published in 2007) approached more than 2,400 companies; and it now seems CDP will be repeated over the coming years also further extending the number of companies covered.

In the FT500 set, that was included in all five years, response rates have grown considerably over the years, from 227 companies (46 per cent) in 2003, 287 (59 per cent) in 2004, 351 (71 per cent) in 2005, 362 (72 per cent) in 2006, and 383 (77 per cent) in 2007. In other words, the vast majority of FT500 companies are now using CDP as a mechanism for carbon disclosure. Yet, these numbers also show that the increase in responses from 2003 to 2005 has levelled off since. With regard to responses to CDP, five categories can be distinguished: companies that filled out the questionnaire and gave permission for public disclosure through the Internet; filled out the questionnaire but restricted disclosure to the collaborating institutional investors; provided information mostly referring to their sustain-ability report; answered CDP but declined to participate; and companies that did not respond at all. Figure 4.4 shows the trends in each category over the first four years of CDP.

To explore geographical spread and type of sector of reporting companies we added together the public and restricted disclosure categories. As Figure 4.5 indi-cates, in terms of numbers North American companies using CDP for carbon disclosure initially scored lower than European companies, but they surpassed them by 2005 (it must be noted that the North American sub-sample predomin-antly consists of US companies). However, percentages tell a different story. North American companies went from 30 per cent response in 2003 to 44 per cent, 61 per cent and 66 per cent in the following years, respectively. Response in Europe has been much higher as it moved from 74 per cent in 2003 to just below 90 per cent in the following years. What Figure 4.5 also shows is that large companies from developing countries are starting to enter the FT500, and also address climate change, with 13 responding companies in 2006 compared to only

6 See <http://www.cdproject.net>.

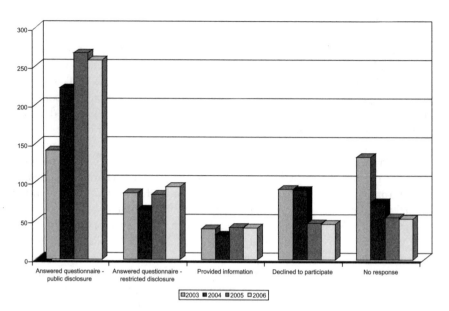

Figure 4.4 Carbon disclosures through Carbon Disclosure Project 2003–2006.

Source: Based on CDP (2003, 2004, 2005, 2006)

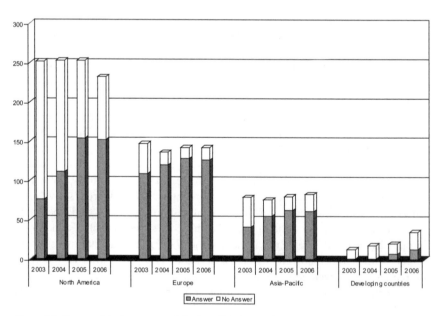

Figure 4.5 Geographical patterns of Carbon Disclosure Project 2003–2006.

Source: Based on CDP (2003, 2004, 2005, 2006)

1 in 2003. To explore sectoral patterns we differentiated between manufacturing companies (Figure 4.6) and service companies (Figure 4.7). Regarding manufacturing the overall picture is quite similar to the SEC filings, with utilities and to a lesser extent oil and gas as front runners in reporting, although on the whole companies are more active in using CDP. There are also some differences, however, as a much higher percentage of automotive and chemical companies are using CDP. Finally, as Figure 4.7 points out, service companies generally report less often, but there is an upward trend here as well. Unlike SEC disclosures, insurance companies are more actively reporting via CDP, which can be explained from the activity of European insurance companies which are way ahead of their US counterparts (as included in the FoE studies) in their communication about climate change.

4.3.2 Explaining climate change disclosure patterns

What the patterns in carbon disclosures show is that communicating corporate policy regarding climate change through these avenues is a way of responding to political, social and investor pressure. First, the transparency that a company provides to stakeholders is highly influenced by the position of a company's home country vis-à-vis the Kyoto Protocol. Even for companies based in non-ratifying countries, but with considerable operations in ratifying host countries, the position of the home country is decisive (Freedman and Jaggi, 2005). This is particularly

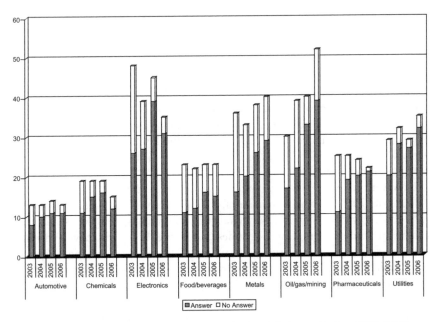

Figure 4.6 Sectoral patterns in manufacturing (Carbon Disclosure Project 2003–2006).

Source: Based on CDP (2003, 2004, 2005, 2006)

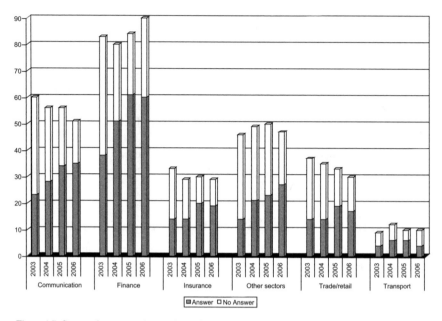

Figure 4.7 Sectoral patterns in services (Carbon Disclosure Project 2003–2006).

Source: Based on CDP (2003, 2004, 2005, 2006)

seen in disclosure in SEC filings, where over the complete period of five years the majority of US companies has been lagging behind non-US companies. However, disclosure patterns of CDP show a slightly different dynamic over this period. Back in 2003 when the CDP questionnaire was first sent out, the results still corresponded with the widely diverging positions on climate change across the regions. The rejection of the Protocol by the Bush Government clearly had its effect on US companies. By contrast, the fact that the EU ratified the Protocol at an early stage led to a more positive stance on the part of European companies. The Japanese government only ratified after some hesitation and has been less outspoken on the subject than the EU, resulting in a more modest position of Japanese companies as well.

However, in spite of the transatlantic policy gap, after 2004 the disclosure patterns of CDP show that companies from the different regions have converged considerably, with US companies catching up with Japanese companies, and both gaining ground on European companies (see Figure 4.5). This convergence not only stands out against disclosure patterns in SEC filings, but also against trends in sustainability reporting, where US companies lag behind Europe and Japan (Kolk, 2005, 2008). A probable explanation is that carbon disclosure via CDP is a relatively low cost and issue-focused way for companies to show that they are taking climate change seriously, especially in a context with much emerging local interest in the topic. Integrating this issue in financial and non/financial reports means that it has to compete with many other issues that are material to the financial bottom line of a company. Moreover, sustainability and CSR reports are not always published on an annual basis, resulting in a much longer time lag in reflecting the most recent state of play.

As a consequence, it seems that the companies that report via CDP can more quickly reflect on and adapt to most recent developments in the climate change arena. This has had the convergent effect seen in carbon disclosure through CDP. As practically all FT500 companies which answer CDP are operating internationally, they not only feel home-country, but also some host-country pressure (e.g. due to the EU ETS). It has therefore been much easier for US companies to catch up in disclosing through this communication channel. Whether this convergence goes beyond communication and also leads to the same level of quality in carbon disclosure is still a question, though. Implementing more sophisticated accounting and reporting systems for GHGs will involve much higher costs, which might lead to a longer continuation of a home-country bias. Therefore, it may not be until the moment that they have to prepare for emissions trading in their home countries that US and Japanese companies will reach the same level of carbon disclosure as their European counterparts. Nevertheless, the convergence in CDP also demonstrates that merely looking at government stances on climate change does not tell the full story. Even though the US Federal Government still has not come up with any clear-cut regulations to curb the emission of GHGs, US companies have caught up considerably in their carbon disclosure. One explanation for this trend is, as we showed in Chapter 2, that an increasing number of US states has filled the gap left by the Federal Government, by introducing climate policies on a state-level (Rabe, 2004). As this is currently taking the shape of regional emissions trading initiatives, increased carbon disclosure by US companies can also be seen as a response to the fact that forthcoming regulations will require establishing GHG accounting and reporting mechanisms to engage in carbon trading. In other words, adopting internal control and communication systems to account for GHG emissions is a pre-emptive move for preparing for future regulation and/or responding to other forms of social and political pressure.

Another explanation for this convergence is that, particularly in the US, (institutional) investors have stepped up pressure on publicly listed companies to disclose such climate change-related information (Monks *et al*, 2004). While shareholder pressure had some influence on the process of setting targets, as noted above, the impact on disclosure is much more apparent. There are several potential reasons why shareholders have become more interested in climate change. First, the impact of shareholder pressure on carbon disclosure is part of a broader movement where a mainstreaming of socially responsible investment has been taking place (Sparkes and Cowton, 2004). As a result, those involved in insurance, banking and investing have started to pay attention to the risks and opportunities of climate change. The year 2006 saw, for example, and as mentioned in section 4.2.1, a report on corporate governance and climate change that ranked the 100 world's largest companies on the extent to which they integrate climate change in their governance practices and strategic planning (Cogan,

2006). Second, climate change received most support amongst the CSR proposals filed by shareholders in the US in the period 2001 to 2003 (Monks *et al*, 2004). In subsequent years, the numbers have still been increasing: from 22 filed in 2004 in the US, to 43 in 2007.[7] In that sense, current interest seems a culmination of a mainstreaming effort that started originally within the (more niche) socially responsible investment community, and with only a few companies that recognised the need to do something on climate change. A third reason that may explain increased shareholder interest is the passing of the Sarbanes-Oxley Act in 2002. This Act requires companies to put in place internal control systems for identifying and reporting material risks. Consequently, shareholders have more rights in demanding information about factors that pose such material risks, of which climate change can be one (Chan-Fishel, 2003).

4.4 CONCLUDING REMARKS

This chapter examined the several mechanisms companies have implemented with the aim to effectively control GHG emissions internally and disclose information on the risks and opportunities of climate change to investors and other external stakeholders. It is apparent that the whole set of business practices for tracking and disclosing climate change-related information has seen great development in the past few years. However, producing reliable information about corporate approaches to climate change still remains a very challenging task. Regarding all three types of practices discussed in this chapter – emissions inventories, emissions reduction targets, and carbon disclosure – there is a lack of standardisation and many options for companies (see Table 4.1) to choose an approach that fits their situation best. While this offers dilemmas for companies, it is also complicating matters for external stakeholders such as investors, regulators and NGOs who would like to compare different companies on their carbon footprint. While regulatory and shareholder pressures are likely to play a role in moving towards a more limited set of agreed-upon methodologies for emissions measurement and disclosure, as put forward by international bodies, there will still be room for managerial discretion on these matters in the years to come. Insight into such operational dimensions of carbon control is helpful as a background for the more strategic decision making related to climate change that will be dealt with next.

---

7 For more information, see <http://www.incr.com>, <http://www.ceres.org>, or <http://www.cdproject.net>.

Part II

Strategic options for business

5 Business strategies for climate change

Emissions measurement, target setting and reporting, as discussed in the previous chapter, are generally considered to be the initial activities in a company's response to climate change. A common next step is evaluating and implementing options for the reduction of greenhouse gas (GHG) emissions in order to reach the aspirations expressed by the climate change targets. For most companies this means deploying a range of relatively 'easy-to-implement' activities that involve some basic technological and behavioural changes (Hoffman, 2006). Examples of such technological changes include measures to improve energy efficiency and reduce energy consumption such as improving insulation of company properties, introducing energy management systems aimed at a better management of lighting and heating of buildings, and replacing outdated, energy-inefficient production installations. Options for behavioural changes comprise improving employee awareness of the implications of their use of office equipment such as printers and computers for a company's energy consumption and reducing the carbon impact of business travel (Okereke, 2007). Particularly when climate change functions as an eye-opener by showing that there are previously untapped low-cost options to reduce energy use, reduction activities of this kind form the 'low-hanging fruit' of climate change mitigation (Hoffman, 2006). Overall, such activities are largely operational, and concern the integration of climate change in corporate day-to-day practices.

However, although for many companies becoming responsive to climate change does not go much further than operational improvements, this does not fully reveal the current state of companies' business practices. Corporate activities on climate change are not only a way of becoming more efficient operationally, but are also starting to play a role on a more strategic level (Porter and Reinhardt, 2007). Climate change can have a considerable influence on the value proposition of a company (Porter and Kramer, 2006), inducing it to fundamentally reconfigure business activities to simultaneously reduce climatic impact and enhance the competitive position (Kolk and Pinkse, 2008). At present, a range of strategic responses is emerging to address climate change and reduce GHG emissions through product and process improvements and emissions trading with the aim of creating and/or retaining value. The exact composition of such strategic options is company-specific, depending on the (perceived) risks and opportunities related to climate change, the competitive dynamic of the markets in which a company is active, and the type of regulation and stakeholder pressure relevant for the industry and countries in which it operates (Kolk and Levy, 2004).

This chapter examines GHG emissions-reduction options available to companies, focusing on the strategic responses that have emerged most recently, and identifies the actual patterns of market-oriented actions currently being taken. These business strategies for climate change consist of different combinations of the market components available to managers. We present a typology that shows that under current, rather flexible regulatory regimes (see Chapter 2), managers have the possibility to choose between a greater emphasis on improvements in their business activities through innovation on the one hand and compensatory approaches granted by the emerging carbon market on the other. An innovation strategy can improve a company's assets and competencies as a result of the development of new climate-friendly technologies or services that reduce emissions. Compensation involves the transfer of emissions or emissions-generating activities. Companies can follow these approaches merely on their own or by interacting with external actors, be it other companies in the supply chain or industry, non-governmental organisations (NGOs) or government agencies. Before explaining this typology (in section 5.2), however, we will first give some more background as to the factors that have influenced corporate activities on climate change.

5.1 FACTORS THAT INFLUENCE CORPORATE POSITIONS ON CLIMATE CHANGE

As with many other sustainability issues, developing strategies to reduce the negative impact on climate change and create a lasting impact on competitiveness is a joint influence of external and company-specific factors (Aragón-Correa and Sharma, 2003; Bansal, 2005; Delmas and Toffel, 2004; Kolk and Levy, 2004; Porter and Reinhardt, 2007) (see Table 5.1). The impact of sustainability issues in general and climate change in particular on companies depends to a large extent on external influences including physical effects, such as extreme weather events, rising sea levels, floods, droughts, etc. (Lash and Wellington, 2007), government policy (Rugman and Verbeke, 1998), and pressure from activists, NGOs, local communities and the media (Bansal, 2005; Buysse and Verbeke, 2003; Eesley and Lenox, 2006). As a consequence, an effective response to climate change relies on the way in which a company is able to anticipate critical incidents such as hurricanes, and, more important in the short term, to integrate the interests of the different stakeholders involved with the issue (Hart, 1995; Sharma and Vredenburg, 1998).

In the longer run, strategically adjusting to climate change is essentially a response to the physical effects of climate change. For example, sectors such as agriculture, food processing, fishery and forestry all depend on raw materials that are vulnerable to changing weather patterns (Lash and Wellington, 2007). For a

Table 5.1 Factors that influence corporate positions on climate change

Factor	Some components
External, issue-related factors	• Physical impact relevant to types and location of operations • Government policies and regulation • Stakeholder pressures and perceptions (including investors, consumers, NGOs, society at large)
Industry-related factors	• Industry structure (technological and competitive situation) • Industry growth • Concentration level
Company-specific factors	• Position within the supply chain • Economic situation and market positioning • History of involvement with (technological) alternatives • Degree of (de)centralisation • Degree of internationalisation of top management • Availability and type of internal climate expertise • Corporate culture and managerial perceptions • Capacity to anticipate risks, spread vulnerabilities, and manage stakeholders

[handwritten marginal note: Might be relevant]

food company such as Unilever this means that there is an increased risk of a faltering supply of agricultural products from parts of the world that are hit more often by increased occurrences of drought or storms that lower crop yields. Therefore, Unilever pursues a strategy of manufacturing a range of products that diversifies the risks of extreme weather conditions, and it keeps track of emissions related to energy use by taking the type of energy source into account. Likewise, Coca Cola has started to study potential problems in water availability in parts of the world that may get less precipitation in coming decades (Lash and Wellington, 2007). Physical risks also affect firms that have operations in vulnerable areas (e.g. coastal regions), such as oil and gas companies with oil rigs in hurricane-prone areas such as the Caribbean. Ultimately, increased physical risks of climate change will have an adverse effect on the insurance industry, because they will be called upon when companies incur damages from extreme weather. It will come as no surprise, then, that the world's largest reinsurance companies – Swiss Re and Munich Re – were amongst the first to acknowledge the strategic risks of climate change (Dlugolecki and Keykhah, 2002).

However, in the shorter run, a corporate strategic response is not confined to adjustments in anticipation of the physical impact of climate change, but particularly a reaction to social, economic and political pressures (Kolk and Pinkse, 2004). Most notably, climate change has incited considerable political and regulatory machinery, with the Kyoto Protocol and the EU emissions trading scheme as the main outcomes so far. Climate change regulation is both viewed as a business risk and an opportunity. Which perspective a company holds depends on a wide variety of factors, including the industries and countries in which it operates. Typical industries that perceive it as a risk are the oil and gas industry, the automotive sector, and utilities (Ernst & Young, 2008). This is not surprising in view of the fact that emissions reduction regulation is mainly directed at these industries. In the current design of the European Union emissions trading scheme (EU ETS), for example, energy activities, the production and processing of metals, the mineral industry, and the pulp and paper sector are subject to a cap on greenhouse gas emissions (see Chapter 6).

Still, government regulation is sometimes also viewed as an opportunity. Strict regulation favours companies that have already started to take account of climate change in a relatively early phase and potentially crowd out companies that show a poor record with regard to emissions reductions (Levy, 1997). It might also be an opportunity for financial companies, which can assist customers that are affected by such regulation through facilitating their emissions trading activities or financing carbon offset projects for them. Another factor that influences regulatory impact is the geographic spread of a company. While it is quite clear for companies located in the EU what the regulatory impact is, in other countries where climate change regulation is still in a developmental state, such as the US, Canada and Japan, the regulatory impact is more uncertain. Since current investment decisions in installations such as coal-fired power plants will become very costly if regulations are implemented in the near future, regulations will already influence corporate strategy even before they have actually been implemented (Lash and Wellington, 2007).

Climate change has also become a social issue in the sense that people are starting to worry more about the impact on their living conditions. The worldwide box-office success of Al Gore's movie 'An Inconvenient Truth' is the clearest example of this. Correspondingly, NGOs and activists have also stepped up their pressure on companies to deal with the issue of climate change (Boiral, 2006). Not acting on climate change could therefore very well constitute a reputational risk (Hoffman, 2005); or, particularly in the US, a litigation risk (Lash and Wellington, 2007). In the past few years, public opinion in many countries has tilted towards a feeling that companies really should do something about climate change (for more details see the overview of public opinion polls in Chapter 1). Many activities in the field of climate change are therefore initiated to prevent loss of face vis-à-vis the public at large.

However, if maintaining reputation is the main driver, this could lead to climate change activities that reflect legitimacy-seeking behaviour only. The consequence may be that no structural changes will occur (Meyer and Rowan, 1977; Suchman, 1995). If this is the case companies merely pursue measures that satisfy stakeholder requests in the short run, but do not lead to emissions reductions in the long run. To illustrate, while 87 per cent of the companies that answered the Carbon Disclosure Project (CDP) claimed that they take climate change seriously, only 48 per cent had also implemented an emissions reduction programme (CDP, 2006). In other words, there are apparently quite a number of companies that have used the issue to 'greenwash' their public image by taking some small-scale symbolic actions which are broadly communicated (Ramus and Montiel, 2005). Without a doubt several multi-stakeholder partnerships on climate change that we identified in Chapter 3, are used for greenwashing purposes as well, as it is relatively easy to free-ride on the green credentials of some of the front-running companies that take part in a partnership as well (King and Lenox, 2000) or use the brand of renowned NGOs for marketing purposes (Van Huijstee *et al*, 2007). In the Netherlands, for example, electricity producer Essent has a partnership with WWF, and uses their Panda label in marketing campaigns, but proposed to build new coal-fired power plants against the will of this NGO anyway.

While social and political pressures are important for companies in drawing their attention to the issue, climate change has, unlike many other environmental issues, a more dominant strategic impact, because it is also driven by market pressures (Hoffman, 2005). Increased attention for climate change makes consumers more aware of the climatic impact of their purchasing behaviour (Bonini *et al*, 2008), which sets in motion a market transition towards the production of less carbon-intensive products and services. A backlash from consumers against companies that have a negative impact on the climate is particularly risky for environmentally sensitive markets or markets where brand value plays an important role in retaining customers (Lash and Wellington, 2007).

In addition, investors fear that if companies in which they invest are not taking action this could lead to unmanageable financial risks. They thus put pressure on companies to minimise these risks, which means that companies which are lagging behind in their carbon management may be excluded from certain sources of capital. At first only oil and gas and electricity companies were hit by climate change-related shareholders resolutions in this way (Monks *et al*, 2004). However, the *Financial Times* reported in March 2008 that institutional investors are broadening their scope and now also target airlines (e.g. US Airways and Southwest Airlines) and major banks (e.g. Citigroup) that finance carbon-intensive activities such as coal mining (Birchall, 2008).

Besides, the rise of the carbon market has put a price on CO_2 emissions, thus creating a new commodity. This new commodity in turn affects trading patterns in closely related commodities such as coal and natural gas, as it has an impact on the operation costs of power plants (Paolella and Taschini, 2006). Finally, there is market pressure from technological change and innovations by competitors or other companies with products within the same value chain (Okereke, 2007). For example, the development of new (bio)fuels means that car and aeroplane producers need to modify their designs accordingly; or vice-versa, when automotive companies induce technological change, for example by planning to use hydrogen as a fuel, this has implications for fuel suppliers.

It is also important to note that managerial perceptions play a role in companies' responses as well (Levy and Kolk, 2002). In other words, for the type of activities that companies pursue, it matters whether climate change is viewed as the physical impact of weather-related events, forthcoming climate change regulation, or an issue that attracts considerable societal concern (Kolk and Pinkse, 2004). What further complicates an understanding of corporate strategic responses is the fact that climate change does not form an isolated driver for organisational change (Berkhout *et al*, 2006); many other 'internal' drivers play a role as well, such as firms' objective to increase profits, and the particular industry setting should be reckoned with as well. Reducing the impact of or vulnerability to climate change may not always be the primary objective of firms to adjust to climate change.

For example, while in the case of the insurance industry, business responses will be linked to management of weather-related risks (Dlugolecki and Keykhah, 2002), for energy-related industries – e.g. the oil and gas industry, automotives, and electric utilities – it is more likely in anticipation of new government regulation (e.g. the EU ETS) or market pressure from competitors who already follow a more climate-friendly course (Levy and Kolk, 2002). For various other low-carbon industries, the main reason for adapting business practices to climate change may well lie in the fact that it attracts considerable attention from the public and media. Moreover, what further strengthens market transitions towards less carbon-intensive activities is the fact that worry about climate change is also closely entwined with rising energy prices (Okereke, 2007). A 2008 Ernst & Young report of the 10 most important strategic business risks did include climate change in position nine, but the strategic risk from energy shocks ranked even higher in position six (Ernst & Young, 2008).

So type of industry and industry structure play a role in the process of developing a competitive climate change strategy. Whether there are opportunities to create a market for new technologies depends, for example, on industry growth (Russo and Fouts, 1997), and the concentration level of an industry. The industry dynamic, in which companies are involved in the interaction with their competitors, also affects their behaviour vis-à-vis climate change. Companies compete for external funding on the best conditions, and want to increase market share, attract new customers and talented staff, and maintain good relations with investors. This leads to continuous efforts to be more 'attractive' and agile than competitors. Companies closely watch the behaviour of competitors, with a tendency to 'follow the leader' (cf. Knickerbocker, 1973) or to jump on the bandwagon (cf. Abrahamson and Rosenkopf, 1993), regardless or even despite of the fact that this may imply inefficiencies or losses. The clearest example is the automobile industry, where major companies are following Toyota's (first) move towards hybrid vehicles, even when they are not sure whether this will become more than a niche market only. This behaviour is particularly pervasive in highly concentrated markets, dominated by a few large multinationals (Kolk and Levy, 2004). However, there may also be a simple lack of knowledge about what the 'winning' approach will be. This is notable in the oil industry where companies follow different routes regarding (future) energy sources that they all seem to be exploring (Sæverud and Skjærseth, 2007).

Besides the industry, the position of a company in the supply chain stipulates the nature of the core products and services and the responsiveness of customers to the climate change issue. Rethinking product design or developing new products or services is particularly valuable for companies that operate closer to markets for the end-consumer, where differentiation pays off. Companies that are positioned higher up in the supply chain generally produce commodities instead of consumer products and do not have the same opportunity to differentiate their products. It is the dependency on environmentally-conscious consumers and the possibility of changing a product that will have a bearing on the climate strategy in consumer-oriented industries. Whether the customer is an individual or another business will also affect the decision on developing a climate strategy. Whereas business customers are less known for demanding environmentally friendly products, when they choose to do so, their demand will create more leverage, as they are more powerful as a customer. In recent years, for example, companies like Wal-Mart and McDonalds, which used to have rather bad track records on sustainability, have started to demand more sustainable products, thus creating immense pressure on companies supplying the goods that these two companies sell to the end-consumer. If a company directly sells to end-consumers instead, this used to lead to a niche strategy, because the willingness to pay for environmentally sound products was limited to a group of environmentally conscious consumers (Reinhardt, 1998). However, the increased consumer awareness of climate change in recent years may start to lead to a change in this respect, now creating the opportunity to service mass-markets with climate-friendly products as well (Bonini *et al*, 2008).

There are other company-specific factors that shape the specific approach taken. This includes, for example, top management commitment and the degree of internationalisation of top management (Levy and Kolk, 2002). The fact that BP became climate change 'front runner' in the oil industry was for a large part on account of the leadership role taken by John Browne, BP's CEO until May 2007. Similarly, the shift in leadership of ExxonMobil in January 2006 from Lee Raymond to Rex Tillerson appears to have led to a softening stance of this company. Also organisational structure plays a role as this determines for a large part how the strategic planning process takes shape and to what extent addressing an issue like climate change is a centralised or decentralised decision. In addition, organisational culture and a company's specific history shape the perception of climate change. One of the reasons that ExxonMobil has been rather reluctant to invest in renewable energy sources was because it made huge losses on such investments in the 1980s when the Reagan administration suddenly stopped granting large subsidies instigated by the preceding president, Carter. This, combined with the fact that decision authority had been highly centralised as well, left hardly any room for local initiatives that went against the reactive stance of the top of the company at all (Kolk and Levy, 2004).

Whether or not climate change becomes a strategic issue depends in the end on how it is perceived to affect the main value proposition of a company (Porter and Reinhardt, 2007). Even though companies typically emphasise the business opportunities related to climate change rather than the risks (Kolk and Pinkse, 2004), it is not always the case that climate change is necessarily an issue of strategic importance to a company as well (Porter and Kramer, 2006). Nevertheless, the corporate emphasis on the business opportunities in relation to climate change is not that surprising as it reflects the overall trend that 'win-win' views have started to prevail (Kolk, 2000; Porter and Van der Linde, 1995; Walley and Whitehead, 1994). Of course not all companies have adopted this win-win mentality in the same way. On the one hand, the approach may be that the climate change is evaluated just as any other business issue, which means that it has to compete (at some stage) with other investment opportunities on the same financial criteria. On the other hand, the moral case for climate change may prevail, which means that climate-related activities are pursued, preferably but not necessarily to make a profit (Berger *et al*, 2007).

Typical examples of business opportunities from climate change are benefits from changes in (energy) costs, a potential for creating new markets and the development of new technologies (Hoffman, 2005). Perspectives on the kind of opportunities of climate change are obviously mixed, and depend upon company-specific attributes (Levy and Kolk, 2002). If the effect of emissions trading is that energy prices rise even further than they had already done due to other geopolitical developments, this firstly poses a risk for companies that are energy intensive. Only when companies have the technologies available to actually reduce emissions, will it be associated with savings from less energy use, and thus seen as a potential opportunity instead. A creation of new markets for low-carbon products and services is also seen as an opportunity by many as it pushes sales of products and services that have the potential to lower GHG emissions. However, it is not always easy to tap new markets for energy-efficient products because it may very well require large investments in innovative and new technologies, when no 'easy-to-implement' technologies are available. Likewise, higher demand for green electricity helps utilities that have an energy portfolio with a relatively large share of natural gas, renewable energy sources, and, more controversially, nuclear power (e.g. Electricité de France). But a fundamental switch in the portfolio of energy sources is a very slow and costly process, because historical investments have to be depreciated first, which usually takes around 30 years (Grubb, 2004).

To summarise, then, there are so many external, industry and company-specific factors that have a bearing on the way in which a climate change strategy evolves, that it is very difficult to predict the specific approach that companies will follow. What is more, there is not only a great diversity in drivers for climate strategy development, but companies also have a host of strategic options to choose from; to these we will pay more attention in the second half of this chapter.

5.2 STRATEGIC OPTIONS FOR ADDRESSING CLIMATE CHANGE

5.2.1 A typology of climate change strategies

To understand the kind of climate change strategies that have emerged in recent years, in this section we will examine the range of strategic GHG reduction options available to companies. Basically, corporate strategies for climate change consist of different combinations of market components, where companies not only have the option to deal with climate change by changing internal processes, but also involve external actors in the organisational environment in their strategies.

The fact that external influences are often significant in first drawing companies' attention to climate change is clearly reflected in the emerging strategies as well. For example, the relatively flexible policies on climate change across the world give companies the opportunity to comply with the goals set by the government in co-operation with third parties. Such co-operative efforts can take place within a company's own supply chain, but can also move beyond the supply chain. This is seen in the formation of partnerships among competitors, and between companies and NGOs to develop and market low-emissions technologies (see Chapter 3).

In addition, emissions trading schemes play a key role in current climate policy, which opens up a whole new array of ways to comply with the regulatory or voluntary targets set for emissions reduction (see Chapters 4 and 6). Consequently, companies have a choice between on the one hand pursuing product- or process-oriented improvements and on the other hand emissions trading. To some extent, this could be seen as a corporate decision related to 'make' or 'buy' emissions reductions. Peculiar to the issue of climate change is, however, that companies can also do both: they can achieve some reductions internally and buy the balance; moreover, it is also possible that companies 'make and sell'. Such a 'make and sell' strategy particularly fits those companies that can reduce emissions at a relatively low cost and sell the ensuing surplus of emissions credits at a profit.

Corporate strategic responses to climate change can be captured by considering the make and/or buy/sell decision on the one hand, and the degree to which this involves interaction with other companies, on the other. When these two aspects are combined, the strategic options can be set out in a matrix with two dimensions: the main aim (strategic intent) and the form of organisation (degree of interaction). In the resulting typology (see Figure 5.1), six strategic options surface that can be part of a more comprehensive strategy for climate change (in which companies combine several options). The vertical axis of the typology is relatively straightforward, since it differentiates the degree to which companies choose interaction with others to reach their objectives. The typology distinguishes three organisational levels: the individual company (internal), companies' own supply chain (vertical), and interaction with companies outside the supply chain (competitors or companies in different sectors – horizontal).

	Main aim	
Organization	*Innovation*	*Compensation*
Internal (company)	Process improvement (1)	Internal transfer of emissions credits (2)
Vertical (supply chain)	Product development (3)	Supply chain measures (4)
Horizontal (beyond the supply chain)	New product/market combinations (5)	Acquisition of emissions credits (6)

Figure 5.1 Strategic options for climate change.

The horizontal axis deals with differences regarding the main aim of corporate climate strategies. Companies can focus merely on innovation with regard to their own business activities or on compensation. Innovation involves the development of new environmental technologies or services to reduce emissions. The main difference with compensation lies in the fact that innovation fundamentally improves a company's technological capabilities (see also Chapter 7). For example, oil company Royal Dutch/Shell develops solar energy not only to reduce emissions, but also to secure its competitive position in the long run by acquiring new capabilities. Compensation leaves a company's own technological capabilities unaltered; companies use low-emissions and emissions-reduction technologies developed by others.

A company that takes action with regard to climate change does not necessarily adopt all measures identified in the typology, but it is likely that they will use combinations of the different cells. Which of the options will become part of a more comprehensive climate change strategy is likely to depend on managerial perceptions of the issue, as outlined above. Managers that perceive climate change as a business risk may have a tendency to rely on compensatory options. Compensation does not require processes of organisational change to the same extent as the implementation of innovative measures because it does not fundamentally change current process and product technology. It may therefore fit companies that want to avert possible risks in a less strenuous way. Focusing on improvements in business activities may be more apt for those companies that have a clearer view of the opportunities of climate policy. These companies are willing to take the risk of large-scale investments for the development of new environmental technologies, partly because they believe that their long-term survival depends on it.

5.2.2 Innovation

Innovation is a prime orientation on business activities that are directed at the production process (cell 1 in Figure 5.1) or at products (cell 3). Process improvements frequently encompass energy reduction (and/or higher energy efficiency), as most process improvements are aimed at the reduction of CO_2; generally seen as the main greenhouse gas. For low energy users, such as telecommunications, electronics, insurance and the financial sector, which do not generate large amounts of CO_2 emissions, the most important measure is the implementation of management programmes for energy conservation (for example, good housekeeping systems that control heating and reduce electricity use). This is often combined with a programme to increase staff awareness of energy conservation and restrictions on business travel. However, the relatively low energy-intensity of production activities also means that their potential to mitigate climate change is more limited. A moderate user of energy like the IT industry has more possibilities. Companies like Google and IBM, for example, have announced they will significantly increase energy efficiency of their data centres.

By contrast, energy-intensive industries have more options, but also experience greater external pressure to reduce CO_2 emissions. In industries such as chemicals, mining, metals, utilities, and oil and gas, new energy-efficient technologies are developed and implemented to achieve reductions. Process improvements can also involve measures to diminish the use of other GHGs. For example, semiconductor producers take initiatives to optimise their production process in order to reduce the emission of perfluorinated compounds (PFCs), a greenhouse gas with a high climatic impact. In agriculture, waste management, and the oil and gas industry the release of methane (CH_4) is an important aspect of climate change strategies. The oil and gas industry can prevent CH_4 emissions by not using gas venting, and either switch to gas flaring (which is not optimal as it causes CO_2 emissions instead) or capture CH_4 and transform it to more productive uses with gas-to-liquid (GTL) technologies.

A supply-chain orientation to innovation is frequently taken by companies in automotives, chemicals, mining and electronics. They can focus on realising emissions reductions of existing products and/or developing new (energy-efficient) products. Many companies in these industries stress that, even though they can sufficiently reduce their own emissions, the impact of their products and services is much larger, and that this therefore seems a better way to reduce GHG emissions. Taking responsibility for emissions caused by the use of products is, for example, done through life-cycle analysis of major products. Companies such as BMW, General Electric, IBM and Unilever use such life-cycle programmes to integrate GHG emissions in the design phase of their products. For Unilever, the climatic impact of its home products strongly depends on household behaviour (e.g. the temperature at which laundry is washed). As a result, the company uses product design based on life-cycle analysis to enable a decrease of household energy consumption. In addition, it has programmes to increase consumer awareness. Computer hardware and electronic companies also follow an approach of improving their products' energy efficiency to help customers reduce emissions. An example is Dell's advertisements regarding the energy-reducing impact of its computer systems, thus enabling customers to diminish their energy use.

Still, as we have seen in Chapter 4, the vast majority of companies do not take into account emissions from the use of products or services, as this depends on uncontrollable factors like consumer behaviour. The main argument purported is that use of products and services does not lead to any significant emissions. This used to be specifically pervasive in service-oriented companies such as finance and insurance, but it has proven to be contestable. That is to say, this trend has been tilting in recent years as more and more reports have been published on the responsibility of the finance and insurance sectors to consider the climatic consequences of asset management (see Allianz/WWF, 2005, 2006). These studies show that there are considerable opportunities for financial companies for product innovation, for example, by developing products to hedge or insure against carbon risks.

In addition to these internal and supply-chain approaches, companies may use the option of drawing upon organisational capabilities as well, by exploring new product/market combinations (Figure 5.1, cell 5). A possible way to enter new markets is by becoming involved in a strategic alliance or another form of co-operation with other companies. The co-operation between many of the major oil and automobile companies in the California Fuel Cell Partnership (including Ford, GM, Toyota, Chevron, BP, Shell and many others) to develop fuel cells is a case in point of developing a whole new market based on hydrogen as a major fuel. Another example is Stora Enso, a Finnish paper, packaging and forest products company, which is using by-products of its core business to enter a new market for biofuels. In the production process of paper and forest products, Stora Enso also produces large amounts of sawmill and logging residues, which are used for the production of biodiesel in a demonstration plant as part of a joint venture with Finnish oil company Neste Oil. In this way, what used to be a waste product is now actively harvested to serve the purpose of entering new markets. Climate policy in the form of emissions trading may also induce companies to position their products and services outside traditional markets. For example, Barclays has become a broker in the carbon market, thus helping to arrange the sale of emissions credits from companies that have a surplus to those that are short on credits.

5.2.3 Compensation

Different from innovation, compensation includes internal transfer of emissions (Figure 5.1, cell 2), supply chain measures (cell 4), or acquisition of emissions credits through emissions trading or participation in offset projects (cell 6). Compensation means that companies do not primarily aim to reduce GHG emissions, but merely focus on transferring emissions or emissions-generating activities within the company or to other companies. With regard to emissions-reducing technologies, companies that pursue compensatory approaches act as a passive, arm's length actor because they do not participate in the innovation process themselves. The option to offset emissions is mainly the result of the fact that emissions trading has emerged as the main policy instrument to combat climate change.

Internally oriented compensation particularly fits large companies that operate across borders. These companies can alleviate government pressure to mitigate climate change by transferring high-emissions activities to locations where stringent reduction plans are not (yet) in place. To what extent companies actually pursue this route depends a lot on the capital intensity of an industry. For example, the European steel industry has consistently complained about the regulatory burden of the EU ETS, and threatened to relocate steel mills to countries like China and India. However, in response to environmental regulation, relocation is used more regularly as a threat that is not carried out subsequently (Jaffe *et al*, 1995). What is more likely is that companies use internal or external carbon markets to carry out internal trades, transferring emissions credits between business units. BP and Shell have pioneered this option by setting up internal trading schemes, but this was not without problems (see Chapter 4; Victor and House, 2006). With its maturation and extending spread, it is now much easier to use the external carbon market and follow a policy of considering other business units as preferred trading partners. Integrating targets for emissions into investment decisions for new projects is also a form of internal compensation that fits companies active in a single country only. Another way of internal compensation is maintaining a diversified portfolio of products and services. This is particularly manifest in the car industry where one way of complying with stricter emissions standards is to introduce lighter vehicles to compensate for the excess emissions of the heavier vehicles in a company's product portfolio. To illustrate, for German company Daimler, known for producing large-sized cars under the Mercedes brand, the lightweight Smart helps in easing the regulatory pressure from the forthcoming mandatory European automobile emissions standards.

Supply chain measures for compensation aim to avoid the need for emissions cuts within the company. A company instead seeks to find solutions to ensure that activities and sources of high emissions are carried out elsewhere in the supply chain or that emissions are reduced further up the supply chain. The most common supply-chain measure is monitoring the carbon-intensity of supplied materials or suppliers. For example, Dell requires its most important suppliers to disclose information on their carbon emissions, because if they fail to do so Dell will no longer do business with them. However, the intensity by which suppliers are engaged in a company's own climate change strategy differs considerably. Some companies perform sampled monitoring of a limited number of large suppliers only, while others have detailed emissions targets and guidelines for all their suppliers. It must be noted that GHG emissions are not always that prominent in supplier selection; a number of companies select their suppliers based on more general grounds such as environmental programmes and ISO 14001 certification. For example, BMW expects suppliers to maintain the same environmental standards; UK-based utility Centrica has formed partnerships with suppliers to increase understanding of the complete supply chain.

Another supply chain measure is replacing inputs with a high potential for emissions by those with lower emissions. One way of doing this is substituting fossil fuels with carbon-free renewable energy sources. In non-carbon-intensive sectors, such as telecommunications and service-oriented sectors, this requires procurement of electricity and heating generated from clean energy sources. An example is the 2004 commitment by British Telecom to only purchase electricity that is generated by renewable sources and combined heat and power plants. More recently, in 2007, Google put pressure on electricity producers in a similar way, requiring them to generate at least one-fifth of electricity from renewable energy sources. For companies that use fuels directly for combustion purposes, fuel switching has a much larger impact, however, because it requires a radical change in the production process (for example, through the installation of combined heat and power generators). For utilities and chemical companies, for example, fuel switching means that coal-fired plants have to be replaced by gas-fired plants or divested altogether, which is often merely viewed as a measure of last resort. It should be noted, though, that since substitution of raw materials in many instances requires an adjustment in existing production facilities, this involves some innovation as well. Companies can also subcontract or outsource certain high-emissions activities such as transportation and distribution to reduce emissions internally while increasing those of business partners. In terms of environmental effectiveness, outsourcing has no benefit on an economy-wide scale, unless the subcontractor has specific capabilities, for example in logistics, that makes the whole distribution process more efficient than would be the case had the outsourcing company done it internally.

Finally, companies can also move beyond the supply chain and achieve reductions by interacting with others, either by buying emissions credits or by other forms of offsets, for example through the Clean Development Mechanism (CDM) or Joint Implementation (JI). By acting as a buyer on the carbon market, a company can balance its excess emissions. Similarly, offset projects designed under the Kyoto Protocol enable a company to attain and transfer credits by partnering with companies or governments in locations (for example, developing countries) where reductions can be achieved with less effort. It must be noted that alongside the regulatory-driven carbon market, a voluntary carbon market has developed (Gillenwater *et al*, 2007; see Chapter 6). Even though this does not have the same size, the voluntary market (consisting of the Chicago Climate Exchange (CCX) and the Over the Counter (OTC) offset market) had reached a US$91 million volume in 2007. Not surprisingly, the majority of companies active in this voluntary market are based in the US, as a regulatory carbon market is still lacking there (Hamilton *et al*, 2007). In the classification of Figure 5.1, offset projects are not considered to be innovative because they usually merely rely on the transfer of existing technologies instead of on the development of new ones.

5.2.4 Combining innovation and compensation: a carbon-neutral strategy

A recent trend that nicely illustrates the interaction between innovation and compensation as a means to reduce GHG emissions is the carbon-neutral concept. According to the Carbon Trust (2006: 15), 'carbon neutrality is achieved when emissions from a product, activity or a whole organisation are netted off, either through the purchase of an equivalent number of offsets or through a combination of emissions reduction and offsetting'. Carbon neutrality has become rather popular amongst service-oriented companies, such as financial institutions, media and IT companies. One of the first multinationals that announced its plans to become carbon neutral was Swiss Re, in 2003. At the end of 2004, it was followed by HSBC, a pledge which received critical acclaim and led many banks, including Barclays, Credit Suisse, Goldman Sachs, National Australia Bank and Toronto-Dominion Bank, to follow suit (Wright, 2006). Companies in the other sectors – for example, BSkyB, News Corp, PwC, Marks and Spencer, Reckitt Benckiser, Yahoo, Google, and TNT – have formulated similar programmes to become carbon neutral as well.

Carbon neutrality is appealing because it is a concept which is easy to understand and therefore also good to use for communication purposes. In other words, it can be an effective strategy to attract customers without having to explain the technical details of specific CO_2 targets. However, in actual practice it runs into many of the same problems as any other emissions target, such as determining the corporate carbon footprint, a baseline and a business-as-usual scenario (see Chapter 4). Moreover, it only seems fit for companies with relatively low direct emissions – it is hard to imagine an oil company becoming carbon neutral. Carbon neutrality is rather difficult because it is near to impossible to cut back on all energy consumption with internal measures. The Carbon Trust, for example, advises companies to first reduce direct internal emissions, which is equivalent to an innovative approach aimed at process improvements (Figure 5.1, cell 1). However, as it seems improbable to trim down such internal emissions to zero, companies are also recommended to resort to some form of compensation. The 'recommended' subsequent step is a supply-chain approach where companies aim at a cutback in indirect emissions (cell 4). For HSBC, for example, this meant the implementation of a scheme to purchase green power (Wright, 2006). Still, as not all emissions come from energy consumption, e.g. business travel, after these two stages companies typically still have a positive emissions balance. Completely netting off emissions therefore often also involves acquiring some type of emissions credits (cell 6) in the (voluntary) carbon market (Harvey, 2007b).

However, the whole idea of carbon neutrality has been fiercely criticised (see Gillenwater *et al*, 2007; Revkin, 2007). Opponents do not really disapprove of internal and supply-chain measures, but rather the fact that the concept generally relies on buying offsets. The problem is that, particularly in the voluntary carbon market, there are many different types of compensation schemes available, which are not all that reliable. Moreover, the main type of compensation that offset retailers such as the CarbonNeutral Company have on offer is via investments in tree-planting programmes. The climatic impact of such programmes has been debated because tree plantations may come in the place of primary forest, thereby leading to a net increase in GHG emissions instead of a reduction. Moreover, it is not always clear whether the carbon offset projects lead to additional reductions from what would have been achieved otherwise. In the voluntary carbon market, monitoring to verify that claimed reductions are really achieved is often lacking. And even if projects are monitored, there is still no agreed-upon monitoring method. Furthermore, if property rights are not well-defined, emissions credits might be sold more than once (Gillenwater *et al*, 2007). Besides all these potential failures of the voluntary carbon market in delivering actual emissions reductions, there is also the issue of which emissions will be netted off. Most banks that become carbon neutral compensate their internal emissions, but do not go one step further in also neutralising the climatic impact of their financial investments, where their impact is much higher. This has been acknowledged by HSBC, which, although it does not take their investment into account in becoming carbon neutral, creates awareness among clients and requires disclosure of GHG emissions in their project finance activities (Wright, 2006).

Hence, despite the attractiveness of carbon neutrality for marketing purposes, companies that claim to be carbon neutral run a reputation risk as it could be seen as greenwashing. A potential 'solution' to this risk is by only acquiring offsets in the UN-led carbon market, for example by investing in emissions-reducing projects that live up to an NGO-endorsed monitoring standard such as the WWF Gold Standard for CDM and JI projects.

5.3 CONCLUDING REMARKS

This chapter analysed the kind of options available to companies in developing their climate change strategy. The typology that we presented shows that there are various strategic options from which managers can choose in addressing the market components related to the issue of climate change, and that current strategies consist of different combinations of these market possibilities. Existing managerial discretion, resulting from perceptions of the risks and/or opportunities related to climate change, leads companies, also those active in one and the same sector, to choose different approaches. Further development can be expected in the next few years, since ongoing government, stakeholder and shareholder pressure will encourage companies to explore the full range of options, and adapt their climate change strategy in response to changes in external and company-specific factors. In the next two chapters we will explain the two main aims of climate change strategies identified in the typology. Chapter 6 first elaborates on compensation and discusses emissions trading, while Chapter 7 examines which capabilities companies might develop in response to climate change and how far-reaching the influence of climate change is on core business strategies.

6 Carbon trading as (compliance) strategy

The emergence of carbon emissions trading has been important in increasing the strategic relevance of climate change for business: companies had to respond and develop strategies on how to deal with this new market-based policy instrument. Emissions trading has predominantly been implemented in the form of a cap-and-trade system: companies get a limited amount of allowances to emit greenhouse gases (GHGs), but are allowed to trade these with other market participants. This is an appealing approach, first because it gives carbon a price. It thus translates the adverse impact of business on the global climate into financial figures, enabling companies to take account of climate change in business and investment decisions (Egenhofer, 2007; Hoffmann, 2007). Secondly, even though a cap is put on emissions externally, emissions trading is a market-based instrument that does not stipulate by what means companies should stay within the limit. As a consequence, companies have flexibility in complying with a regulatory scheme based on emissions trading, which enhances incorporating carbon management activities into overall strategy (Kolk and Pinkse, 2005a). And, lastly, emissions trading creates a whole new financial market. This market for carbon is strongly linked to other commodity markets – for example, oil, coal and gas – and the price of emissions allowances also has an impact on sourcing policies of energy. As a result, managing climate change is not only the domain of environmental managers but also starts to involve those with expertise in financial and other commodity markets.

Notwithstanding the appeal of emissions trading, it is also a very complex and new kind of business practice. Consequently, strategic responses to emissions trading show the many different faces of multinational corporations (MNCs) in the international arena (Eden and Lenway, 2001). On the one hand, companies fulfil a positive economic role by becoming active traders of emissions allowances/credits and generating additional emissions abatement credits to sell in the carbon market. Moreover, they have done what companies are particularly good at, that is, creating new (carbon) markets, linking different domestic markets (for example by creating Clean Development Mechanism (CDM) credits to trade in the European Union emissions trading scheme (EU ETS)), and acting as agents of change by diffusing new abatement technologies across the world. On the other hand, however, they have also played a political role. MNCs have lobbied extensively to water down the requirements set upon them by emissions trading schemes. As a result, doubts have been raised whether emissions trading schemes actually contribute to the well-being of our planet or just lead to high profits for smart traders (Convery and Redmond, 2007; Egenhofer, 2007; Hepburn, 2007; Sijm *et al*, 2006).

What complicates matters even further is not only that MNCs tend to respond using different economic and political tactics simultaneously (Baron, 1995; Levy and Kolk, 2002), but they are also facing a whole variety of (emergent) emissions trading schemes with different rules. Political disagreements in negotiating the Kyoto Protocol have made a global institutional framework for climate change mitigation, accepted by all countries, problematic (Grubb *et al*, 1999). Hence, Kyoto's intergovernmental emissions trading regime has not been implemented on a global level as of yet, which has induced great diversity worldwide regarding the specific types of trading schemes that emerged to enable trading between companies (see Chapter 2). In Europe, a regulatory approach has prevailed and emissions trading has been established as mandatory government policy using the cap-and-trade approach: the EU ETS. By contrast, in the US and Australia, emissions trading has come up on a smaller scale at the sub-national level, sometimes as a public initiative (e.g. the Regional Greenhouse Gas Initiative (RGGI) and the New South Wales Greenhouse Gas Abatement Scheme (NSW GGAS), but with the establishment of the Chicago Climate Exchange also as a private, voluntary arrangement. In the non-European industrialised countries that ratified Kyoto to date no emissions trading schemes have yet been implemented on a national level. While currently Japan and Australia seem to be moving into this direction, in Canada this is still highly uncertain. Nevertheless, companies from these countries can use the other Kyoto mechanisms – Clean Development Mechanism (CDM) and Joint Implementation (JI) – to reduce emissions via projects in developing countries or economies in transition respectively. Thus, while climate change is still a global issue in its causes, manifestations and implications, and international policy regimes exist, the institutional forms of corporate-level emissions trading differ significantly across countries.

This chapter examines corporate responses to newly created emissions trading schemes and associated offset projects, in the process also outlining the peculiarities of the carbon market and its various components. We will consider how the turbulent developments that the maturing carbon market went through in recent years have led to opportunities for MNCs to use this market for compensatory purposes and/or (re)shape the rules of emissions trading. Section 6.1 first discusses the economic principles underlying emissions trading and the basic rules and characteristics of the emerging carbon market. Subsequently, we will examine how companies have responded strategically, first more generally (section 6.2) and then more specifically, looking at respectively carbon market participation under regulatory constraints (section 6.3) and without (strict) regulatory constraints (section 6.4). In this way, all major trading and offset initiatives are examined in more detail.

6.1 THE EMERGENCE OF THE CARBON MARKET

6.1.1 Economic principles of emissions trading

Environmental economists have long exalted the introduction of a cap-and-trade type of emissions trading scheme to reduce GHG emissions and combat climate change (Hahn and Stavins, 1992; Woerdman, 2004). The main economic argument is that to achieve the same level of environmental effectiveness, emissions trading is relatively more cost-effective. It relies on the efficiency of the price mechanism to reduce emissions where it has the lowest costs. The theoretical proposition underlying this reasoning is that a market-based mechanism such as emissions trading allocates the responsibility to control emissions to those actors that cause the environmental problem. In contrast to a command-and-control approach in which the regulator prescribes which type of technology has to be used to reduce emissions, emissions trading gives companies more flexibility (Hahn and Stavins, 1992). Thus a cap-and-trade system creates an incentive to use reduction technologies that fit a company's existing business practices. It encourages companies to use their specific knowledge and expertise to control emissions, without being 'hindered' by prescribed approaches from regulators that have much less insight into company practices, products and markets (Tietenberg, 1990).

The working of an emissions trading scheme depends on a great number of factors related to its design. This first of all involves the coverage (global, regional, local; which industries) that determines the size of the market, and thus the price of allowances and the volume traded (Springer, 2003). For example, when the US would be part of a global trading scheme, demand for emissions allowances, and thus the allowance price, would be much higher compared with a trading scheme without global coverage (Den Elzen and de Moor, 2002). An important issue with respect to sectoral coverage is whether a trading scheme aims at controlling GHG emissions of producers and importers of fossil fuels (an upstream approach) or at consumers of fossil fuels (a downstream approach) (Sorrell and Sijm, 2003). Notably, most trading schemes, including the EU ETS, focus on downstream emissions and thus cover a broad range of industries (Boemare and Quirion, 2002).

Second, the allocation method of allowances is crucial, since it affects industries' and companies' initial position in the carbon market and the costs associated with trading (Klepper and Peterson, 2004). The two foremost allocation methods are auctioning of allowances and 'grandfathering' (Tietenberg, 1990), in which allowances are allocated free of charge based on past emissions or a benchmarking procedure (Boemare and Quirion, 2002). With regard to economic welfare, auctioning is seen as superior to grandfathering because it generates an economic rent (the revenue of the auction) that can be redistributed to society (Tietenberg, 1990). Moreover, grandfathering also inhibits the incentive to develop environmental innovations and creates disadvantages for new entrants to a market (Boemare and Quirion, 2002). However, auctioning is less favourable for participating industries because not only does it lead to costs to control emissions, but also to costs to acquire allowances in the auction (Tietenberg, 1990). These additional costs are the main reason that the EU ETS has predominantly used grandfathering so far, as it is basically a way of buying industry acceptance (Egenhofer, 2007).

Finally, the length of time and the intertemporal flexibility built into the scheme are also important since they have an impact on planning and investment decisions and on costs. The possibility of banking or borrowing emissions allowances, for example, allows participants to choose the optimal, most cost-effective moment for compliance (Boemare and Quirion, 2002). Banking creates 'temporal hot spots' because it allows participants to take advantage of the current opportunities to reduce emissions for compliance in later periods. One of the problems of banking is that it can discourage participants to further reduce emissions when they have already banked a considerable amount of allowances. However, the absence of banking discourages participants to reduce emissions beyond the allocated level (Kruger and Pizer, 2004). Borrowing is more controversial because it can delay compliance indefinitely (Boemare and Quirion, 2002).

In summary, economic design factors have a considerable influence on the implementation process of an emissions trading scheme and on the types of companies that are most likely to become active in the carbon market. Currently only a relatively limited number of companies worldwide are compelled by regulation to participate. For companies not directly affected by the introduction of a trading scheme, participation is a voluntary initiative not motivated by incentives for compliance. However, involvement in and development of an emissions trading scheme not only depends on the 'right' economic design, but also on the politics surrounding this process (Hahn and Stavins, 1992). Due to political bargaining and the fact that many interest groups try to have an influence, actual trading schemes deviate considerably from the optimal design suggested by economic theory (Boemare and Quirion, 2002; Markussen and Svendsen, 2005).

6.1.2 The carbon market: an internationally emergent institution

The rise of emissions trading has led to a new set of rules which governs how companies 'should' deal with climate change and GHG emissions. Basically, an emissions trading scheme is a new type of institution,[1] which sets boundaries on the amount of GHGs that companies can emit into the atmosphere and defines how this burden is shared among market participants through a price mechanism. Moreover, as not all sectors of an economy are included in an emissions trading scheme (e.g. transportation in the case of the EU ETS), the quantity of allowances allocated determines automatically the burden sharing between trading and non-trading sectors in achieving the economy-wide Kyoto target. If the emissions

---

1   An institution has been defined in the literature as a set of rules that constrains organisations and individuals in conducting their activities (Ingram and Clay, 2000).

trading scheme cap is not stringent, for example due to over-allocation of allowances, this will put additional pressure on non-trading sectors to reduce emissions as they will have to cover a larger share of the total Kyoto burden (Convery and Redmond, 2007; Egenhofer, 2007).

Nevertheless, what has been crucial for the way companies have responded to emissions trading schemes is the fact that it is also an 'emergent institution'. Due to their novelty, emissions trading schemes still lack the level of legitimacy that established institutions have gained over the years, which means that they are not yet widely accepted and still miss the same 'taken-for-grantedness' (Henisz and Zelner, 2005; Scott, 1995; Suchman, 1995). The main emissions trading scheme that currently exists, the EU ETS, directly results from European climate change regulation to comply with the Kyoto targets. But even though regulatory developments in Europe and other parts of the world point in the direction of emissions trading as the predominant way to deal with this topic, such pressure is not necessarily enough to also lead to full institutionalisation of emissions trading as a business practice as well (Hoffman, 1999; Scott, 1995).

An important implication of the 'emergent' status is that an emissions trading scheme is still subject to pressures for change, because the rules are not yet set in stone. In addition, an emergent institution often lacks the support of vested interests that favour the status quo (of carbon not priced on the market). To illustrate, despite widespread support of a considerable number of carbon-intensive companies, including powerful oil multinationals such as BP and Shell, emissions trading has been widely opposed as well (Christiansen and Wettestad, 2003; Gulbrandsen and Andresen, 2004; Markussen and Svendsen, 2005). European steel and chemical industries, for example, lobbied heavily against the launch of the EU ETS (Markussen and Svendsen, 2005). The fact that the development of climate change policy and emissions trading schemes has taken place in a fairly disorderly way in which many different interest groups have tried to have their say has several consequences (Levy and Egan, 2003). On the one hand, it has created opportunities for companies (and other interest groups) to exert pressure on regulators implementing a trading scheme (cf. Lawrence, 1999; Zucker, 1987) in an attempt to change the rules to their benefit. This is openly acknowledged by some companies; Shell, for example, notes in its answers to CDP that 'As governments develop trading systems and allocation plans are drawn up, firms have the opportunity to influence the direction of these developments'. On the other hand, a high inclination for change has also increased uncertainty about the permanence of the institution. Companies doubt whether newly formed trading schemes will remain the same henceforth, which means that there is a significant risk of investing in a business practice that is not here to stay (Henisz and Zelner, 2005).

Although the carbon market has initially been shaped on an international level in negotiating the Kyoto Protocol (Grubb *et al*, 1999), there is still substantial variation internationally regarding the specifics of trading schemes and the progress made in their implementation. Instead of becoming a uniform global institution, emissions trading has seen a trickle-down trajectory (Djelic and Quack, 2003) and has eventually been reshaped to fit climate and energy policies on regional, national, and sub-national levels, creating a whole variety of new 'local' institutions (Maguire and Hardy, 2006). The EU ETS is currently the most well-known example of a regional trading scheme that enables emissions reduction transfers between companies. While its success has been debated, it has given an impetus to the international dispersion of similar cap-and-trade schemes across the globe (Egenhofer, 2007). In Australia emissions trading has recently received more support at the federal level (Griffiths *et al*, 2007). After the Labour Party won the election at the end of 2007, Australia ratified and announced plans to launch a national emissions trading scheme no later than 2010. The year 2007 also saw the launch of the Australia Climate Exchange, the first emissions trading platform in the country. Japan's environment minister announced in March 2008 that his country intends to implement an emissions trading scheme after the Kyoto Protocol expires in 2012. However, no details were given about the exact start of such a domestic cap-and-trade system as it depends on support from the public and industry as well as on moves of other countries regarding emissions trading (Fujioka, 2008). Even in the US, which did not ratify Kyoto, the political debate to set up a federal level emissions trading scheme aimed at companies gained momentum in 2007 (Reinaud and Philibert, 2007), but the exact outcome will depend on the new administration.

Nevertheless, even though it will take some time for all industrial countries to implement similar cap-and-trade schemes as the EU ETS (the most mature scheme), there are now already various other trading schemes (almost) in place (or under development). There is a concomitant variety in the level of constraint they put on companies. Most current schemes are of a public nature, with the implication that once companies fall under a scheme they cannot opt out (Ingram and Silverman, 2002). This includes the EU ETS, its predecessors that were set up some years earlier in the UK (suspended in March 2007) and Denmark (suspended at the end of 2004), the Regional Greenhouse Gas Initiative in the Northeast of the US, and Australia's New South Wales Greenhouse Gas Abatement Scheme. However, due to their different geographical coverage, not all these public schemes produce the same strong constraint on multinationals. The EU ETS clearly stands out as it has been created on a regional European level and affects a broad range of MNC subsidiaries from different sectors. Nonetheless, the impact of the EU ETS is not equal for all MNCs in the EU. It depends on the number of eligible installations that are located in the EU. And because the exact rules for trading and enforcement have been delegated to EU Member States through National Allocation Plans (Ellerman and Buchner, 2008), it also depends on the specific country in which installations are located.

Still, because the other schemes merely apply to national or sub-national levels, they usually affect a smaller number of MNC affiliates compared to the EU ETS. In the US and Australia, for example, the formation of trading schemes has seen a dynamic which is best characterised as a trickle-up trajectory (Djelic and Quack, 2003). State-level authorities tried to bypass their federal governments by introducing emissions trading schemes on a sub-national level with the aim of influencing climate policy on a federal level (Engel, 2006). Whereas in

Australia the state of New South Wales has created a trading scheme unilaterally, in the US several states have chosen to take a multilateral approach by setting up the RGGI (Engel, 2006; Rabe, 2006) and the Western Climate Initiative (Reinaud and Philibert, 2007). The RGGI is in its formative years and is only set to start in January 2009 (Hamilton *et al*, 2007), while the Western Climate Initiative is still in the phase of a proposal without clear details (Reinaud and Philibert, 2007). The US-based trading schemes therefore currently only form an anticipated constraint.

The first examples of private forms of emissions trading were the internal schemes that BP and Royal Dutch/Shell implemented. However, these schemes never moved beyond the pilot phase and were suspended at the end of 2001 and 2002, respectively. The most prominent private scheme for emissions trading is the Chicago Climate Exchange (CCX), which is located in the US. The constraint it sets is different from the public trading schemes because companies choose to be part of it on a voluntary basis. Nevertheless, once a company participates, the impact of CCX is not negligible, since the voluntary commitment is legally binding and is enforced by the CCX itself as well as the National Association of Securities Dealers (Yang, 2006).

Besides cap-and-trade systems, Kyoto's project-based mechanisms – CDM and JI – are other significant components of the global carbon market. Of these two project-based mechanisms, CDM has become the most important in terms of trading volume (Lecocq and Ambrosi, 2007). CDM functions as a public scheme because the rules are determined between a participant's home and host country as well as the United Nations; together they decide about the legality of CDM projects through the CDM Executive Board (Haites and Yamin, 2000). However, CDM does not create a constraint because investing in CDM projects is voluntary (Haites and Yamin, 2000). Instead of a constraint it is more likely to act as a way of taking the edge off the regulatory pressure of cap-and-trade systems that allow the use of CDM for compliance. CDM enables companies to reduce emissions by taking advantage of the 'low-hanging fruit' available in developing countries, thus avoiding more costly investments in more advanced technologies in a domestic context (Hepburn, 2007). However, the uncertain nature of the policy situation once Kyoto has ended (2012), and thus of the role of CDM, is also starting to affect the attractiveness of becoming involved in CDM as the process from start to approval takes quite some time.

Finally, apart from CCX, the remainder of the voluntary carbon market is made up of carbon offset projects that do not involve an official exchange (therefore this market is also referred to as the over-the-counter (OTC) market (Hamilton *et al*, 2007)). Companies use this voluntary offset market to show the public that they achieve their self-commitments (see Chapter 4), and, for example, become carbon neutral (see Chapter 5). In other words, interest in these types of voluntary projects is not part of a regulatory compliance strategy. However, this lack of regulatory pressure has not stopped this market from growing considerably in the past few years. Nevertheless, there are some problems regarding legitimacy of this market, because there are no agreed-upon standards for the quality of voluntary offset projects (Hamilton *et al*, 2007). One advantage of the voluntary market, though, is that it supplies finance to small community projects in developing countries, something which CDM cannot achieve as its transaction costs are too high. This implies that the contribution to sustainable development of voluntary projects might be considerably larger than CDM (Hepburn, 2007).

Table 6.1 shows the size of the global carbon market divided between compliance markets (EU ETS, NSW, UK ETS), project-based markets (CDM, JI), and voluntary markets (CCX, OTC offset market). The global carbon market shows clear growth, as was mostly notable from 2005 to 2006 when it took off. In 2007 global carbon markets grew even further compared to 2006, by 80 per cent (Røine *et al*, 2008). EU ETS by far accounts for the largest share of the carbon market, with a market value of US\$24.4 billion in 2006 (compared to US\$7.9 billion in 2005) (Capoor and Ambrosi, 2007); in 2007, it experienced an additional increase of around 60 per cent (Røine *et al*, 2008). The importance of the EU ETS also stems from figures that show that it held 62 per cent of the physical global carbon market and 70 per cent of the financial market by early 2008 (Røine *et al*, 2008). Almost all of the remainder of the markets (respectively 35 per cent and 29 per cent) is covered by CDM, that also demonstrates large growth, although from a much lower base (Røine *et al*, 2008): the combined value of CDM amounted to US\$5.3 billion and JI to US\$141 million in 2006 (2005 figures were US\$2.6 billion and US\$68 million respectively; Capoor and Ambrosi, 2007). Although not mature yet, experts assess the global carbon market as more mature than before, and as leading to cost-effective, but modest emissions reductions (Ellerman and Buchner, 2008; Røine and Hasselknippe, 2007).

Table 6.1 Trading and market value of the global carbon market 2006

	Trading volume in Million tonnes CO$_2$		*Market value in Million US\$*	
	2005	2006	2005	2006
Compliance markets				
EU ETS	362	1017	7218	18143
NSW GGAS	6	20	59	225
UK ETS	0	N/A	1	N/A
Project-based markets				
CDM	397	523	1985	3349
CDM 2nd	4	40	50	571
JI	28	21	96	95
Voluntary markets				
CCX	1	10	3	38
OTC offset market	N/A	24	N/A	91

Source: Based on Capoor and Ambrosi (2007); Hamilton *et al*, (2007); Røine and Hasselknippe (2007)

6.2 CORPORATE STRATEGIES IN AN EMERGING CARBON MARKET

The strategic choice for a company on how to position the organisation in the global carbon market is particularly complex in the case of multinationals as they operate across borders. The main reason is that an MNC's strategic context reflects a duality – a global context and multiple local contexts – which has been the subject of extensive study (cf. Kostova, 1999; Kostova and Roth, 2002; Rosenzweig and Singh, 1991; Sundaram and Black, 1992; Westney, 1993). Moreover, MNCs frequently have a highly diversified portfolio of activities and thus belong to several industries simultaneously and participate in diverse (geographical) markets. As a consequence an MNC often faces conflicting pressures, which can lead to ambiguities on how to act in a fairly consistent way as a player in global and local markets (Westney, 1993). In the carbon market, MNCs may follow a global approach to minimise costs or exploit possible opportunities from co-ordinated action in emissions trading schemes. In other words, with an increasing number of large MNCs advocating a global approach to climate change – within individual sectors and/or via a long-term overarching global climate change regime – companies may increasingly adopt a more unified, less diversified strategy in this respect as well. However, the variety of trading schemes adopted by governments could also justify a more multidomestic, country-by-country or regional approach to cope with, and/or profit from, existing differences (cf. Bartlett and Ghoshal, 1989; Rugman and Verbeke, 2004). This would fall in line with the diversity of perceptions regarding the need to act on climate change, as well as the different political, geographical and economic realities that have shaped governments' behaviour on the issue.

Hence, MNCs have the option to follow various routes in responding to the emerging carbon market; a distinction can be made between a compliance, avoidance and bargaining strategy (Boddewyn and Brewer, 1994). A compliance strategy implies that a company responds by giving in to external pressure and incorporates the organisational practice to anticipate particular benefits that may be gained in the future. With an avoidance strategy a company tries to prevent conforming to external pressure, for example by relocating production activities (Oliver, 1991). Lastly, a bargaining strategy has the aim of more actively shaping the institutions that exert the pressure. Through 'political' activities such as lobbying and partnerships, a company attempts to steer the direction in which the rules evolve. The type of approach taken – compliance, avoidance or bargaining – will differ by country where an MNC has production sites. An MNC's bargaining power is not equal vis-à-vis home and host country governments. In their home country MNCs typically have a much stronger foothold in the policymaking process, also because this country generally benefits more from their activities (Baron, 1997). Moreover, it is difficult for MNCs to develop a global strategy in response to local pressures, because contexts may vary considerably, and it requires much flexibility and bargaining power to persuade many different host-country governments to take their interests into account (Baron, 1995).

rall, the way in which a company responds to the carbon market depends
ether it faces or expects to be facing a high regulatory constraint. Due to
iphical) variance in corporate bargaining power, another factor of influence is to what extent companies recognise the opportunities that can be gained
in the carbon market. Figure 6.1 presents a framework that combines these
two dimensions – expected regulatory constraint and opportunity recognition –
leading to a matrix that shows four scenarios for strategic responses to emissions
trading schemes. The types of responses resemble similar strategies that have
already been identified in the literature (see Suchman, 1995; Oliver, 1991). The
first strategy is to conform to regulatory pressures and accept a trading scheme as
it is. In the framework this corresponds to a company that is a conformist (cell 1).
In this scenario a company expects to be constrained by regulation, but does not
see many opportunities in changing the regulation and merely abides by existing
rules and norms. The second strategy is to select one local strategic context in
particular, which allows the company to continue business-as-usual (Suchman,
1995). This corresponds to an evader scenario (cell 2); it is a scenario where the
regulatory constraints are weak without clear opportunities to change these either.
Many companies currently still have the option not to belong to a strategic context that centres on emissions trading. Yet, even without feeling a constraint,
companies can choose otherwise when they recognise opportunities to gain from
emissions trading.

The other two scenarios in the framework correspond to a strategy where
companies recognise such opportunities and try to influence regulation through
bargaining behaviour (Suchman, 1995; Oliver, 1991). The difference between
the two scenarios, however, is the different motives companies in each scenario
have to enact their environment. The entrepreneur (cell 3) has a direct interest
in the functioning of the trading scheme because the company expects to be
constrained by it, if not now, then in the future. The entrepreneur seizes the
opportunity to change regulation in a way that alleviates the pressure and

		Opportunity Recognition	
		Low	High
Expected Regulatory Constraint	High	1 Conformist	3 Entrepreneur
	Low	2 Evader	4 Arbitrageur

Figure 6.1 Scenarios for strategic responses to regulatory constraints.

Put in my theors & analyse it for each country

improves regulatory efficiency (Fligstein, 1997), at least with regard to its own interests. In contrast, the arbitrageur (cell 4) does not have a direct interest in the efficiency of the trading scheme as it only faces a weak constraint, but sees opportunities to gain from it in another way, be it financially or strategically. The arbitrageur gains from the unintended consequences that go with building a new institution by using it for purposes it was not created for in the first place (Fligstein, 1997). It is the fact that emissions trading has created an open market for emissions reductions that distinguishes it from other forms of environmental regulation. It basically opens up the possibility of involvement of parties not affected by the regulation itself.

It must be noted that an MNC does not necessarily fit only one of the scenarios of the framework. Because most MNCs are geographically scattered organisations, it may well be that they play varying roles in different countries (Levy and Kolk, 2002). This sometimes reflects divergent regulatory settings in home (headquarters) versus host (subsidiary) settings, while levels of decentralisation and subsidiary autonomy may also play a role. An MNC can, for instance, simultaneously be a conformist in the EU ETS and an evader or entrepreneur regarding the US schemes. Besides, timing also has a bearing on the response to emissions trading. Particularly with regard to the trading schemes that are still being developed, the permanence of the rules is highly ambiguous. Accordingly, this uncertainty about an institution's permanence may affect the intensity of a company's response; leading to the adoption of more superficial activities that are not accompanied by strong internal organisational support structures (Jiang and Bansal, 2003; Milstein *et al*, 2002). For example, when the government is still unclear about the definite proposal for a trading scheme (e.g. in Japan, Canada, Australia and the US) a company could decide to invest in a limited number of eye-catching offset projects, but avoid setting up an internal team or department to become active in the carbon market on a day-to-day basis.

To get more insight into how MNCs approach the carbon market, we have analysed in what way Global 500 companies, which have reported their climate change activities to the Carbon Disclosure Project, are active in the carbon market.[2] In addition, we have looked at findings from recent studies on the development of the global carbon market (e.g. Capoor and Ambrosi, 2007; Convery *et al*, 2008; Convery and Redmond, 2007; Reinaud and Philibert, 2007; Røine and Hasselknippe, 2007; Røine *et al*, 2008) to put things into the right perspective and outline corporate activities and perceptions. Subsequent sections will focus on, respectively, carbon market participation under regulatory constraints (6.3) and without (strict) regulatory constraints (6.4).

---

2   For this analysis, we took the fourth CDP survey, of which findings were released in September 2006, as our starting point. This provided insight into climate change activities of 331 of the largest companies worldwide that are listed in the Financial Times Global 500. The actual collection of full data and analysis of these companies' carbon market activities took place in the period January–April 2007. Examination of more general carbon market information was finished late April 2008.

6.3 CARBON MARKET PARTICIPATION UNDER REGULATORY CONSTRAINTS

6.3.1 The European Union emissions trading scheme

As noted above already, the most prominent emissions trading scheme that is currently up and running is the EU ETS. The EU ETS targets industrial installations, including energy activities (combustion installations exceeding 20 megawatt, oil refineries, coke ovens), production and processing of ferrous metals, mineral industry (installations for cement, glass and ceramic products), and pulp and paper production plants (EC, 2003). The scheme thus primarily affects energy producers (including electric utilities), metals, cement, pulp and paper. However, because large combustion installations are also covered, other industries with energy-intensive activities, for example automotives and food processing, also require permits and were allocated allowances. Interestingly, aluminium and chemical industries are exempted from the EU ETS, supposedly due to their strong lobbying activities (Butzengeiger *et al*, 2003; Markussen and Svendsen, 2005). Overall, the EU ETS covers 13,000 installations and 45 per cent of the CO_2 emissions in the EU (Klepper and Peterson, 2004).

As Figure 6.2 shows, trading volumes have seen a steady increase since the EU ETS commenced in 2005. The EU ETS began with a pilot phase (2005–2007) and will be fully operational in the second phase (2008–2012); this is in line with the first commitment period of the Kyoto Protocol. The main aim of the pilot phase was to get the emissions trading scheme on track, and implement all institutional and financial structures (Convery and Redmond, 2007), such as electronic

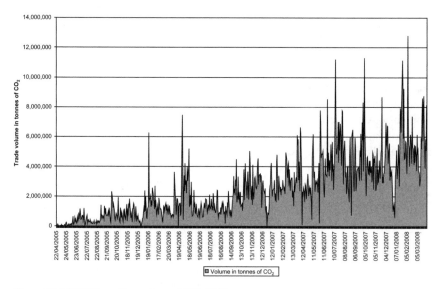

Figure 6.2 EU ETS trading volume 2005–2008.

Source: Based on European Climate Exchange trade volume data

registries (to register and trade allocated allowances) and financial exchanges on which allowances are traded (Convery *et al*, 2008). Moreover, at the start of 2008, it also became clear that the EU aims to continue the trading scheme beyond 2012, as a proposal for a third phase was unveiled (2013–2020). The number of allowances allocated to companies is different for each phase, while the general aim was to further restrict total allowances in each consecutive trading period. How many allowances each industry receives is set out in the national allocation plan (NAP), which means that burden sharing among trading sectors differs between EU Member States (possibly with consequences for competitiveness within Europe).

Not surprisingly, our analysis shows that most MNCs in the sample have their emissions trading activities linked to the EU ETS. Many are directly involved in the EU ETS because they are subject to a cap on their emissions and have been allocated allowances. As Figure 6.3 shows, 72 companies of the 331 that we analysed participate directly in the EU ETS (22 per cent of the sample). European companies form the majority with 51 having one or more eligible installations. Even so, 19 US firms are also covered, but not a single Asian firm in the sample is directly impacted by the EU ETS. If the EU ETS is to be effective it should create a strong constraint, as its goal is to bring down GHG emissions, and since enforcement is stringent, non-compliance would lead to severe penalties. In the first phase companies had to pay a fine of €40 for each metric tonne of CO_2 emitted for which no allowance can be handed over at the end of the year; this amount increased to €100 in the second phase (Convery and Redmond, 2007).

Corporate responses to the CDP questionnaire reflect the view that the EU ETS forms a carbon constraint. With some exceptions, companies with eligible

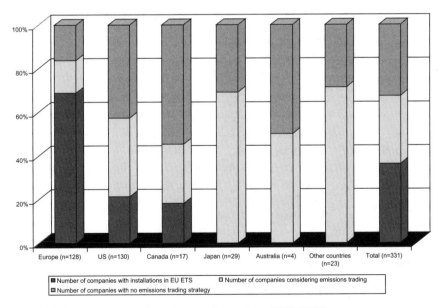

Figure 6.3 Country patterns for carbon market activity (2005–2006).

installations cannot circumvent the EU ETS; the scheme forces them to take their emissions into consideration. Enforcement is also taken seriously; a considerable number mention that they expect to avoid paying non-compliance fines. Correspondingly, compliance is the most often-cited motive for dealing with the EU ETS. Swiss cement company Holcim at the time noted, for example, that their 'priorities for the EU-ETS for 2005–07 are compliance management – i.e. internal and external balancing of emissions and allowances – and learning to use the system as it is conceptually intended to be used'. And they stated that they 'do not engage in speculative trading'. The belief that trading is merely for compliance and not speculation is shared by several other MNCs. ExxonMobil does not consider 'trading emission allowances as a business' and Repsol remarks that its 'participation in the market is orientated to low cost compliance and not to speculation'. Minimising the cost of compliance is an often-heard argument, closely linked to companies buying allowances when they fear a shortage at the end of the trading period. Nevertheless, speculation did occur in the EU ETS; in 2006 several European and US hedge funds entered the European carbon market for speculative reasons (Convery and Redmond, 2007).

Nevertheless, the fact that 22 per cent of the sample has installations under the EU ETS does not necessarily mean that they are also actively engaged in buying and/or selling allowances. A closer look sheds a different light on the intensity by which MNCs have embarked upon emissions trading. At the start of 2005, approximately 20 companies were active in the EU ETS (Convery and Redmond, 2007). Several factors explain why this number of companies actively buying or selling allowances was so low. To begin with, companies can already be affected by some other regulation that shows overlap with the EU ETS (a provision that has been used by quite a few UK companies; Reinaud and Philibert, 2007). For example, Cadbury Schweppes has tried to 'opt out', calling upon its participation in the UK's Climate Change Agreement, while Johnson & Johnson is exempted from trading in Belgium thanks to an 'energy covenant'. Another reason for exemption is that governments also try to protect the competitive position of their national industries and prevent relocation to countries outside the Kyoto Protocol (Bailey, 2007). For example, aluminium companies were exempted because it is difficult for this industry to absorb any cost increases from the EU ETS, as the price of aluminium is determined on international commodity markets (Egenhofer, 2007; Kruger and Pizer, 2004). Many others have refrained from trading for other reasons. One justification companies give for a 'no-trading strategy' is that they own a few installations only. Even if they have a surplus of allowances, they believe the administration and verification costs of selling them are generally too high compared with potential revenues.

However, the most important reason is that it has turned out that in the first allocation period (2005–2007) there was simply no necessity to buy because of considerable over-allocation of allowances (Convery and Redmond, 2007; Egenhofer, 2007). As Figure 6.4 shows, almost all EU Member States, with the exception of Austria, Spain, Italy, Ireland and the UK, had allocations that were above recent emissions, running as high as 45 per cent for Lithuania. Collectively, allowances

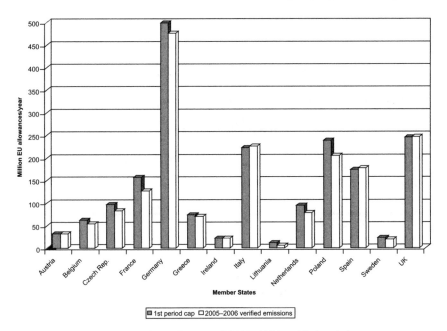

Figure 6.4 The gap between Phase I caps and 2005–2006 verified emissions.

Source: Based on data from EEA (2007)

allocated by EU Member States were 3 per cent above recent emissions (EEA, 2007). As a result, the caps set by the NAPs were only leading Member States to digress from their Kyoto commitments instead of closing the gap between actual emissions and Kyoto targets. Furthermore, the upward trend of 'business-as-usual' scenarios[3] is hardly dampened by the allocation in the first phase of the EU ETS.

Companies have played an important role in the over-allocation. As hardly any historical emissions data were available, governments have been relying on self-reported company data to determine business-as-usual projections, which has opened the door to bargaining behaviour (Grubb *et al*, 2005). Even though there was a comment period open to all stakeholder groups (e.g. NGOs, non-affected industries and customer representatives), due to time constraints only key players of affected industries have been able to influence the final outcome of the negotiation process. Accordingly, this process has been described as 'repeated iteration between government and industry, in which data were obtained, verified, and refined, while various principles of allocation were applied, until a solution which the government and the affected firms could accept was reached' (Ellerman and Buchner, 2007: 72). Some companies openly acknowledge that their political activities had an influence on the design of the first phase of the EU ETS. Italian

---

3   A business-as-usual scenario is used as baseline to calculate what the allocation of allowances should be.

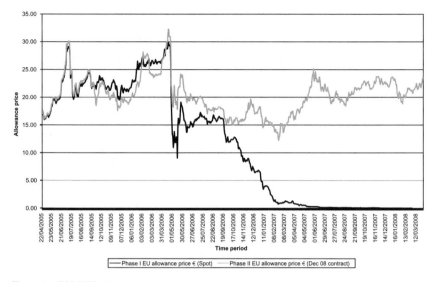

Figure 6.5 EU ETS allowance price development.

Source: Based on European Climate Exchange EU allowance price data

oil company ENI, for example, asserts that it 'has played a proactive role in the process for the definition of the Italian National Allocation Plan and it has supported rational allocation methodologies in line with the Kyoto targets'. However, in general MNCs are not really transparent about their activities in climate change politics (Kolk and Pinkse, 2007a). More indirect activities are more easily observed; for example, quite a few companies raise their membership of industry and trade associations that might have considerable influence on the on-going process of developing the EU ETS.

The over-allocation in the first phase has severely damaged the reputation of the EU ETS. For example, while primary fundamentals such as weather conditions and fuel prices (particularly the gas-to-coal ratio)[4] should determine the EU allowance price to enable predictability, as this would stimulate companies to incorporate the carbon price in investment decisions (Egenhofer, 2007), during the first two trading years, political decisions turned out to be more decisive (Røine and Hasselknippe, 2007). What has been critical in this respect is the incident that happened in April–May 2006. The EU would publish the first verified emissions data on 15 May, but several Member States already disclosed their information prior to that date (Convery and Redmond, 2007). As this information confirmed that many countries had allocated too many allowances, the allowance price dropped dramatically (see Figure 6.5). Even though the phase I allowance price recovered somewhat in the months thereafter, a related design

4   The relationship is that when coal becomes more prominent compared to gas, emissions increase and so will the price of emission allowances.

problem caused the price to further slide away below €1 in the course of 2007. The reason was that phase I allowances could not be banked to use in the second phase and the only companies short of allowances, utilities, had already hedged their positions at the start of 2007 (Røine and Hasselknippe, 2007). In other words, in the third year there was simply no sufficient demand left for first phase allowances. By that time, however, market activity was taken over by trading of allowances valid for the second phase (see Figure 6.5; Convery and Redmond, 2007).

The fact that there has been a considerable trading volume and that the allowance price has moved around €20 on average shows that it is not the case that the trading provision of the EU ETS has not been used at all. The most active players in the first two years of the EU ETS were utilities (e.g. RWE, E.ON, Centrica, Scottish Power and Electrabel) and large banks (e.g. Barclays, Merrill Lynch, BNP, and Fortis). Utilities have become engaged in emissions trading because this industry has most clearly faced a regulatory constraint due to the EU ETS. This is reflected by the fact that utilities received by far the largest share of all allowances in the EU ETS (55 per cent of all EU ETS allowances for the first phase; Hasselknippe and Røine, 2006). To illustrate, the top five recipients of allowances only included utilities: RWE, Vattenfall, Enel, E.ON and EDF. Still, despite the fact that a company such as RWE received approximately 5.9 per cent of all EU allowances, this share is not large enough for an individual company to exercise market power (Convery and Redmond, 2007). This is not to say, however, that no market power has been exercised at all (Convery *et al*, 2008).

It has been suggested by carbon market analysts that there might have been collusion between Europe's largest electricity companies (Egenhofer, 2007). Even though utilities are the major buyers in the market as they were the only ones short of allowances (Røine and Hasselknippe, 2007), they did not raise the alarm that on the whole the first phase had seen massive over-allocation. They had no reason to do so because high allowance prices lead to high electricity prices, which, due to a lack of price elasticity, can be passed through to customers, creating windfall profits for the utilities (Sijm *et al*, 2006). It will come as no surprise, then, that utilities also continue to show their 'entrepreneurial' stake by engaging in the debate on what happens to the EU ETS after 2012, when the first commitment period of the Kyoto Protocol expires. For example, E.ON wants a continuation of the EU ETS in its current form to create more certainty for their long-term investments, and, together with RWE, prefers a global framework to minimise the costs of reducing emissions.

Large purchasers of electricity, for example chemical, pharmaceutical and steel companies, have complained openly about the fact that electricity companies have passed through the price of allowances to their customers. In other words, for these energy-intensive industries the regulatory constraint of the EU ETS was not so much a result of a shortage of EU allowances, but rather soaring electricity prices. European steel company Arcelor, for example, stated the following:

> The allocation of CO_2 credits per country, and even per region, runs counter to the worldwide approach of large sectors such as steel. Furthermore, the

steel industry's major efforts to reduce greenhouse gases were not taken into account by the authorities. The existing system that can be called a 'cap and trade' system is anti-competitive. Arcelor has participated to the works of several international roundtables, like the OECD roundtable that took place last June 2005, to elaborate new rules for a global governance of global warming, by proposing a new approach based on the 'baseline and trade' concept, which means the CO_2 emissions quotas should be set in function of the average CO_2 emissions of a given sector which will help the best performing companies to invest in R&D and increase their production levels and the worst performers to update their process to use more efficient and cleaner production process.

Mexican cement company Cemex warned of the consequences of 'leaking effects', meaning that energy-intensive industries move their production facilities to countries that do not have an emissions target under the Kyoto Protocol. To prevent this from happening Cemex calls for a change in the EU ETS to become 'a more efficient emission trading scheme' and it thus hopes 'that the current design will be improved in the near future.' Choosing a strategy of avoidance in the rather drastic form of relocating production is sometimes mentioned, usually as a threat to influence policy makers. In a web-based survey amongst 2,250 respondents, published early 2007, only a 'handful' referred to relocation, while compliance (via the EU ETS in the first instance, and both internal abatement and CDM/JI as second) prevailed (Røine and Hasselknippe, 2007). A more specific question to a smaller sample of 380 companies, all covered by the EU ETS, of which results became available in April 2008, showed that 83 per cent had not considered relocation, but that the remainder were either considering it (around 12 per cent) or had planned or already moved production (Røine *et al*, 2008). To what extent political considerations had played a role in these answers is hard to judge. It may be a reflection, though, of the fact that the second phase is somewhat less lenient than the first one (see below).

However, apart from the dominant players, for most companies directly affected by the EU ETS in the first phase, trading entailed occasional transactions, instead of continuous involvement. For example, Volvo mentioned that their trading 'is limited to get the allowances needed.' Purchase of allowances is typically for compliance, but not many mentioned that they had done so already. Although there are more companies that reported a surplus of allowances, only a few explicitly stated having sold excess allowances. Before selling their surplus, it seems that many MNCs first balance their allowance accounts on a corporate level. In other words, the EU ETS enables MNCs to trade across Member States but within their own organisations to deal with regulatory differences across the EU (a form of internal compensation, see Figure 5.1 in Chapter 5). Reluctance to sell excess emissions has also particularly been a characteristic of the first one-and-a-half years of the EU ETS – before the market collapsed late April 2006. At that time, information about the need for additional allowances was still poor but an overall shortage was expected. This led to a relatively high carbon price (see Figure 6.5) because utilities were demanding more allowances to compensate for high natural

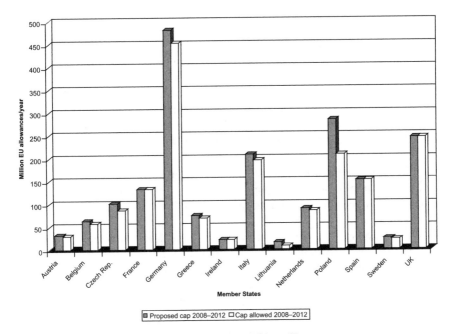

Figure 6.6 The gap between proposed and allowed Phase II caps

Source: Based on data from EEA (2007)

gas prices, while market players with excess allowances wanted to sell due to uncertainty about the direction that market was heading (Convery *et al*, 2008).

Because over-allocation was the Achilles heel of the first phase of the EU ETS, the European Commission has made some changes for the second phase. As Figure 6.6 illustrates, the European Commission has adjusted the proposed cap of almost every Member State downward. Moreover, it has allowed a higher proportion of allowances (10 per cent compared to 5 per cent in the pilot phase) to be auctioned.[5] Not all Member States will use this auctioning provision, however: only Germany, the UK, the Netherlands, Ireland, Hungary, Lithuania, Austria and Belgium have expressed the intention to use it, and then specifically to put a break on the windfall profits of utilities. Nevertheless, there are some doubts whether there will be enough auctioning to prevent windfall profits altogether (Point Carbon, 2008a). For the longer term, the EU plans to revise the EU ETS and further increase the use of auctioning for allocation of allowances. However, this revision has already led to resistance from European industry. As head of the business lobby group European Roundtable of Industrialists (ERT), Royal Dutch/Shell's CEO Jeroen van der Veer sent a letter to EU commissioner Gunter Verheugen, warning against an extension of auctioning as it would harm the

5   In addition, other changes are that airlines will be included from 2011 onwards, and that banking between the second and third phase will be possible (Capoor and Ambrosi, 2007).

competitiveness of European industry (Hollinger, 2008). This clearly illustrates that MNCs keep pursuing two kinds of strategies simultaneously: a market and a political response (Kolk and Pinkse, 2004).

In conclusion, what can be said about the contribution of the EU ETS to climate change mitigation, and what is the impact on the competitiveness of European business? These questions have hardly been investigated yet, partly because it is still rather difficult to measure such environmental and economic impacts of emissions trading, and also because the EU ETS was launched only a few years ago. What is more, it is very difficult to establish whether significant abatement has occurred, since it will never be known what would have happened without the EU ETS (Ellerman and Buchner, 2008), and because economic growth and new entrants to emitting industries cloud the picture. Nevertheless, there are some positive indications that there has been abatement in the first two years of the EU ETS, although it was very limited. The fact that a significant price has been paid for CO_2 allowances suggests that at least electric utilities have factored in the cost of carbon in their investment decisions (Hoffmann, 2007). Moreover, while verified emissions increased slightly, these are largely explained by the fundamentals, fuel prices, production growth and weather (Røine *et al*, 2008). It has been suggested as well that it was not only due to over-allocation that verified emissions turned out be lower than total allocation, but also because companies have managed to reduce emissions – something that would not have occurred without the EU ETS (Convery *et al*, 2008; Ellerman and Buchner, 2008). The European Commission claims that the lack of real emissions reductions in the first phase will change as a result of the reforms for the second phase.

Finally, even though evidence suggests that the carbon price has been integrated in corporate decision making, the extent that it also stimulated technological change appears to be more limited. Findings from research in the German electricity industry suggests that the EU ETS has induced utilities to make short-term investments (e.g. retrofits), but it failed to affect long-term investment in new (coal-fired) power plants (Hoffmann, 2007). One explanation for this is that the absence of banking from the first to the second period has deferred companies from making such changes to their long-term investment policy (Convery *et al*, 2008; Egenhofer, 2007). Still, even though the EU ETS has not worked to its full potential yet as to environmental effectiveness, what companies have been warning the public about – that the EU ETS would harm competitiveness – has not happened either. Research to date has not been able to establish a relation between carbon prices and competitiveness. However, it must be noted that industrial sectors such as cement, steel and refining were not facing full regulatory pressure yet, because they had been over-allocated and were profiting from high commodity prices in this same period (Convery *et al*, 2008).

6.3.2 Alternatives for the EU ETS

While the EU ETS makes up most of the currently existing carbon market, there are some alternatives as regards compliance markets. Other trading schemes that create a regulatory constraint include the New South Wales Greenhouse Gas Abatement Scheme (NSW GGAS), the UK emissions trading scheme (UK ETS) and the Regional Greenhouse Gas Initiative (RGGI). As Table 6.1 shows, the NSW GGAS is the second largest compliance market. This trading scheme works slightly differently than the EU ETS as it is a 'baseline-and-credit' scheme, which works with performance against mandatory intensity targets (or benchmarks) instead of an absolute cap combined with allocated allowances. The goal of the scheme is to improve emissions intensity of electricity which is used or supplied by participants. To comply with the intensity target companies can pursue four types of reduction activities to generate the required volume of New South Wales Greenhouse Gas Abatement Certificates (NGACs): low-emissions generation of electricity (including cogeneration) or improvements in emissions intensity of existing generation activities; activities that result in reduced consumption of electricity; activities carried out by elective participants that reduce on-site emissions not directly related to electricity consumption; and carbon capture from the atmosphere in forests (NSW, 2007). Renewable Energy Certificates (see Chapter 2) generated to comply with the mandatory renewable energy target (MRET) can also be used in the NSW GGAS, but CDM or JI credits are not allowed (Capoor and Ambrosi, 2007).

The NSW GGAS has seen a substantial growth recently as the volume of NGACs traded increased from 6 million in 2005 to 20 million in 2006. Still this only involved a modest number of 669 transactions in 2006 (Røine and Hasselknippe, 2007). As already mentioned in Chapter 2, the NSW GGAS is mandatory for electricity generators, retailers and large market customers, but voluntary for other types of companies. In 2007 all participants were in compliance and had mainly created certificates by cleaner generation (70 per cent) and measures leading to reduced use of electricity (25 per cent). While there has been oversupply of certificates in 2006 this is likely to change in coming years because companies can hedge their future positions by carrying certificates forward as they are bankable. Moreover, according to most projections, supply will fall short of demand around 2008 (NSW, 2007). Regarding the companies in the CDP sample, only the Australian bank ANZ mentions trading activity, as it has developed capabilities in the MRET scheme which it then used to also take part in the NSW GGAS. Besides, telecom company Telstra has explored the possibilities of this scheme. The reason for low involvement of Global 500 companies is the fact that most NSW GGAS participants are likely to be active in a domestic context only (e.g. local electricity companies). The main uncertainty regarding the NSW GGAS is what will happen when the Federal Australian Government introduces a cap-and-trade scheme on a national level (start announced for 2010). It currently seems that even though New South Wales had plans to extend the scheme at least until 2020, it will end when the National Emissions Trading Scheme begins.[6]

---

6   See <http://www.greenhousegas.nsw.gov.au> for recent news updates on the NSW GGAS.

Another local scheme is the UK emissions trading scheme, which started in March 2002. Participating companies have mainly used it to take early action in preparation for the EU ETS. In the UK ETS, companies could participate in several ways, but for the majority trading was directly linked to the Climate Change Levy, a tax on industrial and commercial energy consumption (Boemare and Quirion 2002). Remarkably, the Levy did not cover electricity producers, which as a consequence did not experience any pressure to participate; they could only engage voluntarily in reduction projects (Roeser and Jackson 2002; Rosenzweig *et al* 2002). Companies participating in the UK trading scheme were temporarily exempted (until the end of 2006) from joining the EU ETS. In the CDP sample eight companies mentioned their participation in the UK ETS. This included four UK-based companies (Barclays, GlaxoSmithKline, Tesco, and Unilever), while the remainder consisted of subsidiaries from multinationals based in the US (e.g. Wal-Mart, Ford, and Motorola) and Japan (e.g. Mitsubishi). Most of these companies were compliance-oriented, had exceeded their target, and were able to sell excess emissions. What explains the relatively low participation in the UK ETS is the fact that it ended in March 2007, as it was superseded by the EU ETS. On the whole there has been limited trading activity in the UK ETS with the exception of its final months, as companies had to make sure that they were in compliance for the final deadline in March 2007. The major drawback of the UK ETS was its short timespan, which put off companies to make investments with a longer amortisation period than five years, as it was quite clear that this scheme would not continue in the same form after the opt-out possibility for the EU ETS had ended (Capoor and Ambrosi, 2007).

Finally, amongst the US-based trading schemes that are yet to start, the RGGI is the only one where trading rules have already been determined. The RGGI is an initiative of the governor of the state of New York, who proposed the trading scheme in April 2003. Currently, the RGGI includes 10 North-eastern and Mid-Atlantic States including Connecticut, Delaware, Maine, Maryland, Massachusetts, New Jersey, New Hampshire, New York, Rhode Island and Vermont. In its formative years it has seen some states (e.g. Massachusetts and Rhode Island) dropping out (allegedly due to corporate lobbying), and re-entering in a later stage (Jones and Levy, 2007). The main aim of RGGI is to put a cap on emissions generated by power plants (generators of 25MW or larger). It will start in 2009 with a three-year compliance period, but is planned to continue at least until 2018 (RGGI, 2007). The cap for the first six years will be to stabilise CO_2 emissions; only in the final four years (2015–2018) will the cap be constrained with 2.5 per cent each year, thus adding up to a 10 per cent reduction in 2019 (Selin and VanDeveer, 2007). What sets the RGGI apart from the EU ETS is the way of allocating allowances; they will almost completely be auctioned instead of given away for free. Moreover, it also allows banking of allowances for the complete period of its intended existence (2009–2018). In addition, this scheme permits the use of offsets which have been created in any of the RGGI-states or any other US state that has signed an agreement. The offset projects have to live up to a strict standard, and currently only some types of projects are eligible (NSW, 2007);

still, it opens the door to reduction activities in sectors other than the electricity industry (Jones and Levy, 2007).

To what extent the RGGI will put a regulatory constraint on electric utilities is still open to discussion. Preliminary analyses of the stringency of the cap suggest that there will be excess allowances available at its start (Point Carbon, 2008b). What is more, the low price of Regional Greenhouse gas Allowances (RGAs), which would be a consequence of such over-allocation, will also lower the regulatory constraint substantially for subsequent years, as companies can bank excess allowances. The prediction in April 2008 was that the allowances that can be banked in the first years will not be depleted until 2015, when the cap is lowered for the first time. Regarding the RGGI, companies have predominantly used bargaining strategies (e.g. leading to temporary withdrawal of Massachusetts) as this scheme was still in its formative years. For example, Suez Energy North America (SENA) mentioned that it was 'actively tracking and participating in the development of US climate change legislation, such as the RGGI. While SENA supports linkage with international programs such as Kyoto, it appears that offset programs for the next few years will be limited to the US'. The main concern for companies concerning the RGGI has been the risk of 'emissions leakage' to neighbouring states (Engel, 2006). The reason is that the RGGI creates discrepancies between states within the US, as not all states in the country are subject to similar regulatory constraints. To illustrate, US utility PSEG, which has a lot of its operations in the North-eastern states, argues the following in response to CDP:

> PSEG is, however, very concerned about 'leakage'. Leakage refers to the market imbalance created by requiring generators within the RGGI region to internalize costs of emitting CO_2, whereas generators located outside of the region, but connected on the same electric grid, are not burdened with the same costs. Generators outside of the RGGI region will be able to operate at a comparatively lower cost and sell this energy into the RGGI region. This could place generators inside the RGGI region at an economic disadvantage while at the same time not reducing overall emissions of CO_2. The RGGI States have convened an 'Imports and Leakage' workgroup, of which PSEG is a participant, to consider options for controlling leakage.

Moreover, the RGGI faces comparable political uncertainty as the NSW GGAS, since it might be possible that a federal trading scheme will be implemented after 2012. If this is the case then prices of RGAs could fall tremendously, as happened in the first phase of the EU ETS, unless reductions achieved under the RGGI will be rewarded in a federal scheme (Point Carbon, 2008b). In other words, what developments in all three 'local' trading schemes show is that 'success' highly depends on policy developments at higher governmental levels. An adverse effect of this uncertainty is that these trading schemes will not motivate companies to make long-term investments in emissions reduction (Capoor and Ambrosi, 2007).

6.4 CARBON MARKET PARTICIPATION WITHOUT (STRICT) REGULATORY CONSTRAINTS

6.4.1 Voluntary participation in compliance markets

There are currently many situations in which companies only face limited (or no) regulatory constraints, because there is no (strict) emissions trading regime. The majority of companies in the EU, for example, are simply not affected by the EU ETS, either because they do not have energy-intensive activities (i.e. the increases in the cost of electricity are minimal in the context of the company's overall cost base) or they have no production sites in the EU. This scenario applies even more to those companies with no operations at all within the EU. For these companies, the compliance requirements that apply to companies covered by the EU ETS are clearly not relevant. It is interesting to note that the manner in which these companies engage with public policy seems quite different to those covered by the EU ETS. For these companies, the drivers for their bargaining activities are the potential business opportunities that emissions trading may present or the desire to avoid costs or mandatory regulation in the future. It is also relevant to note that many of these companies are taking action to profit from such (emerging) schemes through voluntarily participating in schemes, either for financial benefit or because participation in such programmes helps develop organisational capabilities or improve corporate image (Kolk and Pinkse, 2008). In relation to the burnishing of corporate image, a number of these companies have highlighted their positive role in promoting emissions reductions or, in the case of the EU ETS, developing the scheme.

The fact that emissions trading has created an open market for emissions reductions distinguishes it from other forms of environmental regulation, opening up the possibility of the involvement of parties not affected by the regulation itself. The financial sector is an important example here as it profits from other companies' lack of knowledge of emissions trading, while it can use experience from trading in other areas. In other words, although banks were not allocated allowances themselves, they trade on behalf of their clients, and see opportunities in the carbon market to influence the trading rules to their advantage. Such opportunities to exploit the EU ETS are due to its novelty and size. Most companies lack the experience to trade a commodity such as emissions allowances and need the expertise of financial middlemen to participate (Pinkse, 2007). Many banks, mostly European but some US as well, provide services to facilitate trading by clients, for example to buy and sell allowances on their behalf or risk management services. By doing so they help the further development of the EU ETS because, as Fortis argues, trading services have 'the effect of increasing liquidity by allowing many companies to trade small volumes while avoiding the administratively cumbersome setting up of an in-house trading desk'. It is the limited size of the market that augments the role of financial middlemen. British bank Barclays illustrates the role of banks, as it argues the following:

Barclays was the first UK Bank to set-up a carbon-trading desk and we helped shape the development of the EU ETS market (for example in helping create standard contracts and in sharing our own trading experiences with new players).

The Slovakian subsidiary of Belgian bank Dexia goes even one step further as it claims to be the only private actor administering a national allowance registry, thereby taking up a public role.

In their CDP responses, some major banks involved in trading also mentioned their role in helping design allocation plans for the second phase of the EU ETS as well as their role in influencing potential schemes in Canada, Japan and the US. For example, they have made recommendations for future phases within the EU ETS, including the introduction of auctioning to prevent windfall profits and create a healthier, more liquid market. While several companies reported to have contributed to the design of new trading schemes, the majority of companies that currently do not face a regulatory constraint reported that they were waiting for more clarity about the exact rules for trading before taking concrete action with regard to potentially upcoming schemes. Companies' attitudes seemed to vary as emissions trading schemes evolved from initial conception, through to voluntary initiatives and then to harder regulatory requirements, at which point their support in principle for emissions trading tended to be heavily qualified by concern about the financial implications for the business.

6.4.2 The Clean Development Mechanism

While carbon trading in the EU ETS is the main route for companies to comply with European regulations, it is not the only route. In addition to the allowances that they received via the EU ETS allocation process, companies can also create emissions credits from the Clean Development Mechanism or Joint Implementation. That is, in October 2004 the EU passed the 'linking directive', enabling companies to use CDM and JI credits to meet the EU ETS obligations (EC, 2004). These project-based markets are currently still dominated by CDM, as about 91 per cent of all primary transactions are from CDM projects (Capoor and Ambrosi, 2007). As already mentioned in Chapter 2, in its initial years CDM was dominated by public participants (e.g. the Dutch Government and the World Bank). Only after the precise rules for CDM became clear with the adoption of the Marrakesh Accords in December 2001 did this project-based market also become more attractive to companies. At first predominantly Japanese companies began to take part in the CDM market, but, after the EU ETS started and the linking directive was passed, this market started to attract European companies as well. This eventually led to an involvement of private companies in 80 per cent of all transactions in 2006 (Lecocq and Ambrosi, 2007), and these 'private' transactions were clearly dominated by European companies with an 86 per cent market share. This was a notable change compared to 2005 when CDM market shares of Japanese and European companies were still of comparable size (Capoor and Ambrosi, 2007).

The types of companies active in the CDM market are fundamentally different, in the sense that CDM participants are more diverse than those participating in compliance markets. One reason for this diversity is of course that a company does not need to have to be allocated allowances to become active in the CDM market. As a result, there are basically three categories of companies active in the CDM market. First, this market has attracted a considerable number of companies, such as banks and speculators, that do not need the credits for compliance, but hope to make a profit by selling these in the secondary CDM market (Lecocq and Ambrosi, 2007). However, as the interest of European companies shows, CDM is also appealing for a second category: companies that face a regulatory constraint, as CDM credits can be used for compliance with the EU ETS (and possibly for other similar schemes in the near future). Nevertheless, instead of creating a regulatory constraint itself, it is more accurate to say that CDM relieves the constraint for those covered by such a regulatory trading scheme. That is also why CDM has been criticised: it offers a passage to avoid regulatory pressure by inflating the number of allowances available for compliance in the EU ETS. As a consequence, CDM can thus slow down corporate initiatives for internal abatement (Røine and Hasselknippe, 2007). The third category consists of companies that currently still face low regulatory constraints on their GHG emissions, but are building a portfolio of credits for compliance in future periods of the EU ETS or any of the other emerging trading schemes in the US, Australia, Canada, or Japan. CDM credits were initially particularly attractive for compliance in the somewhat longer term because at least the trading rules of the EU ETS determine that CDM credits do not expire after the first phase. For the period after 2012 this is uncertain, however.

Not surprisingly, our analysis reveals that CDM is also becoming fairly popular among Global 500 companies. Of the 331 companies in the sample, 90 claim to have or plan to have activities in the CDM market. In terms of geographical origin, the main contrast with the EU ETS is that even though European companies clearly dominate, Japanese companies also take part on a considerable scale. Even if Japanese companies have not yet been confronted with a mandatory scheme in their home country, they use CDM to comply with the voluntary commitments under the Keidanren Voluntary Action Plan (Capoor and Ambrosi, 2007). To what extent announcements of the Japanese, Canadian and Australian national governments about implementing a trading scheme similar to the one in Europe will lead to a rise in demand for CDM credits is debatable, however. This really depends on the degree of uncertainty that companies perceive as to the seriousness of such government announcements. In Japan there are indications that companies indeed believe that the Government will go ahead with a national trading scheme; the fact that the Government has been experimenting with pilot schemes supports this contention. Toshiba argues, for example, that 'we have also started the acquisition of emission credits on the assumption that there will be a change in our business structure and the restriction of the emission cap will be legislated'.

In contrast, Canadian companies have not become serious buyers of CDM credits, notwithstanding the fact that the Canadian Government has regularly presented plans to permit such project-based credits for compliance with domestic climate policy (Capoor and Ambrosi, 2007). In other words, since buying CDM credits requires serious investment with considerable risk, too much regulatory uncertainty appears to act as an impediment to active participation in the CDM market. Canadian oil and gas producer Encana asserts, for example, that it 'does not have any production in the EU and does not currently envision becoming an active participant in any emissions trading scheme beyond that required to maintain compliance with any future Canadian GHG legislation'. Similarly, structural demand from the US is also rather unlikely to increase to any significance soon. The first driving factor would be the RGGI, but companies in this scheme are not allowed to use CDM or JI credits for compliance before the price of an RGGI allowance (RGA) will exceed US\$10, a situation not likely to occur in the first few years (Capoor and Ambrosi, 2007). Still the suggestions made by US and Australian states that they will open their schemes for CDM credits strengthens the belief that the CDM market will be sustained after the Kyoto Protocol expires in 2012 (Røine and Hasselknippe, 2007).

The relative openness of the CDM market compared with the EU ETS leads to a broad interest from companies participating with other motives in mind than compliance alone. This openness has several reasons. Firstly, as mentioned above, companies do not need a permit and allowances to become active. As a result it attracts a great variety of companies, from different countries and industries, which use CDM in many different ways, ranging from regulatory compliance, fulfilling a voluntary commitment, to outright profit-seeking behaviour. For example, many financial institutions are trying to generate CDM credits by financing projects in developing countries that might generate credits as well. US electricity firm Duke Energy exemplifies such profit-seeking behaviour:

> Regarding the CDM, a number of energy projects that Duke Energy is developing in Latin America have the potential to be certified as CDM projects. If this occurs, Duke Energy will be looking to sell whatever credits are generated by the projects.

Another reason is the global dimension of CDM (always entailing projects in developing countries) which makes it attractive to multinationals that are already active in these countries with foreign direct investment (FDI) or have plans to invest here (Arquit Niederberger and Saner, 2005; Ellis *et al*, 2007). FDI can be a stimulant for CDM, because companies with production sites in developing countries see opportunities to further exploit their presence through CDM. If an MNC is planning to invest in GHG-intensive production activities in a developing country, then CDM activities can make it interesting to install extra equipment for abatement. One difficulty in this regard is, however, that according to the additionality rules of CDM an investor has to demonstrate that the abatement is additional to what would have occurred under a business-as-usual scenario. Proving additionality can be quite cumbersome and lead to significant transaction costs as it is often difficult to establish what would have happened in the absence of CDM (Hepburn, 2007). The fact that a project generates CDM credits which can be sold also creates an extra source of finance. Even though it is still unlikely that generating CDM credits will be the sole objective of FDI in developing countries, as an extra source of finance CDM can be used to leverage other investment. CDM will, for example, make it easier to finance projects in energy infrastructure (Ellis *et al*, 2007).

Finally, CDM allows emissions reduction of non-CO_2 sources. In the first few years, projects to abolish highly potent greenhouse gases such as HFC-23 and N_2O have been dominating the CDM market, because the high global warming potential has enabled carbon traders to make huge profits or ease compliance in the home country (exemplified by the Italian utility ENEL's large credit purchase from Chinese HFC-23 projects; Røine and Hasselknippe, 2007). Reducing emissions of HFC-23 gases has mainly been done by encouraging Chinese factories to install end-of-pipe equipment, which is not new and a relatively cheap measure. As a result, by only making a modest capital investment, carbon traders have been able to generate huge amounts of carbon credits that could be sold at a large profit. Besides the easy profits from such HFC-23 abolishment, another reason for the large share of these projects in the CDM market is the fact that additionality is easier to prove for such end-of-pipe technology. In the absence of strict environmental regulations, which is often the case in developing countries, companies have no other incentive for installing such equipment than the CDM credits that it delivers. Additionality is more difficult to establish in the case of projects for the further development of more sustainable sources of energy (Ellis *et al*, 2007). The issue with installing end-of-pipe technology is that HFCs only represent a small part of the problem of the industrial contribution to climate change, as CO_2 and methane are a much greater problem (Hepburn, 2007). Yet, at the end of 2006 HFCs covered almost 60 per cent of all CDM credits, thereby temporarily disrupting this market (Hasselknippe and Røine, 2006). Recently, the balance has tilted more in the direction of renewable energy projects, but the share of HFC-23 projects is still substantial (see Figure 6.7).

The case of HFC-23 also shows a potential harmful consequence of regulating corporate environmental behaviour with a market mechanism. The carbon market motivates companies to reduce emissions in the most cost-effective way. Only if the price of emissions credits is lower than the marginal costs of reducing emissions in-house will companies be stimulated to enter the carbon market (Malueg, 1989). By doing so, they make use of the fact that other participants in the trading scheme have a lower marginal cost for internal abatement. However, as the HFC-23 example shows, credits that can be purchased on the market typically represent reductions achieved from projects that utilise existing (end-of-pipe) technologies (Ellis *et al*, 2007). But the carbon market also aims to spur innovation and motivate firms to invest in more sustainable production technologies that lower GHG emissions. There is thus a sizeable threat that emissions trading is not realising the intended objectives because companies with high

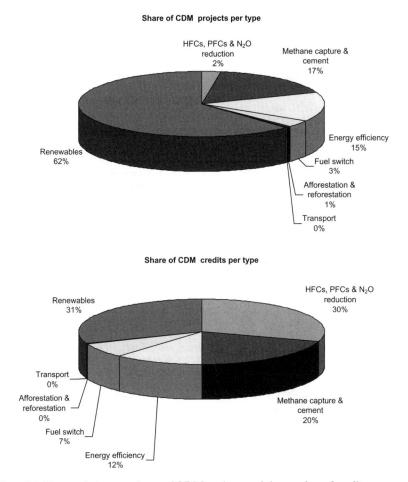

Figure 6.7 The gap between volume of CDM projects and the number of credits.

Source: Based on data from the UNEP Risø CDM Pipeline (the situation on 1 April 2008)

abatement costs are not investing in climate-friendly technologies (Malueg, 1989; Gagelmann and Frondel, 2005).[7]

Due to their dominance on the market, companies also have considerable influence on the way in which the CDM market develops. By embarking upon particular projects that fit into regular business activities and at the same time lead to emissions credits, they are able to influence what constitute legitimate CDM

---

7   It may therefore be wise to also implement climate policies that are technology-specific (Sandén and Azar, 2005). For example, if the EU wants to create a hydrogen economy, it is better to implement specific policy instruments that focus on development of such technologies. If it merely relies on the carbon market with all its problems, it may well be that development of many promising technologies aimed at renewable energy are unnecessarily slowed.

projects. There thus seem to be ample opportunities to play a part in CDM, and many MNCs look at CDM in terms of the opportunities it creates. However, it is difficult to distinguish whether companies actually engage in real activities or merely express their intentions to use this mechanism; it seems that many also just have a go at it. Nevertheless, the fact that enforcement is dispersed over various governmental levels (Haites and Yamin, 2000) cause many corporate initiatives to hardly materialise. With some exceptions, the majority of the 90 companies identified have not yet been able to certify the credits associated with the projects they have set up that might be eligible for CDM. It seems that passing all the hurdles before a CDM project is approved is quite difficult. Matsushita Electric Industrial, for example, states that for a particular project in Malaysia it obtained approval from the Japanese Government, but that it would have to continue 'work aiming at the approval of a Malaysian government and registration to the United Nations in the future'.

There are several ways to circumvent these hurdles. One is to purchase CDM credits on the secondary market from other parties that have taken the effort to deal with all administrative aspects. Given how difficult it is to certify CDM projects, it is not surprising that many projects are still somewhere in the pipeline: they have not reached the final stage yet, or potential sellers keep credits they created for future compliance themselves (in spite of this, and as Table 6.1 shows, the secondary CDM market is growing quite fast). Another option is to participate in a climate fund of which several have been set up by public actors, e.g. World Bank's Prototype Carbon Fund and Japan GHG Reduction Fund, as well as private actors, e.g. Natsource's Greenhouse Gas Credits Aggregation Pool and the European Carbon Fund. Investment in a climate fund seems most sensible when the interest in CDM originates from emissions reduction aims. Japanese firms in particular seem to follow this route as no domestic trading scheme has yet been established in Japan. Many banks have also invested in climate funds to assist their clients in obtaining emissions credits, as the following example of Deutsche Bank illustrates:

> Deutsche Bank has been a pioneer in the field of CDM/JI projects – Deutsche Bank was one of only two banks to invest in the World Bank's groundbreaking Prototype Carbon Fund (PCF) and one of the only banks to participate in the Umbrella Carbon Fund (UCF). We are also involved in several private sector projects in a variety of countries and methodologies.

Finally, like the EU ETS, the CDM market works in a somewhat different way than intended by those who designed it in the first place. At the outset CDM had a dual purpose: to lead to the reduction of GHG emissions in developing countries and to contribute to sustainable development via technology transfer (Ellis *et al*, 2007). There are several reasons why CDM is not completely fulfilling these aims. First, CDM requires from a host country the capacity to install the necessary CDM-related institutions to deal with certification of projects. As only relatively well-developed Asian countries such as China and India possess this capacity, the vast majority of CDM projects take place there, and not in more technology-poor countries in Africa. As a result, CDM follows the same pattern as FDI, thereby further increasing the gap between Africa and other developing countries (Ellis *et al*, 2007). Second, even though recent evidence shows that technology transfers take place in 44 per cent of all CDM projects (Dechezleprêtre *et al*, 2007), such transfers do not necessarily also contribute to sustainable development. The reason is the dominance of projects that aim to abolish industrial gases (e.g. HFC-23 and N_2O). These CDM projects do nothing more than reduce high-potent GHG emissions, but fail to stimulate the local economy, improve health, employment or education (Ellis *et al*, 2007; Hepburn, 2007); this is more likely to occur with projects in renewable technologies. Fortunately the share of renewable energy projects has increased recently (see Figure 6.7).

6.4.3 Voluntary alternatives

Alongside compliance markets and project-based markets, over the last years the voluntary carbon market has grown very fast as well. Historically, the voluntary carbon market precedes compliance markets, as the first voluntary carbon offset already took place in 1989 when US utility AES Corp financed a forestation project in Guatemala to compensate for a new power plant the company had built (Bellassen and Leguet, 2007). However, with the adoption of the Kyoto Protocol and particularly the EU ETS, this voluntary market had apparently lost its appeal to companies. But with the recent rise of public interest in climate change, voluntary offsets are regaining prominence (Hamilton *et al*, 2007). One of the reasons is that, unlike the other market-based mechanisms, the voluntary market is not only used by companies and governmental organisations, but is also open to individual consumers. It is, for example, possible for individuals to offset air travel. Nevertheless, like the CDM market, the voluntary market is currently dominated by corporate players; one estimate is that in 2006 companies were responsible for 80 per cent of the market activity, while the remainder of the activity came from governments (12 per cent), individuals (5 per cent) and NGOs (2 per cent) (Hamilton *et al*, 2007). As mentioned above, the voluntary carbon market basically consists of two components: the Chicago Climate Exchange (CCX) and the Voluntary Offset Market.

The CCX is a collaboration between a number of multinational corporations, local companies, governments and NGOs, which aim to demonstrate that climate change can be managed on a voluntary basis and that emissions trading is a viable mechanism. Participants commit to voluntary reduction targets, with trading of allowances and offsets as options. Geographically, the scheme is restricted to projects on the American continent (Yang, 2006). Although the CCX shows parallels with the EU ETS (e.g. it also has two trading phases and for some time allowed EU allowances for compliance), participation is voluntary and it includes all six GHGs covered by the Kyoto Protocol, not just CO_2. In essence the CCX forms a legally-binding contract, but since it is a private institution the only real penalty that participants face is exclusion from the market (Yang, 2006). To tie as many different types of organisations to it, the CCX allows for three categories of participants: full members, associate members and participating members. Full members are companies which emit a significant amount of GHGs and are the only ones that face a target. For associate members, who are mainly service-related companies with low direct emissions, the CCX is a way of offsetting indirect emissions. Finally, participating members either offer credits from offset projects or provide liquidity as market makers. In size the CCX has grown tenfold from 2005 to 2006 (see Table 6.1) and membership increased from 129 in 2005 to 225 in 2006 (Røine and Hasselknippe, 2007).

From the start the role of multinationals in the CCX has been noteworthy as founding members included American Electric Power, Baxter International, DuPont, Equity Office Properties Trust, Ford Motor Company, International Paper, Manitoba Hydro, MeadWestvaco Corporation, Motorola, STMicroelectronics, Stora Enso North America, Temple-Inland and Waste Management (together with the City of Chicago). Even though the CCX has been designed in a very similar way to regulatory trading schemes, companies' motives to participate in this market are quite different. As the CCX had already started in 2003, it preceded the EU ETS and any other US-based scheme (the regional ones that are likely to be implemented in the coming years). Companies have therefore used the CCX to indirectly prepare for larger schemes that might emerge later. Baxter International mentions, for example, that it 'has had the opportunity to use CCX's trading platform and learn how GHG emissions trading may occur in the international arena'. Thus this company believes that it 'is well positioned to withstand the scrutiny of greater emissions verification and pursue trading as one of our climate change strategies'. Another motive that CCX participants and specifically its founding members point out is that they see the CCX as a vehicle to influence the development of a federal US emissions trading scheme. American Electric Power motivates its active involvement in the CCX as follows:

> AEP has supported CCX in numerous ways, including serving on the board, providing input on the development of the rulebook (including protocols concerning accounting, verification and validation of emission reductions), and by purchasing allowances in the initial CCX auction. We are doing so to demonstrate the cost-effectiveness of reducing emissions by utilizing this market-based instrument. It is our hope that the 'lessons learned' will inform the policy debate on climate change and positively influence the design of greenhouse gas mitigation policies at the international, federal and state levels.

The political undertone of the CCX also deters firms. Electricity company FPL, for example, believes that it is 'not yet representative of what a real regulatory driven greenhouse gas market program will be like', and Occidental Petroleum argues that schemes other than the EU ETS 'offer little business reason for most companies to participate'.

Nevertheless, in its first few years of existence CCX has been successful and seen full compliance of its members as the emissions have consistently been well below the targets (9 per cent in 2003; 12.1 per cent in 2004; 9.7 per cent in 2005; and 5.9 per cent in 2006; CCX, 2007). This is not surprising given the fact that it is a private institution, which leads to a positive selection bias; it only attracts those companies with a strong environmental commitment that can achieve their voluntary binding targets rather easily. However, this is also one of the weaknesses of this private trading scheme: as it is gaining popularity, it will also attract companies lacking a strong environmental commitment, thus making it more vulnerable to opportunistic behaviour (Yang, 2006).

Finally, the other segment of the voluntary carbon market is formed by the offset market. This market for voluntary offsets is completely unregulated, which has some advantages, but also some major drawbacks. The voluntary offset market is by no means a compliance market, but mainly used by companies to burnish their public image. As already discussed in Chapter 5, companies typically enter this market if they have made a pledge to become carbon neutral. Examples are HSBC and BSkyB who made efforts to buy offset from renewable energy projects (e.g. BSkyB has invested in a wind power project in New Zealand). The main advantage of its unregulated nature is that there are less or no rules to abide by, which automatically lowers transaction costs. This improves the accessibility tremendously, both to buyers and sellers. This means that non-profit organisations and individuals can afford to compensate their (in)direct emissions and become buyers. On the supply side, this market opens up possibilities for small-scale community projects, not interesting for CDM, that often also have a more significant contribution to sustainable development. Geographically it does not suffer from the bias towards Asia to the same extent as CDM, as it also covers the poorest regions in the world such as sub-Saharan Africa. One example of a company active in Africa is Imperial Tobacco, which has invested in forest conservation and reforestation schemes. And, since there are no restrictions regarding legitimate emission-reduction technologies, the voluntary offset market can stimulate innovation by allowing experimentation with new, often riskier technologies (Harris, 2007).

However, this lack of standards also makes this market very prone to criticism, and not without reason. It has come to the surface that many offset retailers have entered the market without the intention of making substantial contributions to climate change mitigation (Smith, 2007). For example, the voluntary market has been dominated by forestry projects. This seems due to relatively low transaction costs, the fact that nature conservation groups have been early movers, and the appeal to the public of such initiatives in the sense of 'giving back to nature' (Harris, 2007). However, forestry projects have also been criticised because they can have negative social impacts by displacing people in developing countries, and it is questionable to what extent they actually lead to emissions reductions (they will emit absorbed gases at some stage anyway) (Smith, 2007). What is more, not all offset projects in the voluntary market contribute to sustainable development either, as capture of industrial gases like HFC-23 and N_2O have also taken up a sizeable share of this market (20 per cent in 2006; Hamilton *et al*, 2007). To solve

7 Innovation and capabilities for climate change

The international debate on addressing global climate change and the concomitant reduction of greenhouse gases (GHGs), increasingly points at the role that
business can (and/or should) play. In response companies have taken more
responsibility for their impact on the changing climate. To explain why this
has been the case, Chapter 5 paid attention to the factors that have influenced
corporate activities on climate change, and also outlined strategies available to
companies, which we labelled as compensation and innovation. Chapter 6 subsequently explained compensatory approaches, most notably carbon trading. It
explained companies' activities in this area in the face of a range of emerging
carbon markets, and their peculiarities. However, creating a mature global carbon
market is only the first step to a more fundamental corporate contribution to
GHG emissions reduction. As we mentioned in Chapter 6, even if a carbon
market functions as intended, it would still only be an incentive to take the price
of carbon into account when making investment and other types of corporate
decisions. Only if the incentives and basic rules are correct and companies actually choose abatement (be it internal or in developing countries), will the carbon
market really work. Then there should be a stimulus for underlying innovation
that realises such emissions reductions at the lowest cost.

While companies in carbon-intensive industries receive much attention in the
climate change debate because they are significant emitters, they at the same time
also hold the key to finding (technological) solutions. It is surely the case that
particularly multinational corporations (MNCs) have a huge potential for innovation, which might lead to the development of climate-friendly products and
services (Hall and Vredenburg, 2003). But the question is whether they also take
the effort to invest in climate-friendly technologies, and if so, how far they are
willing to go, especially if this means moving away from technologies they are
familiar with. Even though climate change has been viewed as a market transition
(Hoffman, 2005), the extent to which companies will be co-operative in supporting and enhancing this transition is open to debate. A complete integration of
climate change and a move towards a low-carbon economy ultimately asks for a
competitive reconfiguration (or replacement) of several of the most powerful
industries, namely those that supply fossil fuels and/or have products that demand
massive amounts of fossil fuels (Holdren, 2006).

What is more, compared to compensation, innovation related to climate change is much more novel and in its early stages. Due to the fact that MNCs have been facing a complex international context of continuously changing climate policies, in innovating for climate change MNCs have been rather cautious to take steps in one particular direction. They have clearly doubted the flexibility of climate-induced investments, fearing to make irreversible mistakes (Rugman and Verbeke, 1998). The reason is that innovation depends strongly on long-term investments in research and development (R&D); a process where the outcome is always uncertain. Moreover, climate-friendly technologies will only become a success when companies possess the capabilities of bringing these technologies to the market in the form of products and services and serve (global) mass markets instead of local niche markets only (Gallagher *et al*, 2006; Reinhardt, 1998; Wellington *et al*, 2007). Furthermore, tackling climate change effectively seems to require companies to move away from existing technologies and build new, unrelated capabilities instead. Nevertheless, quite a few early movers, particularly in those sectors most confronted with climate change, have anticipated the ambiguities surrounding climate change by seizing the opportunity to gain a strategic advantage over their rivals (Hoffmann, 2005). It is also an issue from which companies can learn how to anticipate future developments in a context of uncertainty, and exercise leadership that combines societal and strategic concerns.

To understand the potential business contribution in GHG reduction, it is important to shed more light on the way companies build strategic capabilities for climate change mitigation, and particularly to what extent this is or can be linked to their economic 'core' business objectives (Porter and Reinhardt, 2007). We will therefore discuss how corporate climate change activities build on a company's existing capabilities in other areas of its operations and/or may help create new sources of competitive advantage and thus benefit the company's profitability, growth and/or survival. To this end, this chapter explores various aspects of innovation and capabilities for climate change, paying specific attention to MNCs as they are confronted with most complexities. We will first, in section 7.1, give an overview of capabilities that may play a role in the case of climate change, followed by a discussion of some of the key challenges in successfully innovating for climate change. In identifying these challenges, section 7.2 draws attention to the importance of industry peculiarities in determining the degree of innovation that might be possible at all. The impact of climate change capabilities also depends on companies' position in the supply chain and their geographical spread. In explaining these challenges, we will give various examples of industries and companies where innovation and climate change capabilities seem feasible or are emergent.[1]

---

1   For this analysis, we took as our starting point the second and fourth CDP surveys, of which findings were released in September 2004 and September 2006 respectively. The quotes presented in the chapter are from companies' answers to CDP, unless stated otherwise.

7.1 CAPABILITIES UNDERLYING CLIMATE CHANGE STRATEGIES

7.1.1 Valuable capabilities for climate change

Before we analyse capability development induced by global climate change, we first give a conceptualisation of capabilities more broadly. The concept of organisational capabilities has its origin in the field of strategy; an area which has been guided by the question of why some firms are unique and perform better than others, and which factors lead to a sustained competitive advantage (Amit and Schoemaker, 1993; Barney, 1991).[2] The concept itself is based in one of the dominant strategic management theories: the resource-based view. This view posits that competitive advantage is not achieved by choosing certain product market combinations, but by deploying unique resources and capabilities instead. Capabilities have been defined in various ways. One definition conceives a capability as 'a firm's capacity to deploy resources, usually in combination, using organizational processes to effect a desired end' (Amit and Schoemaker, 1993: 35). Another definition states that it is 'a high-level routine (or collection of routines) that, together with its implementing input flows, confers upon an organization's management a set of decision options for producing significant outputs of a particular type' (Winter, 2003: 991). What both definitions basically state is that companies can follow distinctive pathways in creating products and services, but only possess a capability when they do so in a systematic way based on routines that they have developed over time. Capabilities have strategic value because they help companies maintain a first-mover advantage due to the fact that the routine-based nature inhibits instant imitation (Barney, 1991; Nehrt, 1998).

But the question is: how will climate change induce companies to transform existing capabilities or build new capabilities? One way for a proactive approach to climate change to add value is the development of capabilities that are also common in dealing with other social and environmental issues. Proactivity thus relies on anticipating critical incidents such as hurricanes, integrating the interests of the different stakeholders involved with the issue, and building issue-specific knowledge in-house through learning and methods for continuous improvement and innovation (Hart, 1995; Sharma and Vredenburg, 1998). In other words, looking at the activities that companies initiate in response to a sustainability issue gives insight into what extent they develop and/or change capabilities (Aragón-Correa and Sharma, 2003; Eisenhardt and Martin, 2000). Examples of capability development are product differentiation based on

---

2   Within the context of the resource-based view, the term 'sustainable competitive advantage' is used to point at the ability of companies to maintain a competitive advantage over a longer period of time. It is unrelated to sustainability as it is used in the environmental management literature, which instead points at the principle that companies should not be engaged in economic activities that impair long-term well-being of societies and ecosystems. To avoid confusion, we use 'sustained' instead of sustainable when discussing the resource-based perspective.

improving environmental quality for which consumers are willing to pay a premium (Reinhardt, 1998) and in-house development of pollution prevention technologies to lower environmentally induced costs (Christmann, 2000). It must be noted, though, that not all environmental management activities lead to a change in capabilities. For example, many technologies to control pollution, which have been developed in response to environmental regulation, have a negligible effect on competitiveness (Hart, 1995; Russo and Fouts, 1997).

To what extent companies are able to profit from the opportunities from climate change depends on their existing capabilities as well as their flexibility in developing new capabilities. Looking at what companies have already developed internally, it can be said that many have distinctive capabilities for sustainability which may also stimulate the integration of a new issue like climate change. There are several sustainability-specific capabilities that help companies develop a competitive climate change strategy. Since climate change is a rather new issue for most companies, one capability that enhances the development of a climate change strategy is organisational learning (Sharma and Vredenburg, 1998). A company has to learn how the issue affects core business activities, and which strategic adjustments are required to manage these impacts optimally. The availability and type of internal climate expertise is therefore pivotal (Kolk and Levy, 2004).

As many companies still lack sufficient climate expertise, they rely on filling this knowledge gap by accessing climate-specific knowledge outside the boundaries of the company and learn from external partners such as governments, research institutes, non-governmental organisations (NGOs), and consulting firms. There are many examples of MNCs which have ties with universities and research institutes: Suncor funds a Clean Energy Laboratory of the University of British Colombia; ExxonMobil invests in the Global Climate and Energy Project of Stanford University; and Chevron is co-funding the Massachusetts Institute of Technology Joint Program on the Science and Policy for Global Climate Change. Furthermore, Rio Tinto participates in research efforts of the US-based Electric Power Research Institute; while BP, together with Ford, has a partnership with Princeton University, called the Carbon Mitigation Initiative. This initiative has the aim of 'resolving the fundamental scientific, environmental, and technological issues that are likely to influence public acceptance of any proposed solution'; technology for carbon capture and storage is one direction set out.

The embeddedness of a company in broader society influences the extent to which it has access to local knowledge networks. Hence, MNCs with their head-office in a location with much local climate expertise may have a strategic edge over foreign companies that only have subsidiaries in this location, because they are generally more strongly embedded in their home country setting (Levy and Kolk, 2002). Nevertheless, the examples of Rio Tinto and BP show that MNCs can successfully look across borders as well and affiliate with research institutes in host countries. In relation to this, stakeholder integration has also been mentioned as well as a valuable sustainability-specific capability. There are many different types of stakeholders involved in climate change, including regulators, NGOs, investors, suppliers, and consumers. Integrating all these stakeholder perspectives (e.g. with cross-functional management) in the design of processes, products and services is a valuable capability because it is a rather socially complex process (Hart, 1995; Sharma and Vredenburg, 1998). Requests from these stakeholder groups are generally quite different and often even contradictory as well (Jawahar and McLaughlin, 2001).

A demonstrated capability to use methods for continuous improvement and innovation (e.g. total quality management) also enhances climate strategy development, as it helps preventing emissions in the longer run (Hart, 1995; Sharma and Vredenburg, 1998). While initial emissions reductions may be attained rather easily, it becomes increasingly more difficult to achieve additional reductions, as this requires more significant changes in processes and products. Only when companies are able to continuously prevent emissions, which depends on the involvement of a large number of people and the development of tacit skills, can it create a competitive advantage (Hart, 1995). An example of a company facing this problem is Nippon Steel. This company had already substantially improved its energy efficiency some decades ago, because it set a goal of 20 per cent energy savings by 1990 in reaction to the oil shocks of the 1970s. In response to the upsurge of climate change as a policy issue in the 1990s, however, this early target was followed by a 10 per cent reduction of energy consumption to be reached by 2010. However, achieving this new target by internal measures has turned out to be very difficult, which explains why this company has become interested in Clean Development Mechanism (CDM) projects to realise reductions outside the company.

It must be noted, however, that sustainability-specific capabilities are not necessarily the main driver behind a competitive strategy for climate change. A company's climate change strategy is not formulated in isolation but is related to functional strategies, for example product design, R&D, and marketing (Judge and Douglas, 1998). As a consequence, a climate change strategy could just as well build on existing resources and capabilities that bear no relation to sustainability but are complementary nevertheless (Christmann, 2000; Teece, 1986). Actually, it is precisely because climate change affects core business activities more often than other sustainability issues that a strategic response to climate change will build on core capabilities. In other words, it may, for instance, not just be capabilities for continuous improvement and innovation to reduce emissions, but also to improve efficiency of the production process on other dimensions that leads to a competitive climate strategy. More generally, innovation is an important underlying driver, because 'environmental improvements to some extent flow from broader corporate efforts to innovate and implement new and more efficient manufacturing systems and practices' (Florida, 1996: 81). For example, in the automobile industry continuous innovation in improving the performance of car engines tends to lead to fewer emissions as a (usually unintended) by-product as well. Overall this reduction is, however, frequently outbalanced by using more powerful engines for larger cars.

A company's capabilities to control the supply chain will also affect its climate change strategy. A company that has outsourced many non-core activities depends for many of its critical resources on outsiders and will most likely take a proactive approach to supply-chain management to maintain control (Handfield *et al*, 2005). In other words, a company's level of vertical integration determines to what extent it is vulnerable to supplier-related climate risks (Lash and Wellington, 2007). A highly integrated company still has many of its emissions-generating activities, such as resource extraction, electricity generation, and transportation and distribution, within the boundaries of the organisation and is directly responsible for the emissions related to these activities. By contrast, less vertically integrated companies will put more effort into controlling the supply chain to secure the quality of raw material inputs, which will also act as a driver for drawing attention to climate change (Handfield *et al*, 2005). To reduce supply chain risk, companies have started to monitor suppliers' GHG emissions, by integrating emissions into procurement policies and evaluating supplier bids partly based on climatic impacts. Higher energy prices help in this respect to increase attention for energy efficiency and innovative ways to improve this.

7.1.2 Strategic positioning in the dynamic global climate change arena

The above-mentioned capabilities, which apply to sustainability in a more general sense as well, will be valuable for corporate climate strategies. But what sets climate change apart, especially in the case of MNCs, is that its impact is more multi-faceted (Kolk and Levy, 2004). Firstly, it is not a 'purely' environmental issue because it is closely linked to concerns about energy security due to dependence on fossil fuels and oil in particular, and to energy efficiency and management more generally (Gallagher *et al*, 2006; Holdren, 2006; Wellington *et al*, 2007). Secondly, over the years, the strategic impact of climate change has been surrounded with great uncertainty (Brewer, 2005b) (e.g. uncertainty about type, magnitude and timing of the physical impact; about the best technological options to address the issue; as well as about the materialisation of public policies). In response to such uncertainties in the climate change arena, companies are likely to postpone decisions until new options are economically superior as well. Thirdly, the role that climate change plays in MNC strategy is not merely a matter of dealing with local regulation, but usually part of a broader conglomerate of factors involving not only governmental but also societal and market forces, and at different levels, national, regional and/or international. Due to this whole variety of geographically dispersed forces that influence the development of climate change, meeting all stakeholder demands essentially forms a moving target for MNCs. What is expected from MNCs constantly changes because public opinion, regulation, competition and scientific evidence on climate change follow a rather fitful course.

This means that a one-time decision to commit resources and develop related capabilities does not suffice. Instead, companies have to constantly adjust their capabilities for deploying these resources or create new capabilities to stay in line with changes in the climate change arena. In other words, because they face a moving target, *dynamic* capabilities are required. Such dynamic capabilities refer to the competence of companies to renew the configuration of their capabilities to maintain a fit with a changing business context (Teece *et al*, 1997) and can be thought of as value-creating processes such as product development, strategic decision-making and forging alliances (Eisenhardt and Martin, 2000). In other words, to stay responsive to local idiosyncrasies vis-à-vis climate change companies need to keep modifying and transferring capabilities as well as requiring higher-order learning to keep abreast of future developments that can affect key capabilities (Winter, 2003; Zollo and Winter, 2002). Taking a dynamic capabilities perspective can thus help to uncover whether and how climate change incites companies to build climate-specific capabilities or reconfigure their key capabilities that are viewed as the main sources of profitability, growth and survival. It also provides insight into the strategic changes that MNCs implement to tackle climate change and how these differ between geographic locations where an MNC is active.

7.1.3 The industry-specificity of climate change innovation

For most sustainability issues the impact and type of capability development depends on the industry in which a company is active. Legislation to stop ozone depletion, for example, had a strategic impact on the chemical industry but largely no effect on other industries, because the chemical industry was the main source of the harmful emissions (Levy, 1997). Climate change, on the other hand, is likely to have a strategic impact on growth, survival and performance of companies across a much wider range of industries and is more likely to affect core business activities broadly (Hall and Vredenburg, 2003). Nevertheless, companies from different industries are likely to develop different kinds of capabilities. Moreover, the types of organisational processes that are set in motion involve the development of climate-specific capabilities for some companies and the change of key capabilities for others.

One factor that determines how the impact of climate change differs across industries is the technological change that its emergence brings about (Hall and Vredenburg, 2003) as well as the reaction of companies to this change (Helfat and Peteraf, 2003). Climate change may lead to technological change for some industries but not for others, and when it has an effect on technology, it may either enhance or destroy existing capabilities of incumbent firms (Abernathy and Clark, 1985; Tushman and Anderson, 1986). A competence-enhancing discontinuity creates a major change in a company's technology which nevertheless still builds on existing capabilities; while a competence-destroying discontinuity necessitates companies developing completely new capabilities as existing ones have become obsolete (Tushman and Anderson, 1986). It thus depends on a company's existing capabilities whether a technological change is competence-enhancing or destroying (Gatignon *et al*, 2002). Still companies have a choice how to react to technological change (Helfat and Peteraf, 2003); they can, for example, decide to build on existing capabilities, fundamentally change capabilities within the company or acquire new capabilities from outside the company (Gatignon *et al*, 2002; Lavie, 2006).

Climate change as a source of competitive advantage is most likely to occur in high-salience industries such as the oil and gas and automotive industries, that is, those most confronted with the climate issue. Since climate change has the potential to be competence-destroying, it solicits an innovative response to stay competitive in the longer run. In addition, continuous reflection on capability development via internal investments (dynamic capabilities) also seems important for companies specialised in goods or services that are instrumental to mitigating climate change impacts, and more generally to anticipate, influence or respond to public policy and societal developments. This is also relevant for diversified industrial companies such as General Electric and Siemens, which supply energy-related technologies and can thus profit from a competence-enhancing technological change (Gallagher *et al*, 2006).

For the remaining companies, climate change appears not to become a main source of profitability and growth as it neither enhances nor destroys their capabilities. Nevertheless, they may obtain legitimacy from acting visibly and credibly in the field of climate change. For them, there is no compelling reason to develop capabilities internally in managing climate change. Their route for addressing the issue is likely to go through external markets, for example, purchasing greener and productivity-enhancing technologies, adopting externally-developed tools and routines (such as on mitigation, emissions trading, measurement instruments) and 'outsourcing' certain activities to outsiders (who can, for example, take care of lobbying and stakeholder management). In this situation, capabilities may arise from 'internalisation arbitrage', particularly for MNCs (Rugman and Verbeke, 2004; Ghemawat, 2003), when advantage can be obtained from proximity and easy access to multiple external markets that offer such best available practices.

7.2 KEY CHALLENGES FOR CLIMATE CHANGE INNOVATION

Innovating for climate change is a complex decision process because, as mentioned above, this global issue is rather multi-faceted in nature. There are many other factors besides climate change, for example economic development and energy security, which also affect companies' investments in cleaner energy technologies – these are seen as key to addressing climate change. Before we move to the challenges faced by companies, and MNCs in particular, first some insight will be given in the global market for clean energy, which has grown immensely over the past few years. As Figure 7.1 indicates this growth is particularly due to the expansion of wind power (from US$4 billion in 2000 to US$30.1 billion in 2007) and solar photovoltaic (PV) (from US$2.5 billion in 2000 to US$20.3 billion in 2007). Compared to their expansion, the importance of fuel cells has increased

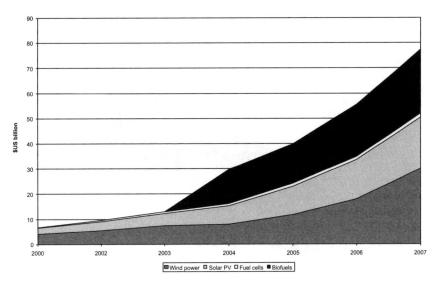

Figure 7.1 The growth of clean energy technologies in the period 2000–2007.

Source: Based on data from Clean Edge

much less (from US$0.2 billion in 2000 to US$1.5 billion in 2007). Biofuels have also seen substantial growth (from US$13.7 billion in 2004 to US$25.4 billion in 2007), but were surpassed in 2007 by wind power as the main form of clean energy (excluding hydro power which is controversial because it often requires a relocation of local communities and has limited capacity for further growth due to site specificity).[3]

Notwithstanding the high growth rates, the total contribution of renewables to global energy supply is still modest. While biomass and hydro power were covering 10 per cent and 2 per cent respectively in 2005, other renewables, including wind and solar power, only accounted for 1 per cent of global energy supply (see Figure 7.2). Companies are facing several challenges (and barriers) that have to be overcome in order to further raise the stake of renewables and to create a significant corporate contribution to a market transition in the direction of a low-carbon economy. If these are not overcome soon, there is a great risk that the transition will either not take place at all or at least not fast enough to keep pace with the adverse physical impacts of a changing climate (Hoffert *et al*, 1998). In the remainder of this chapter, we will discuss five key challenges for climate change innovation, paying specific attention to high-salience industries (automobiles, oil and gas, and electric utilities).

---

3   It must be noted that Clean Edge, which published data on the global market for clean energy annually, only started to report on the size of the global biofuels market from 2004 onwards.

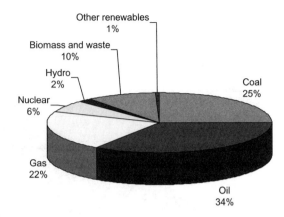

Figure 7.2 Share of clean energy technologies in 2005.
Source: Based on data from the IEA World Energy Outlook 2007

7.2.1 Challenge 1: In search of a silver bullet or scaling up existing technologies

One of the major challenges for climate change innovation is that a real reduction of GHG emissions requires a lower dependence on fossil fuels. Even though energy-efficiency improvements could play an important role in stabilising CO_2 emissions on a global level, it will not be enough to completely ward off the possibility that dangerous CO_2 concentration levels might be reached. To move into safer waters a much greater deployment of low-carbon or carbon-free alternatives is deemed necessary (Hoffert *et al*, 1998). However, for high-impact sectors, such as power generation and transportation, it is not at all clear what should replace the prevailing fossil fuel based technologies. In other words, there is no technological 'silver bullet' solution at the moment. Although non-fossil fuel-based alternatives might lead to a lower climatic impact, it is typically the case that they have other limitations, liabilities and uncertainties (Holdren, 2006) that particularly come to the surface when their deployment is scaled up (Grubb, 2004).

Climate change experts have different views on the most desirable technological trajectories to reach a solution for climate change (cf. Dosi, 1982; Grubb, 2004; Hoffert, 2006). On the one hand, it has been argued that a major investment in (government-led) R&D programmes and international co-operation are necessary because all possible alternatives to the current fossil fuel-based energy infrastructure require large investments in fundamental and applied research (Hoffert *et al*, 1998, 2002). The main idea is that whatever technological trajectory is chosen for power generation (be it continued use of coal or natural gas combined with carbon capture and storage, nuclear, or renewables), this will in all cases call for a radical departure from the existing energy infrastructure and much further research, if these options are to help in significantly reducing carbon emissions. On the other hand, it is stated that there has been too much focus on developing new fundamental scientific, technical and industrial expertise in search of radical solutions, while a significant reduction could also be achieved by scaling up technologies based on existing know-how (Pacala and Socolow, 2004). This approach, which has become known as the 'stabilisation wedges', argues that there will not be one single carbon-free technology that is sufficient to solve the climate change problem on its own; instead it is a portfolio of less ambitious options that will do the job jointly. These options (or wedges) include energy efficiency and conservation measures (e.g. more efficient and reduced use of vehicles, efficient buildings, efficient coal-based power plants); fuel switching (e.g. from coal to natural gas); carbon capture and storage; nuclear power; renewable electricity and fuels (e.g. wind and solar power, and the use of hydrogen and biomass as transportation fuels); and forest and agricultural management (Pacala and Socolow, 2004). Boxes 7.1, 7.2 and 7.3 apply the concept of stabilisation wedges to three of the most carbon-intensive industries: automotives, power generation, and the oil and gas industry.

Box 7.1 Stabilisation wedges in the car industry

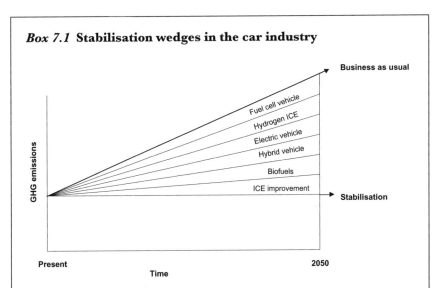

Source: Based on the stabilisation wedges developed by Pacala and Socolow (2004); figure for indicative purposes only

The car industry has several options to reduce CO_2 emissions of the vehicles that it produces. These options range from relatively small adjustments that lead to climate change benefits in the short run to radical innovations that will only have a substantial emissions reduction in the longer run. The low-hanging-fruit can be found in improving fuel efficiency of vehicles that use the currently still dominant internal combustion engine (ICE). One way to do this is by reducing vehicle weight and implementing small innovations like start-and-stop mechanisms to switch off the engine when the car is at standstill. Many car companies are already adopting these kinds of fuel-saving technologies; Volkswagen for example has the BlueMotion line that uses a variety of innovations to save fuel consumption. The more radical options either aim at using different types of fuels, e.g. biofuels, without requiring sweeping changes to the engine, complementing conventional engines with rechargeable energy storage systems to create a hybrid using gasoline and electricity, or completely replacing the engine using a battery only. The most radical option is the fuel cell vehicle which not only uses hydrogen as a fuel, but also creates power with a fuel cell instead of a combustion engine.

Box 7.2 Stabilisation wedges in power generation

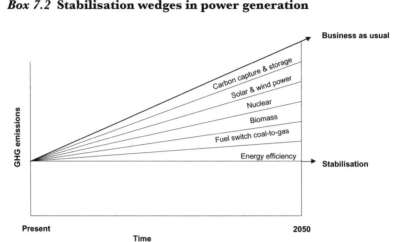

Source: Based on the stabilisation wedges developed by Pacala and Socolow (2004); figure for indicative purposes only

In the short run the easiest way for electric utilities to reduce CO_2 emissions is to improve energy efficiency of conventional coal- or gas-fired power plants. One example is to implement coal gasification technology. Another relatively simple measure is to switch from the use of coal to natural gas in generating electricity. However, to what extent power companies actually choose this option depends much on the relative price difference between the commodity prices of coal and gas. Using biomass alongside a fossil fuel is also a reduction measure that is used on quite a large scale in many countries. More controversial is to expand nuclear generation capacity. This is often not at the discretion of power companies themselves, as it involves a lot of painstaking politics to push for more nuclear energy. For example, German utility RWE often brings up the fact that the German Government does not want to use more nuclear as serious constraint for achieving emissions reduction targets. More sustainable will be to scale up the use of renewable energy sources such as solar and wind power. Finally, if companies (together with governments) would make the necessary investments in a CO_2 pipeline infrastructure, the option of carbon capture and storage might become viable within the next decade as well.

What is remarkable is that both approaches basically call for further development and deployment of the same collection of technologies for energy supply and transportation. However, they diverge in that one puts more emphasis on development and the other on deployment. This difference is important because it has implications for the technological trajectories that companies follow. Translated to the corporate level, this debate on climate change technology comes down to a trade-off for companies between further exploring new technological possibilities and more fully exploiting existing ones (cf. March, 1991). In other words, companies are facing a dilemma whether to search for solutions that still require huge amounts of research and development or choose to scale up existing technologies that have proven themselves (at least in a demonstration phase) (Wellington *et al*, 2007). Such a shift in focus on development or deployment

Box 7.3 **Stabilisation wedges in the oil and gas industry**

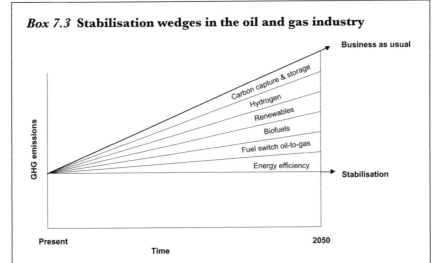

Source: Based on the stabilisation wedges developed by Pacala and Socolow (2004); figure for indicative purposes only

On the face of it, the oil and gas industry has similar options as utilities. The main difference is however that this industry has much higher R&D budgets, which might lead to the expectation that the solutions that it will pursue are more innovative (Grubb, 2004). Nevertheless, many of the short-term measures also include improving energy efficiency, in addition to reducing gas venting and flaring. ExxonMobil is for example using cogeneration plants on a significant scale to cut back on energy costs (Sæverud and Skjærseth, 2007). Many oil companies are also expanding their natural gas segment, partly to diversify away from oil out of fear of oil shortage in the coming decades. What is a bit further away from core business activities is the production of biofuels. In many countries oil companies are already required to mix biofuels with gasoline, but this often just means that they purchase biofuels instead of producing them. Investing in renewables is also used as a way to diversify energy supply and reduce emissions simultaneously, but this still only occurs on a rather small scale. Besides developing various alternative energy sources, the oil industry has also started to invest in hydrogen, an energy carrier instead of source. Finally, oil companies are also investing in carbon capture and storage, and chances for successfully developing this technology for large-scale use is much larger compared with utilities, because oil companies can draw on many of their existing capabilities in CO_2 capture and gas distribution (Stephens, 2006).

means that companies would not only differ in their technological trajectory process-wise, but also in which technological options they will invest. To illustrate, if companies would further invest in renewables they still have a variety of techno-logical options, which have been categorised in three groups (Neuhoff, 2005). Firstly there are the mature technologies – e.g. hydropower, biomass combustion, solar boilers and geothermal technologies – which in specific, beneficial circumstances are already cost-competitive with conventional sources. Secondly, wind and solar PV are seen as emerging technologies, because they are proven as technologies, but not yet cost-competitive due to a lack of market experience. And thirdly, there are renewable technologies that are still in the R&D phase – e.g.

specific forms of solar power, ocean energy and advanced bio-energy – which completely lack market penetration, and largely depend on public R&D programmes for further development (Neuhoff, 2005). It would, for example, depend on the level of risk-taking and need for quick returns whether a company chooses to invest in the relatively mature technologies or in the less well-developed technologies.

The automotive industry clearly illustrates this struggle of choosing between development and deployment. Major players in the car industry for a long time agreed on the idea that hydrogen-powered fuel cells will replace the internal combustion engine in coming decades (Van den Hoed and Vergragt, 2004). The fuel cell vehicle is climate-friendly because it removes direct carbon emissions from cars, using hydrogen as a fuel instead of gasoline or diesel. While the technology was already developed by a company named Ballard in the 1980s, fuel cell technology only took off when Daimler (after teaming up with Ballard) launched two fuel-cell demonstration vehicles in 1994 and 1996, respectively. This led to a concomitant increase in patents on fuel cell technology registered by other car companies. However, the fuel cell vehicle is quite a radical departure from the internal combustion engine. What is more, notwithstanding cost reductions over the past years, the costs of bringing it to the market are still exceptionally high (Hekkert and Van den Hoed, 2004). In other words, for the fuel cell vehicle to become a successful product, it will first need further development.

By contrast, even though the fuel cell vehicle has grabbed the attention in the past decade, a much less radical alternative, the hybrid vehicle, has become far more successful of late. Technologically speaking the hybrid is not as demanding or radical as the fuel cell vehicle. The most popular hybrid is the Toyota Prius, which was introduced into the market in 1997. Toyota's leadership in hybrids is an exemplary case of a company that has been focusing on technology deployment. It was the first to develop the hybrid technology, but the technology particularly became a success because it made good managerial decisions (Helfat and Peteraf, 2003), such as licensing the technology which led others (e.g. Nissan and Ford) to also offer hybrid cars, thereby creating market acceptance (Spencer, 2003). Toyota successfully betted on future contingencies, that is, this company anticipated increasing consumer awareness for fuel prices and the environment, which has spurred the demand for fuel-efficient vehicles. Particularly in the US, it has been easier for the Japanese car companies to position themselves as suppliers of fuel-efficient, clean cars, because traditionally they have had stronger credentials in the small-car segment.

7.2.2 Challenge 2: A competence-enhancing or destroying response to climate change

Whether companies stress development or deployment also depends on the technological change induced by climate change. It is not surprising that companies generally see more opportunities in a competence-enhancing change because this further strengthens their competitive position. If the technological change threatens to destroy existing capabilities of incumbent companies, there will probably be much more resistance. In other words, it is the perception of climate-induced technological change that will have an impact on the process by which companies adapt their capabilities. To analyse how radically companies will change their key capabilities in response to climate change, three capability reconfiguration mechanisms have been discerned: capability evolution, capability transformation, and capability substitution (Lavie, 2006).

Capability evolution is an incremental learning process, which relies on a company's dynamic capabilities to accommodate technological change in a competence-enhancing way. Basically, capability evolution does not replace routines but only modifies and adjusts them by using internal sources of knowledge. As a consequence, path dependencies determine how existing capabilities evolve over time. Through experimentation capabilities change over time, but the way in which they alter depends on a company's particular history and rigidity of existing capability configurations (Lavie, 2006). For incumbents capability evolution may well be the preferred mode of change because it builds on existing capabilities accumulated over time (Dierickx and Cool, 1989). However, companies following this route typically have a rather short-term view on climate change innovation, that is they are looking for new opportunities for their existing products and services.

In particular, sectors such as electric utilities, chemicals, electronics, and metals and manufacturing develop innovations that focus on developing climate-specific capabilities for the near future. Consequently, companies mainly rely on their existing capability configurations. They change some routines, and their capability base slowly evolves in a climate-friendly direction. Electric utilities, for example, draw on their key capabilities in generation, trade and sales of electricity to develop climate-specific capabilities. Most utilities are not involved in the development of renewable energy sources themselves, but instead purchase these from technology suppliers such as General Electric (Grubb, 2004; Marcus and Geffen, 1998). However, quite a few, including American Electric Power, CLP Holdings, Endesa, Exelon, Iberdrola, and Scottish & Southern Energy, are expanding generation capacity that is based on renewable energy sources (e.g. in response to the renewable portfolio standards in the US, or the EU requirements to source 20 per cent from renewables by 2020). Such a reconfiguration of energy sources for electricity production can be competence-enhancing, because utilities use their existing capabilities to market energy to end-users and further exploit their electricity infrastructure (Neuhoff, 2005). Iberdrola, for instance, notes that it has a programme for 'the promotion of electricity produced from renewable energy sources in the internal electricity market, making electricity users aware of the benefits of renewable energies'. Another example of an MNC shifting attention to the climate-friendly attributes of its technology development is General Electric, which launched its Ecomagination campaign. General Electric was already engaged in the development of wind turbines and clean coal technology, but decided to group clean technologies together under one brand and increase investment in these technologies (Harvey, 2005). Depending on the success of marketing its green segment, a conglomerate like General Electric may eventually further expand this strategy. In other words, even though these companies do not change their key capabilities, they respond to climate change by using their existing capabilities to successfully market the low-carbon attributes of their products.

The other two mechanisms have a longer-term orientation, as they take more note of future contingencies (Lavie, 2006). In the case of *capability transformation*, existing capabilities are not completely discarded either, but some of the routines that are part of the capability are modified or newly acquired as a company opens up to external sources of knowledge. In a transformation process the reconfiguration takes place on the level of the capability. Still the capability keeps its function, but does so in a different way because of the change in underlying routines. A capability that is formed through transformation thus consists of past as well as new knowledge and skills (Lavie, 2006) and is at the same time competence-enhancing and competence-destroying (Gatignon *et al*, 2002). Capability transformation is more forward-looking and involves higher-order learning, as not only some of the routines that form the capability change but also the dynamic capabilities that shape the capability (Zollo and Winter, 2002). For example, higher-order learning takes place when companies improve their understanding of climate change, which in turn leads to new R&D activities that make production processes less polluting (Sharma and Vredenburg, 1998). Capability transformation holds quite some promise for the role played by companies in dealing with climate change, because it leaves the function of key capabilities intact while simultaneously enabling them to find ways to help tackle climate change. To illustrate, the launch of the fuel cell vehicle would mean that car producers go through a process of capability transformation. It is a case of transformation because the capability portfolio as a whole keeps its function (producing cars); only the underlying routines will change as a result of the fuel cell technology.

Capability transformation seems to be a more realistic option for companies than *capability substitution*, the third reconfiguration mechanism. Substitution assumes competence-destroying technological change which causes a company's whole portfolio of existing capabilities to become obsolete. This means that the configuration of existing capabilities does not alter, but their value disappears (Lavie, 2006). For substitution to take place a company must acquire a completely new portfolio of capabilities that take the place of the existing one, as no changes are made to the capabilities that lost their value. This basically means that companies have to acquire all new capabilities from outside the company (Lavie, 2006), as it will be difficult, if not impossible, to bring about competence-destroying change from within (Gatignon *et al*, 2002). A major challenge for companies in deciding what course of action to follow is to assess *a priori* what kind of technological discontinuity climate change will trigger, as its actual impact will only be known in retrospect (Tushman and Anderson, 1986).

The major challenge and difficulty of capability substitution is illustrated by developments in the oil and gas industry. Even though oil companies eventually will have to go for a competence-destroying substitution of their portfolio of key capabilities, in what direction this substitution will take place and which technologies will prevail in the coming decades is still unclear. While for the longer term companies such as BP, Chevron, ENI, Royal Dutch/Shell, Suncor, and Total invest in renewable energy sources, others including BHP Billiton, ENI, and Shell also emphasise the development of hydrogen, which is an energy carrier not an energy source. All these developments require a sharper reconfiguration of the existing capability portfolio compared with most industries, such as the car industry. Not only will the underlying technology of the main product – energy – change, but also other processes such as distribution and sales.

However, a renewable energy source such as solar energy hardly builds on existing capabilities in R&D and production. Technologically speaking, producing solar panels is much closer to the semiconductor industry, which has experience with processing silicon, the main raw material for solar panels (Pernick and Wilder, 2007). For example, Applied Materials, the world's largest semi-conductor equipment manufacturer, has made a transition recently towards a more prominent position in solar (Nuttall, 2008). Similarly, although oil companies are investing in wind power, it is a capital good producer such as General Electric that has a capability in producing wind turbines. Moreover, both renewable energy technologies may lead to a system of decentralised energy distribution, and thus threaten centralised energy distribution, currently a key capability of the oil industry. It is thus not surprising that the majority of the oil companies only invest marginally in these renewable technologies. Only BP and Shell have been relatively active through some investments in renewable energy, particularly solar power. Nevertheless, in spite of BP's recent attempt to give this business segment an extra impetus by launching their BP Alternative Energy campaign, its value is still only about 3 per cent of total market capitalisation (Crooks, 2008a).

7.2.3 Challenge 3: Climate-friendly technologies as transition or as final solution

A third challenge with regard to climate change innovation is the transitory nature of technologies. It is clear that in many industries uncertainty about what will become the new dominant technology leads companies to follow different technological trajectories (Anderson and Tushman, 1990; Dosi, 1982). Even though climate change (together with other factors such as energy security) will induce a market transition towards a low-carbon economy in due course, as we argued above, the pace at which it will happen depends on whether companies follow an evolutionary trajectory based on incremental innovations or bet on substitution through radical innovations (Gatignon *et al*, 2002; Lavie, 2006). Moreover, the technological trajectory chosen also determines what will be achieved in terms of emissions reductions. In the long run, the ideal scenario would be an energy and transportation infrastructure that is completely independent of carbon-intensive fossil fuels. However, as the above-mentioned examples illustrate, what companies generally do when confronted with technological change is that they do not fully discard their existing key capabilities, but build on them instead (Unruh, 2000). There is thus a certain level of inertia in the way in which companies adjust their capabilities in response to technological change (Gilbert, 2005; Leonard-Barton, 1992). As a consequence, a climate-induced market shift takes place through transition technologies first (Hekkert and Van den Hoed, 2004). What this often means is that companies deploy technologies that are less carbon-intensive but are not completely carbon-free. One of the main questions is, then, whether technologies that seem to be of a transitory nature at first will not become dominant technologies themselves, thus standing in the way of further development of more radical end solutions.

The most successful innovations in the car industry in terms of market penetration have often been considered as examples of investments in competence-enhancing transition technologies, as the fuel-cell vehicle was long predestined as the ultimate solution (Hekkert and Van de Hoed, 2004). There are several reasons for car companies to first invest in transition technologies: it satisfies short-term demand for fuel-efficient and climate-friendly cars, it helps in establishing a green brand image (Anderson and Gardiner, 2006), and it creates the experience necessary to build the fuel cell vehicle. For example, Ford and BMW have been developing the hydrogen-powered internal combustion engine, which Ford views as 'a "bridging strategy" using existing, proven technologies to deliver the environmental benefits of fuel cells at a fraction of the complexity and cost'. More accepted, however, is hybrid technology, which is illustrated by the following statement from DaimlerChrysler in 2004:

> For the future we view the fuel cell as the technology, which has in the long term the most significant potential of reducing the CO_2-emissions of our products. . . . Today we focus on three steps to reduce CO_2-emissions: the continuous improvement of conventional combustion engines, the hybrid technology as the bridge between the conventional powertrain and the fuel cell as the most efficient technology for reducing CO_2.

Practically all major car companies, including Toyota, Honda, Nissan, Ford, and General Motors, currently offer hybrid cars or plan to do so within the next few years. However, while Toyota and Honda have gained experience by developing the technology in-house for almost a decade, others, including Ford and Nissan, have only quite recently licensed the technology from Toyota (Mackintosh, 2004). Hence, Ford and Nissan are not likely to create a valuable capability in developing hybrid cars because they missed out on the learning curve from developing their own know-how, but merely anticipated a short-term increase in demand for fuel-efficient vehicles due to higher fuel prices. This is illustrated by the fact that Nissan has recently ended the licence agreement and decided to build its own hybrids instead, as the market for hybrids has surged beyond expectation. It now seems that hybrids will stay for a much longer period and might not be a transition after all, but instead an important competitor for the fuel cell vehicle in the long run. This might have serious consequences for the further development of the fuel cell vehicle, because the fuel cell's main advantage compared with the internal combustion engine – that it performs much better in terms of emissions – almost completely fades away compared with hybrids and may not weigh up to the much higher costs of bringing the fuel cell vehicle to the market (Hekkert and Van den Hoed, 2004). What is more, recent success of the hybrid has led to a renewed interest in the electric car as well, even though this technology failed miserably in the 1990s. The reason is that developments in hybrid technology have run parallel with progress in battery technology (e.g. longer lifetime), thus making the electric car more practical as it can cover longer distances. Interestingly, companies that plan to launch electric cars not only include incumbents such as General Motors, Chrysler, Toyota, and Honda (the last two with plug-in hybrids), but also new entrants like California-based Tesla Motors and Fisker Automotive (Makower *et al*, 2008).

Oil and gas companies also invest in competence-enhancing transition technologies. A statement by Shell illustrates the role of transition technologies in the oil industry:

> Given that natural gas has the lowest carbon emissions per unit of energy produced (e.g. electricity) of all the fossil fuels, it offers the world an important bridge to a lower carbon economy as alternative energy technologies are developed and allowed to reach economic maturity.

In the choice for transition technologies many oil and gas companies take their initial capability configurations as a starting point for the development of climate-induced capabilities, thus showing the importance of path dependencies (cf. Helfat, 1997). MNCs that already have a strong position in the production of natural gas, such as BG Group, BP, ENI, ExxonMobil, Halliburton, Norsk Hydro, and Shell, see the changing context due to the emergence of climate change as an opportunity to strengthen this segment of their companies. For example, ExxonMobil considers itself as 'a leading supplier of clean burning natural gas . . . well positioned to contribute to efforts to address greenhouse gas emissions through fuel switching.'

For companies that rely more heavily on the production of coal, climate change is a driver to develop other transition technologies. BHP Billiton and Rio Tinto, which have strong positions in the production of coal, both invest in clean coal technology and technologies to offset emissions by carbon capture and storage (CCS) in underground reservoirs. Oil companies such as Statoil and BP have also started to invest in CCS, although so far mainly in small-scale (experimental) projects; they usually do this co-operatively to spread the risk, thus creating a shared capability. What is appealing about CCS is that it allows carbon-intensive companies to become proactive on climate change, while at the same time continue with their core business activities, even with carbon constraints. Moreover, in terms of technology, oil companies in particular can use much of their existing know-how, as capture technology has already been developed for other purposes in oil refining and gas processing, and they know how to transport CO_2 through pipelines and inject it into underground reservoirs, as this has been used in the US for many years to help with oil production from declining wells (Stephens, 2006). The main problem is, however, that large-scale adoption of CCS would mean that a completely new CO_2 pipeline infrastructure has to be implemented, which will not be cost-effective if the price of carbon is not high enough. This adds to the more generic issue of scaling up, which, even if technologically feasible at some stage, is not commercially viable as of yet, and would require massive subsidies. This brings us to the difficulties of systemic solutions that involve the co-operation of many different private and public partners.

7.2.4 Challenge 4: Positive and negative consequences of systemic climate solutions

One reason why climate change is complex for companies is that in bringing down their own emissions they often need co-operation from others to some extent (Unruh, 2000). In other words, many climate change innovations aim for a more systemic solution, which one company cannot deliver single-handedly. This yields the question of how far companies are willing to go in taking responsibility for climate change, when they need responses from others to achieve a positive outcome. If a company relies on other actors in the value chain, success of climate change innovation depends very much on bargaining power, which has at least three dimensions that need to be considered.

Firstly, when a company has a very strong position in the value chain, this can lead to positive spillover effects to suppliers. Some companies have developed proactive sourcing policies, thus putting pressure on their suppliers. For example, British Telecom and Du Pont have decided to source a significant part of their energy consumption from renewable sources. This creates positive effects because it stimulates their electricity suppliers to put more effort into delivering low-carbon technologies at a cost-competitive price. To illustrate, Du Pont argues that it can have such an impact and motivates its decision as follows:

> We will source 10 per cent of our global energy use in the year 2010 from renewable resources. We are serious about the need for renewable energy to be a part of our future. We are providing a strong 'market signal' that there will be at least one major energy consumer ready to buy; and that we will work with suppliers of renewable energy resources to stimulate their availability at a cost competitive with best available fossil-derived alternatives.

Another example of a company using its bargaining power in a 'positive' way, and one of the more surprising ones given its negative social responsibility credentials, is Wal-Mart. The world largest retailer set several goals to cut back energy use in its stores by 30 per cent and reduce GHG emissions by 30 per cent as well. Wal-Mart's clean energy campaign has not only forced electricity suppliers to deliver more electricity from renewable sources, but has also created opportunities for other suppliers. Wal-Mart has expanded the market for clean trucks, because the company wants to use more hybrid-electric diesel vehicles, and created a bigger market for solar panel producers, as it wants to install solar PV on its stores (Makower *et al*, 2007).

Secondly, notwithstanding the fact that a company has considerable bargaining power, some technological solutions are simply too all-encompassing. As we already saw in Chapter 3, many companies chose to co-operate with other companies to develop new technologies. Many car and oil manufacturers work together with companies that own a specific technology. This usually includes small local niche players and large global competitors. For example, to develop biofuels both DaimlerChrysler and Volkswagen co-operated with Choren industries; a German firm specialised in gasification technology for the production of energy from biomass. Likewise, Ford and DaimlerChrysler both partnered with Canadian niche player Ballard, which developed the fuel cell technology to further improve the fuel cell for use in cars. Two Canadian oil firms, Suncor and Petro-Canada, work with several local firms to develop an infrastructure for fuel cell vehicles and wind energy, respectively. Because the MNCs engaged in these partnerships are not only collaborators on these particular technologies, but also close competitors, it will be difficult to develop a company-specific capability as it is inevitable that at least one competitor owns the same technology. There are more opportunities to create a capability out of collaboration with companies from other industries, because both partners can then use the ensuing technology quite differently in their activities. Dow Chemical and General Motors, for example, work together on the development of fuel cells, each for a different purpose.

Nevertheless, inter-industry co-operation is definitely not always successful. One of the reasons why it is taking the car industry so long to commercialise the fuel cell vehicle is that, on top of the fact that it is difficult and costly to develop this vehicle, it also requires a substitution of fuels at the customer-end of the value chain. The car industry is relying on chemical and oil industries to supply the hydrogen necessary to attract prospective customers. This necessitates a major breakthrough in the production and distribution of hydrogen, which has not occurred yet because it could be a competence-destroying change for suppliers of fossil fuels. As the car industry will not be able to supply the hydrogen itself, it thus faces a major barrier in bringing the fuel cell vehicle to the market. It is basically a chicken-and-egg problem: oil companies will not scale up their hydrogen activities until car companies come with more affordable fuel cell vehicles, while car companies will only launch such models when there is a hydrogen infrastructure (Romm, 2006).

This problem is not so big in the case of biofuels. For instance, several car companies, particularly those from the US, have a fuel strategy aimed at further development of biofuels. Market penetration for biofuels-based (or flex fuel) cars is much easier for several reasons. One is that using biofuels does not have a large impact on R&D and production because it only requires modest changes to the engine of a car, often enabling the use of both biofuels and fossil fuels. What is more, even though car producers need new fuel suppliers for the users of their cars, a shift towards suppliers that produce ethanol and biodiesel instead of petroleum-based fuels is easier because there are already some large and powerful players in the market. For example, for the largest US ethanol producer, Archer Daniels Midland, this technological change in the car industry is competence-enhancing and this company can help push for more support from governments (Harvey *et al*, 2006).

Still, it must be noted that the introduction of biofuels for transportation is seeing a bumpy road as well. The positive impact of biofuels is often doubted, because the emissions-reducing potential depends much on the kind of crops used as raw materials for the production of biofuels. While using sugar as a source of ethanol is more efficient, corn is used on a much larger scale, particularly in the US, because this supports the domestic corn industry instead of the foreign (Brazilian) sugar industry (on which the US levies high import tariffs). Moreover, this so-called first generation of biofuels uses food crops and has been accused of substantially raising food prices. Whether this is true has been contested, though. General Motors' CEO Rick Wagoner, for example, dismissed a UN report on the link between biofuels and food prices as 'shockingly misinformed', as he blames the high oil price instead (Reed, 2008a). Nevertheless, to avoid this debate many companies are now investing in R&D of second-generation biofuels which do not use food crops, but non-food materials instead to produce 'cellulosic' ethanol or synthetic forms of petrol. For example, Shell has set up a joint venture with US-based biotech firm Virent to develop synthetic fuels out of plant sugars (Crooks, 2008b).

Thirdly, powerful companies do not only create positive spillovers; in exercising their power they can also create barriers to a more successful market penetration of climate-friendly technologies. When they co-operate with others in further stimulating climate change innovation the main question for powerful incumbents is to what extent this will contribute to their competitive advantage and not to those of others. While MNCs have the power to use their strength in the value chain to leverage some of their existing capabilities to enter new markets in clean technology, at the same time they can also act as one of the main barriers to a more successful market penetration of low-carbon technologies. The latter may occur when these technologies do not originate from incumbents but from new entrants. This threat of new entrants particularly plays a role when climate change disrupts capabilities throughout the whole value chain (Rothaermel and Hill, 2005; Tripsas, 1997). On the one hand, if MNCs are able to adapt both upstream and downstream activities simultaneously, this will contribute more to a sustained competitive advantage, because such investments will be more difficult to imitate (Verbeke *et al*, 2006), and lead to dynamic capabilities of combining technological (upstream) and nontechnological (downstream) capabilities (Rothaermel and Hill, 2005). On the other hand, it will also be riskier to accommodate the change because MNCs cannot leverage existing capabilities and thus open the door to new entrants. Hence, MNCs may also have an incentive to attempt to obstruct such a change (Tripsas, 1997).

Utilities' vast grip on the existing infrastructure for the transmission and distribution of electricity is a case in point. The system for supply of electricity clearly suffers from a 'carbon lock-in' as technological and market systems surrounding electricity favour generation from fossil fuels (Sandén and Azar, 2005; Unruh, 2000). This carbon lock-in is one of the reasons why it is difficult to scale up the use of renewables for electricity purposes. Technologically speaking, renewables involve intermittent generation instead of constant generation as with coal- or gas-fired power plants. This creates a barrier since existing transmission networks cannot handle intermittent sources of electricity very well, due to the fact that power stations would need more back-up and storage capacity (Neuhoff, 2005). Furthermore, in most parts of the world the market for electricty is now privatised and large utilities often own the transmission network. To reach a mass market of electricity consumers, renewable energy suppliers thus rely on the co-operation of incumbent utilities. However, the barrier lies therein that adjusting the transmission network to enhance access of renewables does not benefit these utilities because besides the transmission network they generally also own the large conventional power plants. Adapting the network would thus open the door to new entrants at the cost of profitability of their own power plants. Governments also further buttress the carbon lock-in as fossil-based energy technologies still receive much higher subsidies than their renewable counterparts (Neuhoff, 2005).

The question then is why are utilities not offering renewables on a larger scale themselves, instead of waiting for new entrants to do this for them? Clearly one of the motives is that they still want to exploit their conventional power plants as these have very long periods for depreciation (30–40 years). Moreover, a switch to renewables would also require innovation from utilities with regard to generation and transmission; not one of their key capabilities (Grubb, 2004). Instead of becoming more innovative with their privatisation, utilities have spent much less on R&D, which fell to very low levels (Margolis and Kammen, 1999). In other words, one of the main challenges for escaping the carbon lock-in is that it requires 'radical innovation in one of the least innovative sectors in the whole economy' (Grubb, 2004: 119).

7.2.5 Challenge 5: Local abatement or a global solution

Developing capabilities to adapt to climate change doesn't necessarily just occur at MNC headquarters, nor can it be assumed to be implemented uniformly throughout the global organisation. The role that climate change plays in MNC strategy is determined by a broad conglomerate of factors involving governmental as well as societal and market forces, working at different geographical levels. There may well be particular geographical factors that are conducive to a climate-induced change in capabilities, but this also means that it benefits the MNC at a specific location only. Climate change creates a geographically disparate and moving target: while it may form a threat in one location, it can be an opportunity in another. Regardless of whether regional or local characteristics are seen as a potential advantage or disadvantage, liability or risk, geographical differences are something to be faced by MNCs, and those companies that excel in doing this are the ones most likely to develop climate-specific capabilities. Hence, learning from climate change does not merely mean that MNCs need dynamic capabilities to cope with technological change; constantly rejuvenating capabilities by being responsive to a wide range of climate change-relevant locational factors is what gives them an edge vis-à-vis competitors as well.

But what are climate change-relevant location-specific factors? In general, these are factors such as strategically beneficial regulations, availability of natural resources, access to markets to sell products and services, factor costs (labour, capital and land), and knowledge-intensive assets such as skilled labour and public infrastructure (Dunning, 1998). For example, because national regulatory responses have varied considerably, with the European Union emissions trading scheme (EU ETS) and the US rejection of the Kyoto Protocol as two extremes, there is a wide variety in climate-related regulations to be reckoned with. In addition, many EU countries and US states have subsidies to stimulate investments in the development of renewable energy technologies (IEA, 2004). Climate change policy in the home country can help MNCs to develop technologies that give them a competitive advantage over their rivals (Porter and van der Linde, 1995). However, host-country locations can also form a potential source of capabilities, as foreign subsidiaries may tap into local external knowledge (Almeida and Phene, 2004). The EU ETS, for example, has implications for home-region companies in particular, but also (potentially) for 'outsiders', host-region MNCs for which the EU is important in terms of production facilities and/or sales (Pinkse, 2007), and/or which compete with EU companies on non-EU markets.

Location-specific factors are not only a result of a country's regulations; the broader institutional framework also plays a role (Makino *et al*, 2004). The presence in the local context of a network of other companies or non-profit organisations that are in the process of developing climate-friendly technologies can be complementary to an MNC's own capability development. Also, higher consumer awareness of climate change can be an incentive as it makes them responsive to green marketing campaigns and products with green(er) qualities. MNCs may benefit from climate-related location-specific advantages either because they already have facilities in this particular location or because they move to these locations in an effort to seek strategic assets to complement their existing capabilities (Dunning, 1998). The locus (or loci) of origin of capability development thus depends on the geographic spread of an MNC, as it is partly determined by the 'local' institutional context.

The impact of geographical factors on the way that MNCs transform existing or develop new capabilities depends to a large extent on the origin of a capability. If an MNC perceives climate change as a global issue, decision-making power on this issue will be at the level of its headquarters. In this case, an MNC believes that the consequences of climate change will have a significant impact on the organisation globally, which is therefore dealt with at the highest management level. Headquarters' support considerably increases MNCs' potential for becoming global leaders in tackling climate change. However, since the worldwide institutionalisation of climate change policies is still quite fragmented, many MNCs may also deal with the issue through their regional centres or national subsidiaries (Husted and Allen, 2006; Rugman, 2005). It then becomes a matter of local responsiveness to climate-related institutional pressures from regulators, NGOs, or the investment community (Brewer, 2005b). The more localised the decision is, however, the less likely it is as well that climate change will have a significant strategic impact on the MNC as a whole, because it will be quite difficult for a local subsidiary to convince MNC headquarters that climate change requires a proactive response. Instead of a global leader, an MNC may then produce local heroes instead.

This is not to say that a local response is of no use at all, however. If, through their subsidiaries, MNCs are located in countries that have been front runners on climate change, they have been facing climate-related pressures for a longer period of time already. This could have enabled them to start learning from the issue from an early stage on. Therefore, if a country initiates new regulations to curb emissions this will probably be a much greater shock to domestic companies than to MNCs. Nonetheless, experience with climate change in a specific location will only create a cross-border advantage if MNCs are able to transfer capabilities from other locations. One of the main challenges relating to the geography of climate-induced capability development, therefore, is whether MNCs will develop different types of location-bound capabilities that fit individual countries, or non-location-bound capabilities that can be transferred and deployed globally (Rugman and Verbeke, 2004). The peculiarities of MNCs particularly arise from the potential to leverage non-location-bound capabilities. Similar or identical procedures for every subsidiary facilitates the exchange of experiences, it breeds internal consistency, enables benchmarking, and is clear to outsiders. Some MNCs, therefore, strive to harmonise their environmental management system and standards at all locations (Christmann, 2004). Yet, the situation in specific countries, for example as a result of stakeholder or government pressure, may create location-bound capabilities as well (related to local responsiveness) (Rugman and Verbeke, 2001). In some cases these can only be used in the country in question; in others they might help to increase MNCs' competitiveness elsewhere.

The transferability of a capability typically depends on the attributes of the knowledge bundles that establish the capability; the higher the tacitness of the knowledge, the less transferable it becomes (Kogut and Zander, 1993). A higher level of tacitness may be due to the extent to which a capability results from linkages with external parties (e.g. governmental bodies, universities, or NGOs). These linkages are in general much better in an MNC's home country (or region), which explains findings that many MNCs are organised on a regional basis (Ghemawat, 2003; Rugman and Verbeke, 2004). Host-country attributes also determine transferability of a capability to a foreign location. Transfer of capabilities to relatively 'distant' countries (Ghemawat, 2001) in terms of dissimilarity of environmental policies usually results in higher adaptation costs of alignment with the institutions of these particular host countries (King and Shaver, 2001; Rugman and Verbeke, 2005). In other words, transfer of environmental best practices is not always without problems (Tsai and Child, 1997). A global approach to environmental management usually relies on advanced technologies, but successfully implementing these in developing countries can be very expensive due to a lack of adequate infrastructure there.

If home-country climate policy stimulates climate-specific R&D that translates into new technological capabilities these would, on the face of it, be non-location-bound. It should be relatively easy to transfer a technology to other geographical locations, regardless of whether it originates from corporate headquarters, a regional centre or a national subsidiary. That is to say, a subsidy or tax break for the development of renewable energy technologies typically only has a function at the start of the technology life cycle; once the technology is incorporated in products it can be redeployed to other locations (Helfat and Peteraf, 2003), thus becoming non-location-bound. Climate-friendly technologies, for example related to hydrogen or fuel cells, are no longer of a tacit nature or tied to external parties such as local governments, and sourcing and production of these technologies can take place anywhere in the world (Rugman and Verbeke, 2004). However, if locational factors continue to be of value further down the life cycle, transferability becomes more difficult. For example, for some specific technologies related to renewable energy, the location of production depends on a country's natural capital. Such geographic site specificity is crucial for hydroelectric and wind power, which require mountainous areas and sufficient wind speed respectively (Russo, 2003). Such a capability cannot simply be redeployed, as it depends on specific attributes of the location (Helfat and Peteraf, 2003).

The same holds for the development of cars that run on biofuels based on flex-fuel technology, which enables the use of ethanol as well as gasoline. Car manufacturers including Ford, Fiat, Volkswagen, and General Motors have first introduced this technology in their Brazilian subsidiaries (Johnson, 2006). The reason is that since the oil crises in the 1970s the Brazilian Government has stimulated local sugar producers to invest in ethanol to reduce dependence on foreign oil, thereby creating a first-mover advantage in ethanol. Currently, a capability in flex-fuel technology is still location-bound in foreign subsidiaries, and occurs when the natural resource necessary for this technology is readily available in this specific location. However, since President Bush announced intentions to also lower the US's dependence on foreign oil in his 2006 State of the Union, interest in ethanol as a fuel has increased in the US as well (Simon, 2006), which has already stimulated the use of ethanol in the US considerably (Makower *et al*, 2008). Such developments may reduce the degree to which capabilities are location-bound.

Nevertheless, most technologies are more likely to strongly depend on location-specific factors when they have further advanced in the life cycle and reached the sales stage. Chevron, for example, states that they 'invest in a variety of renewable and alternative energy technologies and believe that those energy sources will be important in the overall mix of energy for the global economy in the future. But widespread application will depend on many factors, including the rate of technological development, market acceptance, and demonstration of economic viability'. A lack of transferability is thus not necessarily the result of the tacitness of the knowledge on which they are based and local geographical circumstances, but is also linked to the ability of MNCs to create market acceptance for new technologies to realise global sales (Rugman and Verbeke, 2004). In other words, although MNCs may have some influence on market acceptance through marketing campaigns, it also depends on local consumer responsiveness to climate-friendly products and services, and the availability of the necessary public infrastructure.

7.3 CONCLUDING REMARKS

This chapter examined to what extent climate change has the capacity to induce MNCs to become innovative and develop capabilities that not only lead to emissions reductions as such, but also affect companies' profitability, growth and survival. We showed that climate change is an issue that affects a wide range of companies around the world, and that has implications beyond the 'pure' environmental dimensions, being linked to energy security and economic development. Climate change provides a clear opportunity to consider how capabilities can develop and change, in a context where there is considerable attention for this topic, not only by environmentalists and policy makers, but also investors and major multinationals that have become rather active. At the same time, there is also considerable uncertainty and complexity in view of the diversity of contexts and policy responses, which means that capabilities developed in response to this 'moving target' will need constant rejuvenation. The climate change issue can thus give insight into dynamic capabilities, into how MNCs may be able to learn at various fronts, from the issue itself as well as from the way in which it is being dealt with in a range of countries and industries. In addition, we presented five challenges that seem of crucial importance for the ultimate success of climate-induced innovation. At least some of these challenges need to be overcome soon to avert the risk of adverse climate change impacts at some point. Otherwise, the corporate world may be stuck in a similar stalemate that has kept global policy negotiations in a tight grip. In the final chapter we will reflect a little further on some of the dilemmas on the way forward.

Conclusions

8 Dilemmas on the way forward

A concluding chapter in a field so dynamic as climate change which also attempts to look forward, in a sense is like looking in a crystal ball. As we are academics, we will not attempt to predict the future of climate policy and various scenarios that may or may not unfold. Instead, the final pages of this book will briefly point at some of the dilemmas on the way forward in the post-Kyoto setting. Considering the long and complex development of climate change policy over the years (as outlined in Chapter 2), and the complexities surrounding carbon control (Chapter 4) and compensatory approaches such as emissions trading (Chapter 6), it seems safe to assume that a speedy global approach is not very likely. And, even if there would be a breakthrough, then a complicated transition towards such a uniform regime is to be expected. Leaving this speculation aside, however, there are several issues that deserve attention on the basis of our study of business and climate change and its evolution over a period of more than a decade.

First of all, dilemmas abound as to the future shape and set-up of carbon trading. These relate to the organisation of (future) emissions trading schemes, considering on the one hand the interaction between national, regional and international levels, and the industry level on the other. For the coming years, the big question is how the range of emissions trading schemes – regionally in the EU, voluntary local ones in for example the US and Australia, and new federal systems that may be established – can best be harmonised. This also involves the extent to which voluntary markets will associate with compliance markets and how various schemes can be linked. Another main issue that remains is what targets, if any, will apply for developing countries. This will have great bearing on considerations of competitiveness related to companies from different regulatory settings, including 'North' versus 'South'. Although a sector-based global trading system seems to avoid some of the competitive (dis)advantage issues between countries at first sight, developing-country representatives fear that Western (Northern) companies will be better placed to meet standards as they have more resources and technological capabilities. To what degree this will be the case obviously also depends on the rules that will be adopted for such a system.

Awaiting the implementation of the Kyoto Protocol and, subsequently, the outcome of the post-Kyoto negotiations, companies have already played a large role in helping the carbon market develop. They have not only complied with existing regulation, but have also chosen to respond strategically by avoiding such constraints, used their bargaining power to influence actors that enforce new legislation, and acted in voluntary carbon markets to stay ahead or profit from emerging opportunities. In some cases, companies have reaped the benefits of existing gaps in the system. Examples include perverse incentives that enabled or even stimulated utilities to amass windfall profits under the European Union emissions trading scheme (EU ETS) and the generation of large amounts of carbon credits for installing end-of-pipe technologies for HFC-23 emissions reductions within the Clean Development Mechanism (CDM) setting (Chapter 6). The carbon market in that sense has certainly not yet incited widespread innovation and moves towards less carbon-intensive activities, an outcome partly due to limitations in current policies and markets which is reflected in companies' strategies for climate change.

One aspect to be considered in this respect is that company responses (which cover a wide variety of activities as set out in this book, both market and political in nature) sometimes contradict, even within one and the same organisation. Chapter 1 already gave some examples from earlier years related to divergent views on the part of multinationals at the corporate level versus those of subsidiaries (Shell Oil in the US versus other Shell companies; General Motors corporate versus Adam Opel in Germany). In the current setting, there are CEOs representing their companies, for example, pleading in favour of climate change policies while concurrently combating the rules when it comes to actual implementation. Or governments that advocate strict reduction targets but start to protest when the implications for important domestic sectors and/or companies become clear.

For example, prior to the launch of the January 2008 plan by the European Commission to announce more concrete steps to realise a 20 per cent reduction of greenhouse gases (GHGs) by 2020 (compared to 1990 levels), a flurry of lobbying activities to lower ambitions took place, from both governments (including France and Germany) and companies. The latter included the European Round Table of Industrialists' climate and energy working group, chaired by the CEO of Shell, and those sectors scheduled to become subject to stricter rules, most notably heavy industry. This encompassed (well-known) warnings from various affected parties that it would lead to plant closures, relocation of industries to outside the EU and other types of damage to the economy. This example not only shows the contradictions, but also that such lobbying leads to suboptimal outcomes, which explains why some economists advocate a carbon tax. For example, the extent that the EU will be able to reduce free allocation of allowances, which has been labelled as 'a vehicle for delivering covert industrial subsidies to politically favoured industries on a truly epic scale' (Barber, 2008), with companies moving beyond the traditional oppositional stance toward more far-reaching plans than the current state, will determine future effectiveness of emissions trading as a policy instrument.

More generally, to induce abatement and a search for low-carbon solutions, the right incentives should be in place, and one way of doing this is to put a price on carbon. If the carbon market works, there would be a stimulus for innovation that realises emissions reductions at the lowest cost and breaks the carbon lock-in noted in Chapter 7. In the current setting, as outlined in this book (Chapter 6), with carbon trading and partly related offset schemes as main policy instruments, this is definitely not the case yet; carbon trading is now taking place in a wide variety of variants, only a few regulatory and most others voluntary. As a consequence, the existing trading schemes are not yet forming a real carbon constraint for many companies that do have the potential to contribute to climate change innovation. In other words, these forms of compensation have not led to an adequate carbon price so far and thus will not suffice to 'solve' the climate change problem, as consequent emissions reductions have been limited, if they have occurred at all.

Chapter 7 discussed in detail five key challenges that need to be addressed to further innovation and the development of capabilities for climate change. One involved the discussion on the scaling up of existing technologies, in view of the fact that there is no 'silver bullet' solution yet, and how the balance between further technological development and deployment of the existing collection of technologies are best to be found. A related issue is how and in what way climate-friendly solutions can link to and/or build on companies' existing capabilities and further their competitive positions. This is all the more important as choices have to be made on technological trajectories in a market transition towards a low-carbon economy, which may entail incremental or rather more radical innovations. The success or failure of such innovations also depends on companies' bargaining power, in their value chains and vis-à-vis (potential) competitors. This is particularly relevant in the case of multinationals, as climate change is a geographically disparate issue which can form an opportunity for innovation in one place but a threat to corporate activity in another. Depending on the peculiarities of the countries and companies in question, multinationals may adopt a global or a local/regional approach, and try to reap (and transfer) the benefits that are attached to a particular location.

For a profitable and sustained transition towards more environmentally-friendly and less carbon-intensive technologies that foster innovation, in the absence of viable markets and concomitant infrastructure, decisive policy steps are needed as well as behavioural changes. In Chapter 7, this has been referred to as systemic climate solutions that require co-operation between private and public partners, both profit-making and non-profit-making. In that sense, it is about time that the wave of partnerships for climate change that has emerged in recent years (Chapter 3) gets more steam and takes off in a more substantive and co-ordinated manner. There is a large 'chicken-and-egg' problem, though, with parties waiting for one another, and calls to break the deadlock but without clear ideas as to the how. Hardly anyone is taking decisive steps even though quite a number of companies and governments have the ability to do so. Moreover, the role of consumers in tackling climate change should become clearer as well. Seen from an economy-wide perspective, industry is just one of the sectors responsible for a significant amount of GHG emissions; large-scale energy demand also comes from buildings and transportation (Grubb, 2004). Although with regard to these latter two sectors business has a role to play as well, the effectiveness of emissions-reducing initiatives depends to a much greater extent on consumer behaviour (Pinkse and Dommisse, 2008). This creates another 'chicken-and-egg' problem: companies do not supply low-carbon products if they do not sense demand from consumers; while at the same time consumers will not buy more low-carbon alternatives if their choice is still limited. Therefore another dilemma for companies is: how to convince consumers to buy climate-friendly products and services? It now seems that because companies already expect a low demand for 'green' products at the outset, marketing of these products is not taken to its full potential.

There are tradeoffs to be made, at the actor level as indicated above, but also with regard to issues, most notably climate change in relation to, for example, availability of food and water. In recent years, growing interest in biofuels has sparked a discussion on competition for scarce resources, especially harming poor people in low-income countries. In particular the first-generation of biofuels that uses food crops has been targeted for various reasons. Firstly, the environmental benefits (including the emissions-reducing potential) of biofuels are much less than initially expected. This also has to do with the fact that some biofuels consume large quantities of water and/or are grown in areas often deforested for the purpose, thus exacerbating other problems. The only sources that have largely escaped criticism are ethanol from sugar cane as grown in Brazil and those that rely on second-generation technologies and are generated from waste products, using algae for example; although it must be noted that the latter are not commercially viable at this stage yet.

Secondly, there are issues related to poverty and food prices. While higher demand for biofuels can raise rural incomes, also in developing countries, grain-based biofuels in particular may have an upward effect on food prices, especially corn and soyabean. This debate received much attention in 2008 when food prices soared, in a context of surging oil prices (that increase costs of diesel and fertilisers), higher demand (particularly from China), bad harvests, export restrictions, and subsequent speculation in agriculture derivatives markets. While there are different views on whether and how biofuels have impacted food prices (with some denying any influence, and others emphasising the opposite), estimates on its contribution in early 2008 ranged from 10 per cent (Food and Agriculture Organisation) to 20–30 per cent (the International Monetary Fund and the International Food Policy Research Institute) (Blas, 2008).

Interestingly enough, General Motors' CEO dismissed the evidence on the role of biofuels on food prices, as already mentioned in Chapter 7. This obviously has to do with the focus, especially on the part of US car companies, on bio-ethanol as a relatively low-cost means to bring down emissions. There seems to be an underlying belief that the oil industry has an interest in raising doubts about ethanol in order to defend their existing business models – this is at least the suspicion on the part of some car company executives (Reed, 2008b). This provides just an illustration of the stakes involved, especially for companies. What is noteworthy is that the controversy over the science of climate change, which some companies found important a decade ago (see Chapter 1), seems to have been replaced by disagreements on more detailed aspects such as the one on the impact of biofuels on food prices. Corporate interests and the use of arguments on competitiveness have remained stable in a way, although the precise setting in which debates take place has changed considerably over the years, as this book has shown.

The link between climate change on the one hand, and topics such as water, food and poverty on the other, shows that these issue linkages definitely make the discussion and the decision-making process more complicated. What it brings as well, though, is more interest in these other global social and environmental problems, which sometimes tend to receive less media and public attention than climate change. However, this does not mean that issues such as poverty, access to food and water, and other human (social and political) rights are less urgent. While we would not argue for focusing less on climate change, in our view it is important to take the whole range of issues into account, and not only those that are in the public eye and/or have become a strategic concern for managers and policy makers. And although media coverage is not so easy to influence, let alone the public debate, there are other ways (for example via education) in which more balanced attention can be paid to several societal issues with which companies are confronted, particularly in their international operations. Climate change obviously is an example of an issue that affects various functions, including public affairs, communications, marketing, strategy, organisation, accounting and finance. It thus provides a good illustration, also, of how an initially relatively marginal and contested environmental problem has evolved into one of strategic interest with important operational implications, as outlined in this book. Even though we cannot predict how it will develop, this is very likely to remain so in the coming years.

References

Abernathy, W J, and Clark, K B, 1985, 'Innovation: mapping the winds of creative destruction', *Research Policy*, 14: 3–22.

Abrahamson, E, and Rosenkopf, L, 1993, 'Institutional and competitive bandwagons: using mathematical modeling as a tool to explore innovation diffusion', *Academy of Management Review*, 18(3): 487–517.

Allianz/WWF, 2005, *Climate Change and the Financial Sector: an Agenda for Action*, London: Allianz group and WWF.

Allianz/WWF, 2006, *Climate Change and Insurance: an Agenda for Action in the United States*, New York: Allianz Group and WWF.

Almeida, P, and Phene, A, 2004, 'Subsidiaries and knowledge creation: the influence of the MNC and host country on innovation', *Strategic Management Journal*, 25: 847–864.

Amit, R, and Schoemaker, P J H, 1993, 'Strategic assets and organizational rent', *Strategic Management Journal*, 14: 33–46.

An, F, and Sauer, A, 2004, *Comparison of Passenger Vehicle Fuel Economy and Greenhouse Gas Emission Standards around the World*, Arlington, VA: Pew Center on Global Climate Change.

Anderson, M, and Gardiner, D, 2006, *Climate Risk and Energy in the Auto Sector*, Boston, MA: Ceres.

Anderson, P, and Tushman, M L, 1990, 'Technological discontinuities and dominant designs: a cyclical model of technological change', *Administrative Science Quarterly*, 35: 604–633.

Andresen, S, and Agrawala, S, 2002, 'Leaders, pushers and laggards in the making of the climate regime', *Global Environmental Change*, 12: 41–51.

Aragón–Correa, J A, and Sharma, S, 2003, 'A contingent resource-based view of proactive corporate environmental strategy', *Academy of Management Review*, 28(1): 71–88.

Arita, E, 2004, 'Proposed emissions trading, carbon tax set to be hard sell', *The Japan Times*, 7 August.

Arita, E, 2005, 'Working to reach Kyoto goals overseas', *The Japan Times*, 16 February.

Arquit Niederberger, A, and Saner, R, 2005, 'Exploring the relationship between FDI flows and CDM potential', *Transnational Corporations*, 14(1): 1–40.

Arts, B, 2006, 'Non-state actors in global environmental governance – New arrangements beyond the state', in M Koenig-Archibugi, and M Zürn (eds), *New modes of governance in the global system – Exploring publicness, delegation and inclusiveness*: 177–200, Hampshire: Palgrave MacMillan.

Asia-Pacific Partnership, 2006, Charter for the Asia-Pacific Partnership on Clean Development and Climate, retrieved 15 October 2007 from <http://www.asiapacificpartnership.org>.

Bäckstrand, K, 2006, 'Multi-stakeholder partnerships for sustainable development: rethinking legitimacy, accountability and effectiveness', *European Environment*, 16: 290–306.

Bäckstrand, K, 2008, 'Accountability of networked climate governance – the rise of transnational climate partnerships', *Global Environmental Politics*, 8(3): 74–102.

Bailey, I, 2007, 'Neoliberalism, climate governance and the scalar politics of EU emissions trading', *Area*, 39(4): 431–442.

Bansal, P, 2005, 'Evolving sustainably: a longitudinal study of corporate sustainable development', *Strategic Management Journal*, 26: 197–218.

Baranzini, A, Thalmann, P, and Gonseth, C, 2004, 'Swiss climate policy: combining VAs with other instruments under the menace of a CO_2 tax', in A Baranzini, and P Thalmann (eds), *Voluntary Approaches in Climate Policy*: 249–276, Cheltenham: Edward Elgar.

Barber, T, 2008, 'EU urged to use taxes in climate change', *Financial Times*, 21 January.

Barney, J, 1991, 'Firm resources and sustained competitive advantage', *Journal of Management*, 17(1): 99–120.

Baron, D P, 1995, 'Integrated strategy: market and nonmarket components', *California Management Review*, 37(2): 47–65.

Baron, D P, 1997, 'Integrated strategy, trade policy, and global competition', *California Management Review*, 39(2): 145–169.

Bartlett, C A, and Ghoshal, S, 1989, *Managing Across Borders – The Transnational Solution*, Boston: Harvard Business School Press.

Bellassen, V, and Leguet, B, 2007, *The Emergence of Voluntary Carbon Offsetting*, Paris: Caisse des Dépôts – Mission Climat.

Berger, I E, Cunningham, P H, and Drumwright, M E, 2007, 'Mainstreaming corporate social responsibility: developing markets for virtue', *California Management Review*, 49(4): 132–157.

Berkhout, F, Hertin, J, and Gann, D M, 2006, 'Learning to adapt: organisational adaptation to climate change impacts', *Climatic Change*, 78: 135–156.

Biermann, F, Chan, M–S, Mert, A, and Pattberg, P, 2007, *Multi–Stakeholder Partnerships for Sustainable Development: Does the Promise Hold?* Paper presented at the Conference on the Human Dimensions of Global Environmental Change, Amsterdam.

Birchall, J, 2008, 'US airlines pressed on climate change', *Financial Times*, 10 March.

Blas, J, 2008, 'UN says oil rise hits food prices harder', *Financial Times*, 26/27 April.

Blyth, W, and Bosi, M, 2004, *Linking non–EU Domestic Emissions Trading Schemes with the EU Emissions Trading Scheme*, Paris: OECD/IEA.

Bodansky, D, 2001, 'The history of the global climate change regime', in U Luterbacher, and D F Sprinz (eds), *International Relations and Global Climate Change*: 23–40, Cambridge, MA: The MIT Press.

Boddewyn, J J, and Brewer, T L, 1994, 'International-business political behavior: new theoretical directions', *Academy of Management Review*, 19(1): 119–143.

Boehmer–Christiansen, S, 1996, 'The international research enterprise and global environmental change – Climate-change policy as a research process', in J Vogler, and M F Imber (eds), *The Environment and International Relations*: 171–195, London: Routledge.

Boemare, C, and Quirion, P, 2002, 'Implementing greenhouse gas trading in Europe: lessons from economic literature and international experiences', *Ecological Economics*, 43: 213–230.

Boiral, O, 2006, 'Global warming: should companies adopt a proactive strategy?' *Long Range Planning*, 39: 315–330.

Bonardi, J–P, and Keim, G D, 2005, 'Corporate political strategies for widely salient issues', *Academy of Management Review*, 30(3): 555–576.

Bonini, S M J, Hintz, G, and Mendonca, L T, 2008, 'Addressing consumer concerns about climate change', *McKinsey Quarterly*, March 2008.

Börzel, T A, and Risse, T, 2005, 'Public-private partnerships: effective and legitimate tools of transnational governance?', in E Grande, and L W Pauly (eds), *Complex Sovereignty: Reconstituting Political Authority in the Twenty–First Century*: 195–216, Toronto: University of Toronto Press.

Braithwaite, J, and Drahos, P, 2000, *Global Business Regulation*, Cambridge: Cambridge University Press.

Bramley, M, 2007, *Analysis of the Government of Canada's April 2007 Greenhouse Gas Policy Announcement*, retrieved 19 October 2007 from <http://www.pembina.org>.

Brau, R, and Carraro, C, 2004, 'Voluntary approaches as climate policy tools: competition issues and the role of market structure', in A Baranzini, and P Thalmann (eds), *Voluntary Approaches in Climate Policy*: 89–104, Cheltenham: Edward Elgar.

Brewer, T L, 2005a, *Climate Change in the US Government Budget, Funding for Technology and other Programmes, and Implications for EU–US Relations*, Brussels: CEPS.

Brewer, T L, 2005b, 'Global warming and climate change: new issues for business strategy, government policy, and research on business-government relations', in R Grosse (ed), *International Business and Government Relations in the 21st Century*: 147–170, Cambridge: Cambridge University Press.

Brewer, T L, 2006, *Public Opinion on Climate Change Issues in the G–8 and G–5 Countries*, retrieved 16 October 2007 from <http://www.usclimatechange.com>.

Brouhle, K, and Harrington, D R, 2007, 'Firm strategy and the Canadian Voluntary Climate Challenge and Registry', *Business Strategy and the Environment*, forthcoming.

Busby, J, and Ochs, A, 2004, 'From Mars and Venus down to Earth: understanding the transatlantic climate divide', in D Michel (ed), *Climate Policy for the 21st Century: Meeting the Long–term Challenge of Global Warming*: 35–76, Washington: Center for Transatlantic Relations.

Butzengeiger, S, Michaelowa, A, and Bode, S, 2003, 'Europe – a pioneer in greenhouse gas emissions trading, History of rule development and major design elements', *Intereconomics*, 38(4): 219–228.

Buysse, K, and Verbeke, A, 2003, 'Proactive environmental strategies: a stakeholder management perspective', *Strategic Management Journal*, 24: 453–470.

Byrne, J, Hughes, K, Rickerson, W, and Kurdgelashvili, L, 2007, 'American policy conflict in the greenhouse: divergent trends in federal, regional, state, and local green energy and climate change policy', *Energy Policy*, 35: 4555–4573.

Canadian Government (2005), *Project Green, Moving Forward on Climate Change: A Plan for Honouring our Kyoto Commitment*, retrieved on 22 April 2005 from <http://www.climatechange.gc.ca>.

Capoor, K, and Ambrosi, P, 2007, *State and Trends of the Carbon Market 2007*, Washington DC: World Bank.

Carbon Trust, 2006, *The Carbon Trust Three Stage Approach to Developing a Robust Offset Strategy*, London: The Carbon Trust.

CCX, 2007, 2006 *Program-wide True-Up Summary Report*, retrieved on 11 April 2008 from <http://www.chicgoclimatex.com>.

CDP, 2003, *Carbon Disclosure Project 2003*, London: Innovest.

CDP, 2004, *Carbon Disclosure Project 2004*, London: Innovest.

CDP, 2005, *Carbon Disclosure Project 2005*, London: Innovest.

CDP, 2006, *Carbon Disclosure Project 2006 – Global FT500*, London: Innovest.

CDP, 2007, *Carbon Disclosure Project 2007 – Global FT500*, London: Innovest.

Chan-Fishel, M, 2002, *Survey of Climate Change Disclosure in SEC Filings of Automobile, Insurance, Oil and Gas, Petrochemical, and Utilities Companies*, Washington, DC: Friends of the Earth US.

Chan-Fishel, M, 2003, *Second Survey of Climate Change Disclosure in SEC Filings of Automobile, Insurance, Oil and Gas, Petrochemical, and Utilities Companies*, Washington, DC: Friends of the Earth US.

Chan-Fishel, M, 2004, *Third Survey of Climate Change Disclosure in SEC Filings of Automobile, Insurance, Oil and Gas, Petrochemical, and Utilities Companies*, Washington, DC: Friends of the Earth US.

Chan-Fishel, M, 2005, *Fourth Survey of Climate Change Disclosure in SEC Filings of Automobile, Insurance, Oil and Gas, Petrochemical, and Utilities Companies*, Washington, DC: Friends of the Earth US.

Chan-Fishel, M, 2006, *Fifth Survey of Climate Change Disclosure in SEC Filings of Automobile, Insurance, Oil and Gas, Petrochemical, and Utilities Companies*, Washington, DC: Friends of the Earth US.

Child, J, and Tsai, T, 2005, 'The dynamic between firms' environmental strategies and institutional constraints in emerging economies: evidence from China and Taiwan', *Journal of Management Studies*, 42(1): 95–125.

Christiansen, A C, 2003, 'Convergence or divergence? Status and prospects for US climate strategy', *Climate Policy*, 3(4): 343–358.

Christiansen, A C, and Wettestad, J, 2003, 'The EU as a frontrunner on greenhouse gas emissions trading: how did it happen and will the EU succeed?' *Climate Policy*, 3(1): 3–18.

Christmann, P, 2000, 'Effects of "best practices" of environmental management on cost advantage: the role of complementary assets', *Academy of Management Journal*, 43(4): 663–680.

Christmann, P, 2004, 'Multinational companies and the natural environment: determinants of global environmental policy standardization', *Academy of Management Journal*, 47(5): 747–760.

Cogan, D C, 2006, *Corporate Governance and Climate Change: Making the Connection*, Boston, MA: Ceres.

de Coninck, H, Fischer, C, Newell, R G, and Ueno, T, 2007, 'International technology-oriented agreements to address climate change', *RFF Discussion Paper*, 06–50.

Convery, F, Ellerman, D, and de Perthuis, C, 2008, *The European Carbon Market in Action: Lessons from the First Trading Period*, Paris: Caisse des Dépôts – Mission Climat.

Convery, F J, and Redmond, L, 2007, 'Market and price developments in the European Union emissions trading scheme', *Review of Environmental Economics and Policy*, 1(1): 88–111.

Crooks, E, 2008a, 'BP seeks low-carbon payback', *Financial Times*, 28 February.

Crooks, E, 2008b, 'Shell venture sweetens biofuels debate', *Financial Times*, 27 March.

Crowley, K, 2007, 'Is Australia faking it? The Kyoto Protocol and the greenhouse policy challenge', *Global Environmental Politics*, 7(4): 118–139.

Dechezleprêtre, A, Glachant, M, and Ménière, Y, 2007, *The North-South Transfer of Climate-Friendly Technologies through the Clean Development Mechanism*, Paris: Cerna/Écoles des Mines de Paris.

Delmas, M A, and Terlaak, A K, 2001, 'A framework for analyzing environmental voluntary agreements', *California Management Review*, 43(3): 44–63.

Delmas, M, and Terlaak, A, 2002, 'Regulatory commitment to negotiated agreements:

evidence from the United States, Germany, The Netherlands, and France', *Journal of Comparative Policy Analysis: Research and Practice*, 4: 5–29.

Delmas, M A, and Toffel, M W, 2004, 'Stakeholders and environmental management practices: an institutional framework', *Business Strategy and the Environment*, 13: 209–222.

den Elzen, M G J, and de Moor, A P G, 2002, 'Analyzing the Kyoto Protocol under the Marrakesh Accords: economic efficiency and environmental effectiveness', *Ecological Economics*, 43: 141–158.

Depledge, J, and Grubb, M, 2006, 'COP/MOP-1 and COP-11: a breakthrough for the climate change regime?' *Climate Policy*, 5: 553–560.

Dierickx, I, and Cool, K, 1989, 'Asset stock accumulation and sustainability of competitive advantage', *Management Science*, 35(12): 1504–1511.

DiMaggio, P, 1988, 'Interest and agency in institutional theory', in L G Zucker (ed), *Institutional Patterns and Organizations – Culture and Environment*: 3–21, Cambridge, MA: Ballinger Publishing Company.

Djelic, M-L, and Quack, S, 2003, 'Theoretical building blocks for a research agenda linking globalization and institutions', in M-L Djelic, and S Quack (eds), *Globalization and Institutions*: 15–34, Cheltenham: Edward Elgar.

Dlugolecki, A, and Keykhah, M, 2002, 'Climate change and the insurance sector: its role in adaptation and mitigation', *Greener Management International*, 39 (Autumn): 83–98.

Dosi, G, 1982, 'Technological paradigms and technological trajectories', *Research Policy*, 11: 147–162.

Dowell, G, Hart, S L, and Yeung, B, 2000, 'Do corporate global environmental standards create or destroy market value?' *Management Science*, 46(8): 1059–1074.

Dunning, J H, 1998, 'Location and the multinational enterprise: a neglected factor?' *Journal of International Business Studies*, 29(1): 45–66.

EC, 2001, Directive 2001/77/EC of the European Parliament and of the Council of 27 September 2001 on the promotion of electricity produced from renewable energy sources in the internal energy market, *Official Journal of the European Communities*, L 283/33–40.

EC, 2003, Directive 2003/87/EC of the European Parliament and of the Council of 13 October establishing a scheme for greenhouse gas emission allowance trading within the Community and amending Council Directive 96/61/EC, *Official Journal of the European Union*, L 275/32.

EC, 2004, Directive 2004/101/EC of the European Parliament and of the Council of 27 October 2004 amending Directive 2003/87/EC establishing a scheme for greenhouse gas emission allowance trading within the Community, in respect of the Kyoto Protocol's project mechanisms, *Official Journal of the European Union*, L 338/20.

EC, 2006, Directive 2006/32/EC of the European Parliament and of the Council of 5 April 2006 on energy end–use efficiency and energy services and repealing Council Directive 93/76/EEC, *Official Journal of the European Union*, L 114/64.

EC, 2007, Communication for Limiting global climate change to 2° Celsius: The way ahead for 2020 and beyond, *COM(2007) 2 final*, Brussels, 10 January.

Eden, L, and Lenway, S, 2001, 'Introduction to the symposium, Multinationals: the Janus face of globalization', *Journal of International Business Studies*, 32(3): 383–400.

EEA, 2007, *Greenhouse Gas Emission Trends and Projections in Europe 2007 – Tracking Progress towards Kyoto Targets*, Copenhagen: European Environment Agency.

Eesley, C, and Lenox, M J, 2006, 'Firm responses to secondary stakeholder action', *Strategic Management Journal*, 27: 765–781.

Egels–Zandén, N, and Wahlqvist, E, 2007, 'Post-partnership strategies for defining corporate responsibility: the Business Social Compliance Initiative', *Journal of Business Ethics*, 70(2): 175–189.

Egenhofer, C, 2007, 'The making of the EU emissions trading scheme: status, prospects and implications for business', *European Management Journal*, 25(6): 453–463.

Eisenhardt, K M, and Martin, J A, 2000, 'Dynamic capabilities: what are they?' *Strategic Management Journal*, 21: 1105–1121.

Ellerman, A D, and Buchner, B K, 2007, 'The European Union emissions trading scheme: origins, allocation, and early results', *Review of Environmental Economics and Policy*, 1(1): 66–87.

Ellerman, D, and Buchner, B, 2008, 'Over-allocation or abatement? A preliminary analysis of the EU ETS based on the 2005–06 emissions data', *Environmental and Resource Economics*, forthcoming.

Ellis, J, Winkler, H, Corfee–Morlot, J, and Gagnon–Lebrun, F, 2007, 'CDM: taking stock and looking forward', *Energy Policy*, 35: 15–28.

Engel, K H, 2006, 'Mitigating global climate change in the United States: a regional approach', *NYU Environmental Law Journal*, 14(1): 54–85.

Ernst & Young, 2008, *Strategic Business Risk 2008 – The Top 10 Risks for Business*, London: Ernst & Young with Oxford Analytica.

Etzion, D, 2007, 'Research on organizations and the natural environment, 1992–present: a review', *Journal of Management*, 33(4): 637–664.

Exxon, 1998, *Exxon Perspectives*, Irving, TX: Exxon.

ExxonMobil, 2004, *Corporate Citizenship Report*, Irving, TX: ExxonMobil.

Fisher, D R, 2004, *National Governance and the Global Climate Change Regime*, Lanham: Rowman and Littlefield Publishers.

Fligstein, N, 1997, *Fields, Power, and Social Skill: a Critical Analysis of the New Institutionalism*, paper presented at the Conference on Power and Organization of the German Sociological Association, Hamburg, Germany.

Florida, R, 1996, 'Lean and green: the move to environmentally conscious manufacturing', *California Management Review*, 39(1): 80–105.

Ford, 2004, *Corporate Citizenship Report*, Dearborn, MI: Ford.

Ford, 2005, *Ford Report on the Business Impact of Climate Change*, Detroit: Ford Motor Company.

Fransen, T, Bhatia, P, and Hsu, A, 2007, *Measuring to Manage: a Guide to Designing GHG Accounting and Reporting Programs*, Washington, DC and Geneva: WRI/WBCSD.

Fransen, L, and Kolk, A, 2007, 'Global rule-setting for business: a critical analysis of multi–stakeholder standards', *Organization*, 14(5): 667–684.

Freedman, M, and Jaggi, B, 2005, 'Global warming, commitment to the Kyoto protocol, and accounting disclosures by the largest global public firms from polluting industries', *The International Journal of Accounting*, 40: 215–232.

Fujioka, C, 2008, 'Japan seeks to design post-Kyoto emissions-trading program', *International Herald Tribune*, 11 March.

Gagelmann, F, and Frondel, M, 2005, 'The impact of emission trading on innovation – science fiction or reality?' *European Environment*, 15: 203–211.

Gallagher, K S, Holdren, J P, and Sagar, A D, 2006, 'Energy-technology innovation', *Annual Review of Environment and Resources*, 31: 193–237.

Gardiner, D, and Jacobson, L, 2002, 'Will voluntary programs be sufficient to reduce U.S. greenhouse gas emissions? An analysis of the Bush Administration's Global Climate Change Initiative', *Environment*, 44(8): 24–33.

Gatignon, H, Tushman, M L, Smith, W, and Anderson, P, 2002, 'A structural approach to assessing innovation: construct development of innovation locus, type, and characteristics', *Management Science*, 48(9): 1103–1122.

GE, 2005, *GE Launches Ecomagination to Develop Environmental Technologies; Company-Wide Focus on Addressing Pressing Challenges*, Fairfield, CT: General Electric.

Geller, H, Harrington, P, Rosenfeld, A H, Tanishima, S, and Unander, F, 2006, 'Policies for increasing energy efficiency: Thirty years of experience in OECD countries', *Energy Policy*, 34: 556–573.

Ghemawat, P, 2001, 'Distance still matters: the hard reality of global expansion', *Harvard Business Review*, 79(8): 137–147.

Ghemawat, P, 2003, 'Semiglobalization and international business strategy', *Journal of International Business Studies*, 34: 138–152.

Gilbert, C G, 2005, 'Unbundling the structure of inertia: resource versus routine rigidity', *Academy of Management Journal*, 48(5): 741–763.

Gillenwater, M, Broekhoff, D, Trexler, M, Hyman, J, and Fowler, R, 2007, 'Policing the voluntary carbon market', *Nature Reports Climate Change*, 6: 85–87.

Glachant, M, and De Muizon, G, 2007, 'Climate Change Agreements in the United Kingdom: a successful policy experience?' in R D Morgenstern, and W A Pizer (eds), *Reality Check – The Nature and Performance of Voluntary Environmental Programs in the United States, Europe, and Japan*: 64–85, Washington, DC: RFF Press.

Glasbergen, P, 2004, 'The architecture and functioning of Dutch Negotiated Agreements', in A Baranzini, and P Thalmann (eds), *Voluntary Approaches in Climate Policy*: 170–188, Cheltenham: Edward Elgar.

GlobeScan, 2006, *Global Views on Climate Change*, retrieved 10 October 2007 from <http://www.worldpublicopinion.org>.

GlobeScan/BBC/PIPA, 2007, *All Countries Need to Take Major Steps on Climate Change: Global Poll*, retrieved 10 October 2007 from <http://www.worldpublicopinion.org>.

Googins, B K, and Rochlin, S A, 2000, 'Creating the partnership society: understanding the rhetoric and reality of cross-sectoral partnerships', *Business and Society Review*, 105(1): 127–144.

Griffiths, A, Haigh, N, and Rassias, J, 2007, 'A framework for understanding institutional governance systems and climate change: the case of Australia', *European Management Journal*, 25(6): 415–427.

Grubb, M, 2004, 'Technology innovation and climate change policy: an overview of issues and options', *Keio Economic Studies*, 41(2): 103–132.

Grubb, M, Azar, C, and Persson, U M, 2005, 'Allowance allocation in the European emissions trading system: a commentary', *Climate Policy*, 5: 127–136.

Grubb, M, Vrolijk, C, and Brack, D, 1999, *The Kyoto Protocol – A Guide and Assessment*, London: RIIA/Earthscan.

Gulbrandsen, L H, and Andresen, S, 2004, 'NGO influence in the implementation of the Kyoto Protocol: compliance, flexibility mechanisms, and sinks', *Global Environmental Politics*, 4(4): 54–75.

GWPH, 2005, *Kyoto Protocol Target Achievement Plan*, Tokyo: Global Warming Prevention Headquarters.

Haar, L N, and Haar, L, 2006, 'Policy-making under uncertainty: commentary upon the European Union Emissions Trading Scheme', *Energy Policy*, 34: 2615–2629.

Hahn, R W, and Stavins, R N, 1992, 'Economic incentives for environmental protection: integrating theory and practice', *American Economic Review*, 82(2): 464–468.

Haites, E, and Yamin, F, 2000, 'The clean development mechanism: proposal for its operation and governance', *Global Environmental Change*, 10(1): 27–45.

Hall, J, and Vredenburg, H, 2003, 'The challenges of innovating for sustainable development', *MIT Sloan Management Review*, 45(1): 61–68.

Hamilton, K, Bayon, R, Turner, G, and Higgins, D, 2007, *State of the Voluntary Carbon Markets 2007: Picking up Steam*, London/Washington: New Carbon Finance and The Ecosystem Marketplace.

Handfield, R, Sroufe, R, and Walton, S, 2005, 'Integrating environmental management and supply chain strategies', *Business Strategy and the Environment*, 14: 1–19.

Harris, E, 2007, *The Voluntary Carbon Offsets Market: an Analysis of Market Characteristics and Opportunities for Sustainable Development*, London: International Institute for Environment and Development.

Harrison, K, 1999, 'Talking with the donkey: cooperative approaches to environmental protection', *Journal of Industrial Ecology*, 2(3): 51–72.

Harrison, K, 2007, 'The road not taken: climate change policy in Canada and the United States', *Global Environmental Politics*, 7(4): 92–117.

Hart, S L, 1995, 'A natural-resource-based view of the firm', *Academy of Management Review*, 20(4): 986–1014.

Harvey, F, 2005, 'GE looks out for a cleaner profit', *Financial Times*, 1 July.

Harvey, F, 2007a, 'Winds of change beginning to blow', *Financial Times*, 12 October.

Harvey, F, 2007b, 'Next step is "positive" carbon neutrality', *Financial Times*, 7 June.

Harvey, F, Cameron, D, and Beattie, A, 2006, 'Wind changes in favour of biofuels', *Financial Times*, 20 June.

Hasselknippe, H, and Røine, K, 2006, *Carbon 2006, Towards a Truly Global Market*, Oslo: Point Carbon.

Hekkert, M, and Van den Hoed, R, 2004, 'Competing technologies and the struggle towards a new dominant design, The emergence of the hybrid vehicle at the expense of the fuel cell vehicle?' *Greener Management International*, 47 (Autumn): 29–43.

Helfat, C E, 1997, 'Know-how and asset complementarity and dynamic capability accumulation: the case of RandD', *Strategic Management Journal*, 18(5): 339–360.

Helfat, C E, and Peteraf, M A, 2003, 'The dynamic resource-based view: capability lifecycles', *Strategic Management Journal*, 24: 997–1010.

Henisz, W J, and Zelner, B A, 2005, 'Legitimacy, interest group pressures, and change in emergent institutions: the case of foreign investors and host country governments', *Academy of Management Review*, 30(2): 361–382.

Henry, L A, and McIntosh Sundstrom, L, 2007, 'Russia and the Kyoto Protocol: seeking an alignment of interests and image', *Global Environmental Politics*, 7(4): 47–69.

Hepburn, C, 2007, 'Carbon trading: a review of the Kyoto mechanisms', *Annual Review of Environment and Resources*, 32: 375–393.

Hesse, A, 2006, *Climate and Corporations – Right Answers or Wrong Questions? Carbon Disclosure Project Data – Validation, Analysis, Improvements*, Bonn: Germanwatch.

Hoffert, M, 2006, 'An energy revolution for the greenhouse century', *Social Research*, 73(3): 981–1000.

Hoffert, M I, Caldeira, K, Benford, G, Criswell, D R, Green, C, Herzog, H, Jain, A K, Kheshgi, H S, Lackner, K S, Lewis, J S, Lightfoot, H D, Manheimer, W, Mankins, J C, Mauel, M E, Perkins, L J, Schlesinger, M E, Volk, T, and Wigley, T M L, 2002, 'Advanced technology paths to global climate stability: energy for a greenhouse planet', *Science*, 298(5595): 981–987.

Hoffert, M I, Caldeira, K, Jain, A K, Haites, E F, Harvey, L D D, Potter, S D, Schlesinger, M E, Schneider, S H, Watts, R G, Wigley, T M L, and Wuebbles, D J, 1998, 'Energy implications of future stabilization of atmospheric CO_2 content', *Nature* 395: 881–884.

Hoffman, A J, 1999, 'Institutional evolution and change: environmentalism and the U.S. chemical industry', *Academy of Management Journal*, 42(4): 351–371.

Hoffman, A J, 2005, 'Climate change strategy: the business logic behind voluntary greenhouse gas reductions', *California Management Review*, 47(3): 21–46.

Hoffman, A J, 2006, *Getting Ahead of the Curve: Corporate Strategies that Address Climate Change*, Arlington, VA: Pew Center on Global Climate Change.

Hoffmann, V H, 2007, 'EU ETS and investment decisions: the case of the German electricity industry', *European Management Journal*, 25(6): 464–474.

Holdren, J P, 2006, 'The energy innovation imperative: addressing oil dependence, climate change, and other 21st century energy challenges', *Innovations: Technology, Governance, Globalization*, 1(2): 3–23.

Hollinger, P, 2008, 'Industry warns EU on CO_2 proposals', *Financial Times*, 21 January.

Hunt, C, 2004, 'Australia's greenhouse policy', *Australasian Journal of Environmental Management*, 11(2): 156–163.

Husted, B W, and Allen, D B, 2006, 'Corporate social responsibility in the multinational enterprise: strategic and institutional approaches', *Journal of International Business Studies*, 37(6): 838–849.

IEA, 2004, *Renewable energy – Market and policy trends in IEA countries*, Paris: International Energy Agency.

IPCC, 2007a, *Climate change 2007: The Physical Science Basis – Contribution of Working Group I to the Fourth Assessment Report of the IPCC*, Cambridge: Cambridge University Press.

IPCC, 2007b, *Climate Change 2007: Impacts, Adaptation and Vulnerability – Contribution of Working Group II to the Fourth Assessment Report of the IPCC*, Cambridge: Cambridge University Press.

Ingram, P, and Clay, K, 2000, 'The choice-within-constraints institutionalism and implications for sociology', *Annual Review of Sociology*, 26: 525–546.

Ingram, P, and Silverman, B S, 2002, 'Introduction: the new institutionalism in strategic management', in P Ingram, and B S Silverman (eds), *Advances in Strategic Management*, Vol 19: 1–30, Greenwich, CT: JAI Press.

Innovest, 2002, *Value at Risk: Climate Change and the Future of Governance*, Boston: CERES.

Jaffe, A B, Peterson, S R, Portnoy, P R, and Stavins, R N, 1995, 'Environmental regulation and the competitiveness of U.S. manufacturing: what does the evidence tell us?' *Journal of Economic Literature*, 33: 132–163.

Jawahar, I M, and McLaughlin, G L, 2001, 'Toward a descriptive stakeholder theory: an organizational life cycle approach', *Academy of Management Review*, 26(3): 397–414.

Jiang, R J, and Bansal, P, 2003, 'Seeing the need for ISO 14001', *Journal of Management Studies*, 40(4): 1047–1067.

Johnson, E, 2006, 'Flexibility on fuel gives manufacturers an edge', *Financial Times*, 28 February.

Jones, C A, and Levy, D L, 2007, 'North American business strategies towards climate change', *European Management Journal*, 25(6): 428–440.

Judge, W Q, and Douglas, T J, 1998, 'Performance implications of incorporating natural environmental issues into the strategic planning process: an empirical assessment', *Journal of Management Studies*, 35(2): 241–262.

Jung, T Y, Ancha, S, Tamura, K, Sudo, T, Watanabe, R, Shimada, K, and Kimura, H, 2005, *Asian Perspectives on Climate Regime Beyond 2012 – Concerns, Interests and Priorities*, Hayama: Institute for Global Environmental Strategies.

Kameyama, Y, 2004, 'Evaluation and future of the Kyoto Protocol: Japan's perspective', *International Review for Environmental Strategies*, 5(1): 71–82.

Keeling, C D, and Whorf, T P, 2005, 'Atmospheric CO_2 records from sites in the SIO air sampling network', in *Trends: A Compendium of Data on Global Change*, Carbon Dioxide Information Analysis Center, Oak Ridge National Laboratory, U.S. Department of Energy, Oak Ridge, Tenn,, USA.

Kent, A, and Mercer, D, 2006, 'Australia's mandatory renewable energy target (MRET): an assessment', *Energy Policy*, 34: 1046–1062.

Khanna, M, and Ramirez, D T, 2004, 'Effectiveness of voluntary approaches: implications for climate change mitigation', in A Baranzini, and P Thalmann (eds), *Voluntary Approaches in Climate Policy*: 31–66, Cheltenham: Edward Elgar.

King, A A, and Lenox, M J, 2000, 'Industry self-regulation without sanctions: the chemical industry's responsible care program', *Academy of Management Journal*, 43(4): 698–716.

King, A A, and Shaver, J M, 2001, 'Are aliens green? Assessing foreign establishments' environmental conduct in the United States', *Strategic Management Journal*, 22: 1069–1085.

Klepper, G, and Peterson, S, 2004, 'The EU emissions trading scheme allowance prices, trade flows and competitive effects', *European Environment*, 14: 201–218.

Knickerbocker, F T, 1973, *Oligopolistic Reaction and Multinational Enterprise*, Boston: Harvard University.

Knill, C, and Lehmkuhl, D, 2002, 'Private actors and the state: internationalization and changing patterns of governance', *Governance: An International Journal of Policy, Administration, and Institutions*, 15(1): 41–63.

Kogut, B, and Zander, U, 1993, 'Knowledge of the firm and the evolutionary theory of the multinational corporation', *Journal of International Business Studies*, 24(4): 625–645.

Kolk, A, 2000, *Economics of Environmental Management*, Harlow: Financial Times Prentice Hall.

Kolk, A, 2001, 'Multinational enterprises and international climate policy', in B Arts, M Noortmann, and B Reinalda (eds), *Non-State Actors in International Relations*: 211–225, Aldershot: Ashgate.

Kolk, A, 2005, 'Environmental reporting by multinationals from the triad: convergence or divergence?' *Management International Review*, 45(1): 145–166.

Kolk, A, 2008, 'Sustainability, accountability and corporate governance: exploring multinationals' reporting practices', *Business Strategy and the Environment*, 17(1): 1–15.

Kolk, A, and Hoffmann, V H, 2007, 'Business, climate change and emissions trading: taking stock and looking ahead', *European Management Journal*, 25(6): 411–414.

Kolk, A, and Levy, D, 2004, 'Multinationals and global climate change: issue for the automotive and oil industries', in S M Lundan (ed), *Multinationals, Environment and Global Competition*, Vol 9: 171–193, Amsterdam: Elsevier.

Kolk, A, and Pinkse, J, 2004, 'Market strategies for climate change', *European Management Journal*, 22(3): 304–314.

Kolk, A, and Pinkse, J, 2005a, 'Business responses to climate change: identifying emergent strategies', *California Management Review*, 47(3): 6–20.

Kolk, A, and Pinkse, J, 2005b, 'The evolution of multinationals' responses to climate change', in J Hooker, A Kolk, and P Madsen (eds), *Perspectives on International Corporate Responsibility*, Vol 2: 175–190, Charlottesville, Virginia: Philosophy Document Center.

Kolk, A, and Pinkse, J, 2007a, 'Multinationals' political activities on climate change', *Business and Society*, 46(2): 201–228.

Kolk, A, and Pinkse, J, 2007b, 'Towards strategic stakeholder management? Integrating perspectives on sustainability challenges such as corporate responses to climate change', *Corporate Governance*, 7(4): 370–378.

Kolk, A, and Pinkse, J, 2008, 'A perspective on multinational enterprises and climate change: learning from "an inconvenient truth"?' *Journal of International Business Studies*, forthcoming.

Kostova, T, 1999, 'Transnational transfer of strategic organizational practices: a contextual perspective', *Academy of Management Review*, 24(2): 308–324.

Kostova, T, and Roth, K, 2002, 'Adoption of an organizational practice by subsidiaries of multinational corporations: institutional and relational effects', *Academy of Management Journal*, 45(1): 215–233.

KPMG, 1999, *KPMG International Survey of Environmental Reporting 1999*, The Hague: KPMG.

KPMG, 2002, *KPMG International Survey of Corporate Sustainability Reporting 2002*, De Meern: KPMG.

KPMG, 2005, *KPMG International Survey of Corporate Responsibility Reporting 2005*, Amsterdam: KPMG Global Sustainability Services.

Krarup, S, and Millock, K, 2007, 'Evaluation of the Danish Agreements on Industrial Energy Efficiency', in R D Morgenstern, and W A Pizer (eds), *Reality Check – The Nature and Performance of Voluntary Environmental Programs in the United States, Europe, and Japan*: 86–104, Washington, DC: RFF Press.

Kruger, J A, and Pizer, W A, 2004, 'Greenhouse gas trading in Europe – The new grand policy experiment', *Environment*, 46(8): 8–23.

Lash, J, and Wellington, F, 2007, 'Competitive advantage on a warming planet', *Harvard Business Review*, 85(3): 94–102.

Lavie, D, 2006, 'Capability reconfiguration: an analysis of incumbent responses to technological change', *Academy of Management Review*, 31(1): 153–174.

Lawrence, T B, 1999, 'Institutional strategy', *Journal of Management*, 25(2): 161–188.

Lecocq, F, and Ambrosi, P, 2007, 'The Clean Development Mechanism: history, status, and prospects', *Review of Environmental Economics and Policy*, 1(1): 134–151.

Leonard-Barton, D, 1992, 'Core capabilities and core rigidities: a paradox in managing new product development', *Strategic Management Journal*, 13: 11–125.

Levy, D L, 1997, 'Business and international environmental treaties: ozone depletion and climate change', *California Management Review*, 39(3): 54–71.

Levy, D L, and Egan, D, 2003, 'A neo-Gramscian approach to corporate political strategy: conflict and accommodation in the climate change negotiations', *Journal of Management Studies*, 40(4): 803–829.

Levy, D L, and Kolk, A, 2002, 'Strategic responses to global climate change: conflicting pressures on multinationals in the oil industry', *Business and Politics*, 4(3): 275–300.

Lyon, T P, and Maxwell, J W, 2004, 'Public voluntary programmes for mitigating climate change', in A Baranzini, and P Thalmann (eds), *Voluntary Approaches in Climate Policy*: 126–142, Cheltenham, UK: Edward Elgar.

MacGill, I, Outhred, H, and Nolles, K, 2006, 'Some design lessons from market-based greenhouse gas regulation in the restructured Australian electricity industry, *Energy Policy*, 34: 11–25.

Mackintosh, J, 2004, 'Toyota licenses Ford for hybrid engine patent use', *Financial Times*, 10 March.

Maguire, S, and Hardy, C, 2006, 'The emergence of new global institutions: a discursive perspective', *Organization Studies*, 27(1): 7–29.

Makino, S, Isobe, T, and Chan, C M, 2004, 'Does country matter?' *Strategic Management Journal*, 25: 1027–1043.

Makower, J, Pernick, R, and Wilder, C, 2007, *Clean Energy Trends 2007*, San Francisco: Clean Edge.

Makower, J, Pernick, R, and Wilder, C, 2008, *Clean Energy Trends 2008*, San Francisco: Clean Edge.

Malueg, D A, 1989, 'Emission credit trading and the incentive to adopt new pollution abatement technology', *Journal of Environmental Economics and Management*, 16: 52–57.

March, J G, 1991, 'Exploration and exploitation in organizational learning', *Organization Science*, 2(1): 71–87.

Marcus, A, and Geffen, D, 1998, 'The dialectics of competency acquisition: pollution prevention in electric generation', *Strategic Management Journal*, 19: 1145–1168.

Margolick, M, and Russell, D, 2001, *Corporate Greenhouse Gas Reduction Targets*, Arlington, VA: Pew Center on Global Climate Change.

Margolis, R M, and Kammen, D M, 1999, 'Underinvestment: the energy technology and RandD policy challenge', *Science*, 285(5428): 690–692.

Markussen, P, and Svendsen, G T, 2005, 'Industry lobbying and the political economy of GHG trade in the European Union', *Energy Policy*, 33: 245–255.

Mazurkiewicz, P, 2005, 'Corporate self-regulation and multi-stakeholder dialogue', in E Croci (ed), *The Handbook of Environmental Voluntary Agreements*: 31–45, Dordrecht: Springer.

McGee, J, and Taplin, R, 2006, 'The Asia-Pacific Partnership on Clean Development and Climate: A complement or competitor to the Kyoto Protocol?' *Global Change, Peace and Security*, 18(3): 173–192.

Meyer, J W, and Rowan, B, 1977, 'Institutionalized organizations: formal structure as myth and ceremony', *American Journal of Sociology*, 83(2): 340–363.

Milstein, M B, Hart, S L, and York, A S, 2002, 'Coercion breeds variation: the differential impact of isomorphic pressures on environmental strategies', in A J Hoffman, and M J Ventresca (eds), *Organizations, Policy and the Natural Environment, Institutional and Strategic Perspectives*: 151–172, Stanford: Stanford University Press.

Monks, R, Miller, A, and Cook, J, 2004, 'Shareholder activism on environmental issues: a study of proposals at large US corporations (2000–2003)', *Natural Resources Forum*, 28: 317–330.

Morgenstern, R D, and Pizer, W A, (eds), 2007, *Reality Check – The Nature and Performance of Voluntary Environmental Programs in the United States, Europe, and Japan*, Washington, DC: RFF Press.

Nehrt, C, 1998, 'Maintainability of first mover advantages when environmental regulations differ between countries', *Academy of Management Review*, 23(1): 77–97.

Neuhoff, K, 2005, 'Large-scale deployment of renewables for electricity generation', *Oxford Review of Economic Policy*, 21(1): 88–110.

Newell, P, and Paterson, M, 1998, 'A climate for business: global warming, the state and capital', *Review of International Political Economy*, 5(4): 679–703.

Nordhaus, W D, and Yang, Z, 1996, 'A regional dynamic general-equilibrium model of alternative climate-change strategies', *American Economic Review*, 86(4): 741–765.

NSW, 2005, *New South Wales Greenhouse Gas Abatement Scheme*, retrieved on 21 April 2005 from <http://www.greenhousegas.nsw.gov.au>.

NSW, 2007, *Intro to the Greenhouse Gas Reduction Scheme*, retrieved on 8 April 2008 from <http://www.greenhousegas.nsw.gov.au>.

Nuttall, C, 2008, 'Silicon feels the power of the sun', *Financial Times*, 25 March.

OECD, 1999, *Voluntary Approaches for Environmental Policy: An Assessment*, Paris: Organisation for Economic Co-operation and Development.

Oikonomou, V, and Jepma, C J, 2008, 'A framework on interactions of climate and energy policy instruments', *Mitigation and Adaptation Strategies for Global Change*, 13(2): 131–156.

Okereke, C, 2007, 'An exploration of motivations, drivers and barriers to carbon management: the UK FTSE 100', *European Management Journal*, 25(6): 475–486.

Oliver, C, 1991, 'Strategic responses to institutional processes', *Academy of Management Review*, 16(1): 145–179.

Pacala, S, and Socolow, R, 2004, 'Stabilization wedges: solving the climate problem for the next 50 years with current technologies', *Science*, 305(5686): 968–972.

Paolella, M S, and Taschini, L, 2006, 'An econometric analysis of emission trading allowances', *Swiss Finance Institute Research Paper Series*, 6(26): 1–42.

Paterson, M, 1992, 'Global warming', in C Thomas (ed), *The Environment in International Relations*: 155–198, London: The Royal Institute of International Affairs.

Pattberg, P, 2005, 'The institutionalization of private governance: how business and nonprofit organizations agree on transnational rules', *Governance: An International Journal of Policy, Administration, and Institutions*, 18(4): 589–610.

Perego, P, 2005, *Environmental Management Control – An Empirical Study on the Use of Environmental Performance Measures in Management Control Systems*, unpublished PhD dissertation, Radboud Universiteit Nijmegen, Nijmegen.

Pernick, R and Wilder, C, 2007, *The Clean Tech Revolution: The Next Big Growth and Investment Opportunity*, New York: HarperCollins.

Peterson, T D, and Rose, A Z, 2006, 'Reducing conflicts between climate policy and energy policy in the US: the important role of the states', *Energy Policy*, 34(5): 619–631.

Pew Center, 2006, *Summary of COP 12 and COP/MOP 2*, Arlington, VA: Pew Center on Global Climate Change, retrieved 12 October 2007 from <http://www.pewclimate.org>.

Pew Research Center, 2006, *America's Image Slips, but Allies Share U.S. Concerns over Iran, Hamas*, retrieved 10 October 2007 from <http://www.pewglobal.org>.

Philibert, C, 2005, 'The role of technological development and policies in a post-Kyoto climate regime', *Climate Policy*, 5: 291–308.

Phillips, G, 2004, 'Monitoring, verification and accounting of emissions', in C De Jong, and K Walet (eds), *A Guide to Emissions Trading – Risk Management and Business Implications*: 99–119, London: Risk Books.

Pinkse, J, 2007, 'Corporate intentions to participate in emission trading', *Business Strategy and the Environment*, 16(1): 12–25.

Pinkse, J, and Dommisse, M, 2008, 'Overcoming barriers to sustainability: an explanation of residential builders' reluctance to adopt clean technologies', *Business Strategy and the Environment*, forthcoming.

Point Carbon, 2008a, *EU ETS Phase II – The Potential and Scale of Windfall Profits in the Power Sector*, Oslo: Point Carbon/WWF.

Point Carbon, 2008b, *The Regional Greenhouse Gas Initiative: Implications of the First Trades*, Oslo: Point Carbon.

Porter, M E, and van der Linde, C, 1995, 'Green and competitive – Ending the stalemate', *Harvard Business Review*, 73(5): 120–138.

Porter, M E, and Kramer, M R, 2006, 'Strategy and society: the link between competitive advantage and corporate social responsibility', *Harvard Business Review*, 84(12): 78–92.

Porter, M E, and Reinhardt, F L, 2007, 'A strategic approach to climate', *Harvard Business Review*, 85(10): 22–26.

Prakash, A, and Kollman, K, 2004, 'Policy modes, firms, and the natural environment', *Business Strategy and the Environment*, 13: 107–128.

Price, L, 2005, 'Voluntary agreements for energy efficiency or GHG emissions reduction in industry: an assessment of programs around the world', *Proceedings of the 2005 ACEEE*

Summer Study on Energy Efficiency in Industry, Washington, DC: American Council for an Energy-Efficient Economy.

Price, L, and Wang, X, 2007, 'Constraining energy consumption of China's largest industrial enterprises through the Top-1000 Energy-Consuming Enterprise Program', *Proceedings of the 2007 ACEEE Summer Study on Energy Efficiency in Industry*, Washington, DC: American Council for an Energy-Efficient Economy.

Rabe, B G, 2004, *Statehouse and Greenhouse – The Emerging Politics of American Climate Change Policy*, Washington, DC: The Brookings Institution.

Rabe, B, 2006, 'Second generation climate policies in the American states: proliferation, diffusion, and regionalization', *Issues in Governance Studies*, 6: 1–9.

Rabe, B G, 2007, 'Beyond Kyoto: Climate change policy in multilevel governance systems', *Governance: An International Journal of Policy, Administration, and Institutions*, 20(3): 423–444.

Ramus, C A, and Montiel, I, 2005, 'When are corporate environmental policies a form of greenwashing?' *Business and Society*, 44(4): 377–414.

Reed, E, 2008a, 'GM chief hits at UN biofuel data', *Financial Times*, 21 April.

Reed, E, 2008b, 'Alarm and irritation from carmakers over debate', 26/27 April.

Reinaud, J, and Philibert, C, 2007, *Emissions Trading: Trends and Prospects*, Paris: OECD/IEA.

Reinhardt, F L, 1998, 'Environmental product differentiation: implications for corporate strategy', *California Management Review*, 40(4): 43–73.

Reinhardt, F L, 1999, 'Bringing the environment down to earth', *Harvard Business Review*, 77(4): 149–157.

Revkin, A C, 2007, 'Carbon-neutral is hip, but is it green?' *The New York Times*, 29 April.

RGGI, 2007, *Overview of RGGI CO_2 Budget Trading Program*, retrieved on 9 April 2008 from <http://www.rggi.org>.

Roberts, J T, and Parks, B C, 2007, *A Climate of Injustice – Global Inequality, North–South Politics, and Climate Policy*, Cambridge, MA: The MIT Press.

Roeser, F, and Jackson, T, 2002, 'Early experiences with emissions trading in the UK', *Greener Management International*, 39 (Autumn): 43–54.

Røine, K, and Hasselknippe, H, 2007, *Carbon 2007, A New Climate for Carbon Trading*, Oslo: Point Carbon.

Røine, K, Tvinnereim, E, and Hasselknippe, H, 2008, *Carbon 2008, Post-2012 is Now*, Oslo: Point Carbon.

Romm, J, 2006, 'The car and fuel of the future', *Energy Policy*, 34: 2609–2614.

Rondinelli, D A, and London, T, 2003, 'How corporations and environmental groups cooperate: assessing cross-sector alliances and collaborations', *Academy of Management Executive*, 17(1): 61–76.

Rosenzweig, P M, and Singh, J V, 1991, 'Organizational environments and the multi-national enterprise', *Academy of Management Review*, 16(2): 340–361.

Rosenzweig, R, Varilek, M, and Janssen, J, 2002, *The Emerging International Greenhouse Gas market*, Arlington, VA: Pew Center on Global Climate Change.

Rothaermel, F T, and Hill, C W L, 2005, 'Technological discontinuities and comple-mentary assets: a longitudinal study of industry and firm performance', *Organization Science*, 16(1): 52–70.

Rowlands, I H, 1992, 'The international politics of global environmental change', in I H Rowlands, and M Greene (eds), *Global Environmental Change and International Relations*: 19–37, London: MacMillan.

Rowlands, I H, 1995, *The Politics of Global Atmospheric Change*, Manchester: Manchester University Press.

Rowlands, I H, 2005, 'The European directive on renewable electricity: conflicts and compromises', *Energy Policy*, 33: 965–974.

Rugman, A M, 2005, *The Regional Multinationals, MNEs and 'Global' Strategic Management*, Cambridge: Cambridge University Press.

Rugman, A M, and Verbeke, A, 1998, 'Corporate strategies and environmental regulations: an organizing framework', *Strategic Management Journal*, 19: 363–375.

Rugman, A M, and Verbeke, A, 2001, 'Subsidiary-specific advantages in multinational enterprises', *Strategic Management Journal*, 22: 237–250.

Rugman, A M, and Verbeke, A, 2004, 'A perspective on regional and global strategies of multinational enterprises', *Journal of International Business Studies*, 35: 3–18.

Rugman, A M, and Verbeke, A, 2005, 'Towards a theory of regional multinationals: a transaction cost economics approach', *Management International Review*, 45 (Special Issue): 5–17.

Russo, M V, 2003, 'The emergence of sustainable industries: building on natural capital', *Strategic Management Journal*, 24: 317–331.

Russo, M V, and Fouts, P A, 1997, 'A resource-based perspective on corporate environmental performance and profitability', *Academy of Management Journal*, 40(3): 534–559.

Ruth, M, Coelho, D, and Karetnikov, D, 2007, *The US Economic Impacts of Climate Change and the Costs of Inaction*, Maryland: Center for Integrative Environmental Research/ University of Maryland.

Sæverud, I A, and Skjærseth, J B, 2007, 'Oil companies and climate change: inconsistencies between strategy formulation and implementation?' *Global Environmental Politics*, 7(3): 42–62.

Sandén, B A, and Azar, C, 2005, 'Near-term technology policies for long-term climate targets – economy wide versus technology specific approaches', *Energy Policy*, 33: 1557–1576.

Schreurs, M A, 2002, *Environmental Politics in Japan, Germany, and the United States*, Cambridge: Cambridge University Press.

Scott, W R, 1995, *Institutions and Organizations*, Thousand Oaks: Sage Publications.

Selin, H, and VanDeveer, S D, 2007, 'Political science and prediction: what's next for U.S. climate change policy?' *Review of Policy Research*, 24(1): 1–27.

Selsky, J W, and Parker, B, 2005, 'Cross-sector partnerships to address social issues: challenges to theory and practice', *Journal of Management*, 31(6): 849–873.

Sharma, S, and Vredenburg, H, 1998, 'Proactive corporate environmental strategy and the development of competitively valuable organizational capabilities', *Strategic Management Journal*, 19: 729–753.

Shell, 1998, *The Shell Report: Profits and Principles – does there have to be a choice?* London: Shell International.

Siebenhüner, B, 2003, 'The changing role of nation states in international environmental assessments – the case of the IPCC', *Global Environmental Change*, 13: 113–123.

Sijm, J, Neuhoff, K, and Chen, Y, 2006, 'CO_2 cost pass-through and windfall profits in the power sector', *Climate Policy*, 6(1): 49–72.

Simon, B, 2006, 'Bush and car chiefs to push more ethanol use', *Financial Times*, 28 April.

Simons, R, 1994, 'How new top managers use control systems as levers of strategic renewal', *Strategic Management Journal*, 15: 169–189.

Smith, K, 2007, *The Carbon Neutral Myth – Offset Indulgences for your Climate Sins*, Amsterdam: Carbon Trade Watch.

Sorrell, S, and Sijm, J, 2003, 'Carbon trading in the policy mix', *Oxford Review of Economic Policy*, 19(3): 420–437.

Spar, D L, and La Mure, L T, 2003, 'The power of activism: assessing the impact of NGOs on global business', *California Management Review*, 45(3): 78–101.

Sparkes, R and Cowton, C J, 2004, 'The maturing of socially responsible investment: a review of the developing link with corporate social responsibility', *Journal of Business Ethics*, 52: 45–57.

Spencer, J W, 2003, 'Firms' knowledge-sharing strategies in the global innovation system: empirical evidence from the flat panel display industry', *Strategic Management Journal*, 24: 217–233.

Springer, U, 2003, 'The market for tradable GHG permits under the Kyoto Protocol: a survey of model studies', *Energy Economics*, 25: 527–551.

Stafford, E R, Polonsky, M J, and Hartman, C L, 2000, 'Environmental NGO-business collaboration and strategic bridging: a case analysis of the Greenpeace-Foron alliance', *Business Strategy and the Environment*, 9: 122–135.

Stephens, J C, 2006, 'Growing interest in carbon capture and storage (CCS) for climate change mitigation', *Sustainability: Science, Practice, and Policy*, 2(2): 4–13.

Stoett, P, 2006, 'Canada, Kyoto, and the Conservatives: Thinking/moving ahead', in H Selin, and S D VanDeveer (eds), *Climate Change Politics in North America: The State of Play*: 7–16, Washington, DC: The Woodrow Wilson International Center for Scholars.

Streck, C, 2004, 'New partnerships in global environmental policy: the Clean Development Mechanism', *Journal of Environment and Development*, 13(3): 295–322.

Suchman, M C, 1995, 'Managing legitimacy: strategic and institutional approaches', *Academy of Management Review*, 20(3): 571–610.

Sundaram, A K, and Black, J S, 1992, 'The environment and internal organization of multinational enterprises', *Academy of Management Review*, 17(4): 729–757.

Sundin, H, and Ranganathan, J, 2002, 'Managing business greenhouse gas emissions: The Greenhouse Gas Protocol – A strategic and operational tool', *Corporate Environmental Strategy*, 9(2): 137–144.

Teece, D J, 1986, 'Profiting from technological innovation: implications for integration, collaboration, licensing and public policy', *Research Policy*, 15: 285–305.

Teece, D J, Pisano, G, and Shuen, A, 1997, 'Dynamic capabilities and strategic management', *Strategic Management Journal*, 18(7): 509–533.

Thalmann, P, and Baranzini, A, 2004, 'An overview of the economics of voluntary approaches in climate policies', in P Thalmann, and A Baranzini (eds), *Voluntary Approaches in Climate Policy*: 1–30, Cheltenham, UK: Edward Elgar.

Tiberghien, Y, and Schreurs, M A, 2007, 'High noon in Japan: embedded symbolism and post-2001 Kyoto Protocol politics', *Global Environmental Politics*, 7(4): 70–91.

Tietenberg, T H, 1990, 'Economic instruments for environmental regulation', *Oxford Review of Economic Policy*, 6(1): 17–33.

Tietenberg, T, 1998, 'Disclosure strategies for pollution control', *Environmental and Resource Economics*, 11: 587–602.

Tripsas, M, 1997, 'Unraveling the process of creative destruction: complementary assets and incumbent survival in the typesetter industry', *Strategic Management Journal*, 18 (Summer Special Issue): 119–142.

Tsai, T, and Child, J, 1997, 'Strategic responses of multinational corporations to environmental demands', *Journal of General Management*, 23(1): 1–22.

Tushman, M L, and Anderson, P, 1986, 'Technological discontinuities and organizational environments', *Administrative Science Quarterly*, 31: 439–465.

Unruh, G C, 2000, 'Understanding carbon lock-in', *Energy Policy*, 28: 817–830.

Van den Hoed, R, and Vergragt, P J, 2004, 'Institutional change in the automotive industry, Or how fuel cell technology is being institutionalised', *Greener Management International*, 47(Autumn): 45–61.

Van Huijstee, M M, Francken, M, and Leroy, P, 2007, 'Partnerships for sustainable development: a review of current literature', *Environmental Sciences*, 4(2): 75–89.

Verbeke, A, Bowen, F, and Sellers, M, 2006, *Corporate Environmental Strategy: Extending the Natural Resource-Based View of the Firm*, Paper presented at the Annual Meeting of the Academy of Management, Atlanta.

Victor, D G, 2004, *Climate Change: Debating America's Policy Options*, New York: Council on Foreign Relations.

Victor, D G, and House, J C, 2006, 'BP's emissions trading system', *Energy Policy*, 34(15): 2100–2112.

Waddock, S A, 1991, 'A typology of social partnership organizations', *Administration and Society*, 22(4): 480–515.

Wakabayashi, M, and Sugiyama, T, 2007, 'Japan's Keidanren Voluntary Action Plan on the Environment', in R D Morgenstern, and W A Pizer (eds), *Reality Check – The Nature and Performance of Voluntary Environmental Programs in the United States, Europe, and Japan*: 43–63, Washington, DC: RFF Press.

Walley, N, and Whitehead, B, 1994, 'It's not easy being green', *Harvard Business Review*, 72(3): 46–52.

Watanabe, R, 2005, 'Current Japanese climate policy from the perspective of using the Kyoto mechanisms', *Option Survey for Japan to Acquire Credits from Abroad*: 31–63, Hayama: Institute for Global Environmental Strategies.

Weart, S R, 2003, *The Discovery of Global Warming*, Cambridge, MA: Harvard University Press.

Welch, E W, Mazur, A, and Bretschneider, S, 2000, 'Voluntary behavior by electric utilities: levels of adoption and contribution of the Climate Challenge Program to the reduction of carbon dioxide', *Journal of Policy Analysis and Management*, 19(3): 407–425.

Wellington, F, and Sauer, A, 2005, *Framing Climate Risk in Portfolio Management*, Washington DC: CERES and WRI.

Wellington, F, Bradley, R, Childs, B, Rigdon, C, and Pershing, J, 2007, *Scaling Up: Global Technology Deployment to Stabilize Emissions*, Washington DC: World Resources Institute.

Weng, C K, and Boehmer, K, 2006, 'Launching of ISO 14064 for greenhouse gas accounting and verification', *ISO Management Systems* (March–April): 14–16.

Westney, D E, 1993, 'Institutionalization theory and the multinational corporation', in S Ghoshal, and D E Westney (eds), *Organization Theory and the Multinational Corporation*: 53–76, New York: St Martin's Press.

White House, 2002, *Global Climate Change Policy Book*, retrieved on 22 October 2007 from <http://www.whitehouse.gov>.

Winter, S G, 2003, 'Understanding dynamic capabilities', *Strategic Management Journal*, 24: 991–995.

Witte, J M, Streck, C, and Benner, T, 2003, 'The road from Johannesburg: what future for partnerships in global environmental governance?' in T Benner, C Streck, and J M Witte (eds), *Progress or Peril? Networks and Partnerships in Global Environmental Governance, The Post-Johannesburg Agenda*: 59–84, Berlin: Global Public Policy Institute.

Woerdman, E, 2004, 'Path-dependent climate policy: the history and future of emissions trading in Europe', *European Environment*, 14: 261–275.

Wright, C, 2006, 'Carbon neutrality draws praise, raises expectations for HSBC', *Ecosystem Marketplace*, 1 August.

WRI/WBCSD, 2004, *The Greenhouse Gas Protocol – A Corporate Accounting and Reporting Standard* (revised edition), Washington, DC and Geneva: WRI/WBCSD.

Yang, T, 2006, 'The problem of maintaining emissions "caps" in carbon trading programs without federal government involvement: a brief examination of the Chicago Climate Exchange and the Northeast Regional Greenhouse Gas Initiative', *Fordham Environmental Law Journal*, 18(fall): 1–17.

Yaziji, M, 2004, 'Turning gadflies into allies', *Harvard Business Review*, 82(2): 110–115.

Zollo, M, and Winter, S G, 2002, 'Deliberate learning and the evolution of dynamic capabilities', *Organization Science*, 13(3): 339–351.

Zucker, L, 1987, 'Institutional theories and organization', *Annual Review of Sociology*, 13: 443–464.

Index